NO TIME TO WAVE GOODBYE

With an introduction by Michael Caine

In September 1939 millions listened anxiously as the Prime Minister declared that Britain was at war with Germany. When the children of Britain heard the news, most of them were in new homes, far away from their loving parents. The stories of these children – forever known as 'the evacuees' – are gathered here in their own words, as they recount the confusion, excitement and heartache of one of the defining moments of British history.

NO TIME TO WAVE GOODBYE

No Time To Wave Goodbye

by

Ben Wicks

Magna Large Print Books
Long Preston, North Yorkshire,
BD23 4ND, England.

British Library Cataloguing in Publication Data.

Wicks, Ben
    No time to wave goodbye.

      A catalogue record of this book is
      available from the British Library

      ISBN   978-0-7505-3403-1

First published in Great Britain in 1988 by Bloomsbury

Copyright © 1988 by Ben Wicks

Cover illustration © mirrorpix

The moral right of the author has been asserted

Published in Large Print 2011 by arrangement with
Bloomsbury Publishing Ltd.

Magna Large Print is an imprint of Library Magna Books Ltd.

Printed and bound in Great Britain by
T.J. (International) Ltd., Cornwall, PL28 8RW

Contents

*This book is dedicated to children in war,
whose heroism is so often overlooked*

Introduction

The idea behind *No Time to Wave Goodbye* is such a good one that I'm amazed no one has thought of it before. The evacuation of thousands and thousands of youngsters from London when war broke out was a masterpiece of organization. It was also an operation that was to have a profound effect in later life on the children who were uprooted from their homes and, with their Mickey Mouse gas-masks, dispatched to live with strangers in what often amounted to a 'foreign land'.

I know how they felt because I was one of them, a six-year-old cockney more familiar with the smells and sounds of Billingsgate fish market than with manure and birdsong. Certainly I came in for my share of rough treatment from the family who first took me in, but I went on to enjoy some halcyon days over the next six years growing up on a 200-acre farm in Norfolk, which changed me from a young 'city slicker' into the country-lover I am to this day.

The brief definition of 'evacuee' in the

Everyday English Dictionary – 'a person transferred from a vulnerable to a safe area on account of air raids' – may be accurate as a general description, but it gives no inkling of the thousands of stories, both sad and happy, behind that momentous evacuation in the last war. It's good that so many former evacuees, their parents and the people who took them in have spared the time to remember an era so graphically recalled, and in such a worthwhile way, in Ben Wicks's book.

Michael Caine

Acknowledgements

The task of finding people who were part of Britain's evacuation almost 50 years ago was assigned to two remarkable women, who previously had little knowledge of the happening and as such faced an even greater challenge. Without the patience and assistance of two Canadians, Robin and Linnet Fawcett, this book would have been impossible to write.

Each of the thousands of letters we received was read and acknowledged by them. Their sympathetic answers to phone calls prompted many involved in the historic events to reveal stories that were painful and had been deliberately buried. The many invitations they received from families with whom they had made contact was proof of the obvious sincerity they had shown during their initial communications.

Added to their task were months of systematic digging for facts in libraries and Government buildings to trace the beginnings of the evacuation operation and the names of those involved.

Without an incredible amount of work by Penny Phillips, my editor at Bloomsbury Publishing in London, this book would not be appearing in the felicitous form that it now takes. Both her intelligent and sensitive editing of my manuscript and her relentless striving for accuracy have contributed immeasurably to the final outcome.

My agent, Matie Molinero, made many suggestions and my wife, Doreen, once again encouraged a husband whose nose appeared to be constantly buried in never-ending stacks of paper.

Ben Wicks, 1988

Foreword

Six years ago I was being interviewed on a television programme. It was not the first time. As a journalist I have been involved in many stories around the world that were of interest to the media. But this programme was different. The interviewer was concerned with my life as a newsman. Soon we began discussing my early life and I suddenly found myself relating for the first time the story of my days as an evacuee when, as a little boy wearing a large label, I gripped the string of a small brown paper carrier-bag containing my belongings and said goodbye to loving parents. I was to be gone for two years.

Four sets of families took me into their homes, all complete strangers. Some were kind, some were not.

As the interviewer began to dig deeper I began to cry. It was an embarrassing moment. Yet it was to be the same reaction as that of many ex-evacuees whom we contacted during the preparation of this book. Like me, they had successfully buried their experiences deep in the recesses of their minds. Most were telling their story for the first time. Some had been married for more than 30 years and had never told their wives or husbands. Our book became the couch they had never had the courage to lie on.

In an attempt to contact them we wrote letters to the editors of 30 British newspapers. We received more than 8,000 replies by letter and telephone. This same approach was made in Australia, New Zealand, Canada, South Africa and the United States of America, which many of those involved in the remarkable evacuation scheme now call home.

Many were so upset recalling their experiences that they found it difficult to talk. A few laughed so hard that it was impossible for them to speak.

Enclosed with the letters sent to us were photographs of then and now, wedding pictures, reunion pictures and many letters written by evacuees to their parents at the time of their evacuation – all tenderly preserved.

In a few years these people will be gone – the teachers who held the hands of the children; the farmers who watched in astonishment as many children from the nation's poor areas, having watched cows being milked, refused to drink the milk feeling sure that it was in fact urine; the nurses who searched the hair of the children for nits; the incredible foster parents who took the children into their homes and accepted them as part of their families; and, last but not least, the children themselves.

As the historians and popular writers have busied themselves with the exploits of the leaders and heroes of the Second World War, a whole army of witnesses has been completely overlooked – the 11-year-old girl who toured her new village with a pram, looking for pieces of furniture for use in the home her mother had found in a condemned cottage; the little girl who found kindness and understanding with the local prostitute; and those who left the homes of loved ones to find only cruelty and abuse – all ignored then and unknown today.

A wartime Britain once looked to the skies and worshipped Churchill's 'few', as thousands of its children on the ground struggled to survive behind closed curtains. Through their letters and interviews they have now found a voice.

When we set out to lay the groundwork for this book we had intended to document the lives of a number of British people who had obviously suffered as a result of the Second World War. What we found was a key that opened a whole section of contemporary British history that has remained hidden, locked in the hearts of those who took part.

For almost 50 years the evacuation of children and mothers from the preconceived danger areas has been pushed into the background, overshadowed by events of the Second World War that continue to be replayed time and time again. Famous battles, stirring speeches and outstanding heroes have all laid a blanket over a happening that did more to change the face of a nation than a thousand D-Days.

Through the letters we have received the children, foster parents, teachers and all involved at that time have carried us back to another Britain, a Britain of tiny beings who bit their lips and wrote to tell their parents of a new land they had discovered in their own backyard, a country where apples grew on trees and birds sang somewhere other than in wooden cages.

For me, evacuation from the squalor of soot-covered slums provided a view of the outside world. I saw greener pastures and was never again happy with my city environment. Later the Army would provide me with a means of escape. I have now found that I was not alone. Some returned to their homes to stay. Others remained in the countryside they had grown to love. But what of their lives since, and what effect did this happening have?

Many now live in other countries. The independence forced upon them at an early age gave them an education no school could have provided. I, certainly, have followed a path that without evacuation I would have hesitated to tread. My life has been richer.

Wherever those who took part now live, we have attempted to track them down and ask about their lives then and since. Although each and every one has had a different answer, almost all have agreed on one thing: come what may, they would never ever send *their* children away.

And what of Britain? The country owes to all those who took part a debt of gratitude that can never be repaid. The face of Britain was changed for ever. The eyes of many working-class children were opened to the advantages of the few. City and country children found themselves sharing beds. The rules of the class system in Britain began to bend, heralding the introduction of changes desperately needed in a post-war Britain.

An army of children, clutching tiny bags, came out of the dark and pricked a nation's conscience.

The children would never be the same again. Neither would Britain.

Ben Wicks, 1988

PART ONE

The Years Before

1

A Personal Experience

In the early hours of Friday 1 September 1939, German troops made their way across the border into Poland.

At the same time, thousands of children in Britain rubbed their eyes and climbed from their beds. For many it would be years before they climbed back into them. Within hours they were joining the crocodile lines of others making their way to the nearest railway station. Two days later they listened as an angry Prime Minister told the world that Britain was at war with Germany.

Most of the children heard the news from new homes, the homes of 'borrowed parents'. They were and for ever will be known as 'the evacuees', part of the greatest movement of people that Britain has ever experienced. It was a mammoth operation that voluntarily split families apart as hundreds of thousands of children fled an expected large-scale bombing of helpless civilians.

I was 12 years old when I climbed from my bed that fateful morning. Two older sisters grumbled about a brother who constantly whistled first thing in the morning. Life was pretty good for me and I was a happy child. The fact that we were poor was hidden by a majority who were in the same boat. Without television we were spared the constant reminder of what we might have and enjoyed what little we did have. Without a car we were locked into our surroundings and, like most slum-dwellers in large cities, found ourselves anchored to a district of grime-covered buildings.

The summer had been a hot one and our annual visit to the hop-fields of Kent had been a wonderful three weeks. Surrounded by hundreds of other cockney families my mother, my sisters and I had worked in fields that would, in just a few months, become the backdrop for swirling aircraft locked in a theatre of death. From early morning to late at night we'd picked the hops that would later be used in the beer Dad would drink at weekends. Unlike my mother, who was gregarious and loved company, my father was the shyest man I ever knew. The camp-fire singsongs of the hop-fields were not for him. The quiet of the buildings and a newspaper read by gaslight were all he needed.

The approaching war would not be the first he had experienced. Dad had been called into the Army in 1916 and had served in the trenches of France for two years. A victim of one of the first gas attacks of the war, he had suffered ever since. Nightly we would hear the soothing voice of my mother comforting him as he walked back and forth hoping that this would relieve the pain. He never complained and never spoke about his experiences in France except to joke about them. Years later I found two letters pinned together in a small tin box. One was dated 1916 and begged the Army to excuse my father since he was a 'vital part of the company'. The other letter was dated 1919. It was sent to my father on his return and told him how his employers had replaced this 'vital part of the company' and no longer needed his services. It was the only hint I ever had of the hurt that my father may have suffered in his lifetime.

Little did he know on that September morning in 1939 that within hours his only son would be taken away and he would not see him for almost three years. Once again a war would intrude on this gentle man's life and once again it would cause him pain.

Life had not been easy for either of my parents. Long years of unemployment for Dad after the war had made things particularly tough. It was during this period that my twin brother and I had been born. Within hours my brother had died and Dad had been forced to seek the help of our local undertaker, Alf Smith. With typical cockney kindness he had placed my brother between the feet of a woman who had died the night before. In this way it was possible for my brother to have a Christian burial, though where he is buried and with whom is something Alf Smith never did tell Dad.

The building in which we lived, St George's Buildings, was more than 100 years old. It was five storeys high, and on each floor there was a single balcony that ran the length of the building, making it possible to look into the neighbours' windows and check any new additions of furniture. The block of buildings was built in a square with the centre reserved for two huge open rubbish bins. This gave everyone an equal opportunity of smelling the rotting rubbish from the 50 families living there. Rats loved the arrangement and could be seen scurrying back and forth, collecting titbits and carrying them back to their families.

But it was the bugs that I remember most of all. Despite our daily routine of bed-stripping and scrubbing the bed frames with strong disinfectant, they were always back at bedtime, ready to crawl from their hiding-places behind the wallpaper and make their way between the sheets. By dawn my body would be covered in bites and scratched into rivulets of blood. The coming evacuation would bring sadness to many children from Britain's big-city centres, but one thing was sure, for many it would prove a welcome relief from the small pests that fed on the poor of the country during the pre-war years.

Southwark rested on the south side of London Bridge and for hundreds of years had been the refuge for those unfortunates who hunted for shelter in the poorer parts of London. Many turned to crime in order to survive, and found the bridge a useful means of access to where the money could be found and of escape as they hurried back over it clutching their wares, weaving in and out of the alleys before being gobbled up in the narrow streets south of the river.

It was an obvious place to build prisons, and a number had been built in the 1800s. At that time the area was known as the Borough of Clink and the name of the borough stuck as a slang term for prison. It had once been a home for Charles Dickens and his mother when, as a young boy, he had waited with her for his father's release from the Marshalsea debtors' prison.

Almost everywhere, it seemed, a street or turning was stamped with a reminder of the fact that Dickens had lived there. Bob Sawyer had been a medical student at nearby Guy's Hospital, 'a carver and cutter of live people's bodies', as Mrs Raddle calls him in *Pickwick Papers*. The gritty play-ground with three swings and a slide that sat in the shadow of our buildings was in Little Dorrit Court, while Lant Street was the site of the Charles Dickens School that I had once attended.

From that school, after a serious illness that had left me with a cloud on one lung, I had been sent to Stowey House, an open-air school.

As I headed for Stowey House that Friday morning in September 1939, I little dreamed of the changes that were about to take place in my life. I ambled along and, as always, stopped to kneel down and stare into the half-open basement window of the lodging house next door. The three clothes-lines strung along the room were crowded with tramps who had paid their twopence the night before. With their arms over the lines, they slept like human washing hung out to dry, swinging slowly back and forth in rhythm with the snores of their neighbours. At 8.30 a.m. the lodging-house keeper would be down to untie the lines and send them spinning to the floor and out into the street once more. Years later I learned that in that same basement coop one of Britain's great poets, William Henry Davies, had once sat down to write, and from that hot and smelly space of hanging failures, 'What is this life if, full of care, / We have no time to stand and stare?' had been born.

Little had changed since the early 1900s,

and a Dickens roaming the streets of London in September 1939 would, I'm sure, have been disappointed at the lack of progress in the care of the poor.

Now a war was about to take place that would allow a whole generation to escape the fetters of their surroundings. It was to be a war that killed many but at the same time brought to others a taste of a way of life that few of them would have dreamed possible.

The children who were assembled in the grounds of Stowey House that Friday morning were unaware that they were about to see the row of school huts, open to the elements, for the last time. No longer would they sit, fully dressed, attempting to keep warm on the wooden platforms with only a roof to protect them. Built to take advantage of the fresh air deemed essential for the – mostly tubercular – children, the school was situated beside Clapham Common, a wide stretch of park near the centre of London.

The laughter and giggles slowly died as the headmaster took his place on the platform and explained how the war that everyone had hoped would never come was now expected at any time. The evacuation that had been mentioned for months as a possibility was about to become a reality.

As he spoke, teachers throughout the country who had been called back from their summer holidays and were now listening to similar lectures, stood ready to carry out the evacuation exercises they had practised in the months before.

Most children had paid little attention to the rehearsals and had seen them purely as a glorious opportunity to avoid the boredom of the classrooms. Many schools had taken their children to the nearest railway station in an effort to perfect the scheme in preparation for the actual day.

John Bierman, a former foreign correspondent for the BBC and now living in Canada, recalls his experiences as a pupil at one such school:

It was weeks before the start of the war when we were told to bring our gas-mask and some belongings with us to school the next day. When we got to school they attached a label to each of us and then lined us up and off we went down the street to the local railway station. We then turned around and went back to the school. A day or two later the teacher said, 'I want you to write an essay about the dress rehearsal for the evacuation.' I remember writing describing how we marched down to the station and saying how the roads were lined with expectant mothers. I remember this distinctly because the teacher pulled me up on this. 'John Bierman, what do you mean the streets were lined with expectant mothers?'

Well, I thought, she's a bit thick not knowing what expectant meant. There was silence, since the kids in the class were as surprised as I was that she didn't know what the word meant. So I explained to her how there were all these expectant mothers lining the streets, expecting their children to come back home again in a few hours.

As the headmaster of Stowey House finished speaking, an excited babble of voices filled the room. We were going on a train ride, many of us for the first time and, even better, we were going to see the countryside. It was too good to be true. The buzz and whispers gave way to the ring of the headmaster's bell and a loud thump as he slammed the flat of his hand on the desk-top for silence.

All the children were to make their way home to collect a change of clothes, enough food for the journey and their gas-masks, and then report back to the school in two hours.

In major cities throughout Britain the message had been the same. Anxious to get to the fields and streams, hundreds of thousands of children hurried through the grimy, smutty streets, shouting, laughing and skipping as though guided and led by a giant, invisible Pied Piper.

I arrived home to find that my dad had left for work, but my mum was back from her job of cleaning floors at the local bank. (She started at 4.00 a.m., and finished at 9.00 a.m. each morning.) The news of the evacuation was no surprise to her. Although Chamberlain's attempts to appease Hitler had delayed the war, the summer of 1939 had brought the signing of the Nazi-Soviet pact, seen by most people as a signal that the waiting was over. Throughout the month of August recall notices had fallen through the letter-boxes of thousands of Army, Navy and Air Force reservists, and on 31 August the Government had issued orders that the evacuation would begin the following morning.

Those parents who heard the news spent a fearful evening packing their children's belongings in order to give them an early start next day.

2

The Plans are Laid

If the Wright brothers and those who followed had decided to tear up their plans for a machine that would fly, there would have been no reason for a group of men to hurry through the streets of London on a cold December morning in 1924. Their meeting was to affect the lives of hundreds of thousands of British children and prick the conscience of one of the most powerful nations in the world.

The group had good reason to meet. Events over the last 10 years had finally forced their country to realize that it was no longer an island fortress. The stretch of water that for years had been Britain's first line of defence had now been breached. No longer would their country enjoy the luxury of being able to defend itself on the soil of others.

The first shock had arrived as early as 1914. Although the damage resulting from the air attack had amounted to little more than a few broken windows, the bombing raid had done more than anything else to awaken the British to the realization that being masters of the sea was of little value if an enemy was planning to attack from the air.

The war dragged on and the air attacks increased. Zeppelins began slowly lifting themselves into the sky and heading for London. The slow, lumbering balloons lingered over their targets like huge airborne whales and began dropping large numbers of bombs that caused more than just a few windows to be broken. Lives were lost and, as in the Second World War, the damage was particularly severe in the poorer districts of the East End of London. The worst attack was not a Zeppelin raid but the bombing of London in 1917 by 14 twin-engined German Gothas, in which 160 people were killed and more than 400 injured.

By the time the war ended in 1918, German bombers had made 103 raids on Britain and had dropped some 300 tons of high explosives. The casualties had numbered close to 5,000 and had resulted in over 1,400 deaths.

With these facts before them it is hardly surprising that the men attending the meeting in December 1924 concentrated on the defence of the country's population. There was certainly a lot to be discussed and by the 17th meeting, held on 30 March 1925, a firm group was in place. The committee was chaired by John Anderson, a young and brilliant civil servant, and further comprised M.G. Ashmore from the War Office, I.G. Gibbon, an assistant secretary at the Ministry of Health, and M.P.A. Hankey, Secretary of the CID. Since a major concern of the group was the safety of Britain's children, the Chief Inspector of Elementary Schools, H.M. Richards, stood by to give advice.

The substance of the meeting was recorded in a document headed 'Sub-committee on ARP, Vol. 46-1'. The subjects covered were panic, war, the mobilization of school buildings and what was obviously a concern of all Government offices – who was going to pay for what?

Since the Germans had been defeated, they were not mentioned as a possible enemy. Rather, the language used was such that it applied to anyone who might be planning to drop bombs on Britain at some future date. 'Belligerent' seemed to fit the bill and was the word used in discussions referring to a potential enemy: '...it is possible for a "belligerent" to put forth his greatest effort at the outset, that the amount of explosives dropped from aeroplanes in such a case might well exceed in the first 24 hours the whole weight of explosives ... dropped ... in the whole period of the late war.'

One thing on which everyone round the table was agreed was that efficient ways of stopping air attacks had yet to be found and the committee should continue the discussion in acceptance of that fact. All further discussion therefore concentrated on the civilian population who would be, if not the actual targets, living in the target areas. Most of those on the committee were of the opinion that London was the city most likely to be chosen as a target by a 'belligerent' and used this city as a reference.

All agreed that whatever happened, in the

event of war London must be able to continue its job of supplying the needs of the nation. Anyone whose presence in the city threatened to hinder this objective had to be removed beforehand since they would 'merely add to the risk of casualty and to the possibility of confusion'.

Having agreed on the need for evacuation, the committee went on to discuss who would be evacuated. Certainly children were a top priority – but how many? The obvious person to ask was Mr Richards. He began his answer by defining the area of London under discussion. He explained that 1,200,000 public- and elementary-school pupils would be involved, together with a large number of teachers. An enormous amount of housing would be needed to lodge the children and it was observed that one possibility would be to 'evacuate the very poor districts only'. This idea was based on an assumption not that only the poor were going to be the recipients of any objects falling from the sky, but rather that the wealthy would be in a better position to evacuate themselves and their children to wherever they felt was safe. John Anderson, the Chairman, felt that the parents of poor children should also be given the opportunity to go if they could make their own arrangements.

Once again all eyes turned to Richards,

who by now could probably anticipate the responsibility for the safety of thousands of schoolchildren falling squarely on his shoulders. He maintained that maybe it would be best after all to 'keep the children in London and face it out as best we can'. This line of thinking was fairly common, since there had been widespread reports of French children playing close to the front during the war, leading to the notion that children reacted better to bombing than most adults.

In reading the reports of these early meetings it is interesting to note how far-sighted were many of the thoughts voiced by the committee. The concern about the way poor children would be received in their new country homes was in many cases, it transpired, particularly justified. This remark, part of an exchange between Richards and Gibbon, could easily have been made 15 years later in 1940: 'Some of these small children who come from London would not be the kind of children that would be welcomed too ardently, even by patriotic householders.'

Despite the concern felt by the group, Mr Hankey probably expressed the opinion of all when he declared that just in case, it might be a good idea to 'have a scheme up your sleeve'.

The meeting ended with the observation

that 'schools could be used for mobilization purposes since war usually starts in the summer'. This was a strange theory, no doubt founded on the fact that the First World War had been declared in August of 1914.

Since many of the losses on both sides in the last war had resulted from new methods of waging war – gas, tanks and attacks from the air – it was no surprise that speculation ran rampant among the experts as to the number of casualties that could be expected in any future war. Most people envisaged massive fleets of bombers blackening the skies and sending thousands of tons of bombs down on British cities. The civil servants whose responsibility it was to be prepared for such a happening grew more concerned with each passing year.

By the early 1930s a new leader was beginning to emerge in Germany as Hitler and his Nazi party goose-stepped their way into power. The same Germany that had been knocked on its back in 1918 was beginning to climb back to its feet.

The possibility of a war, and with it aerial bombardment, prompted the formation during 1931-33 of more committees to consider air-raid precautions. In March 1931 one such ARP subcommittee met to discuss the defence of the civilian population after an Air Ministry estimate predicted that in the event of war, enemy planes would drop 100 tons of high explosives on the first day, 75 tons on the second day and 50 tons a day from then on for a month. Experts figured that each ton of high explosives would result in 50 casualties. Add to this what would be the horrendous effects of a poison-gas attack and it is easy to see the reason for concern.

Unsurprisingly, the chief cause of anxiety among those involved in the meetings was the panic that would result from future bombing raids, but what was remarkable was a theory put forward suggesting that those most likely to panic would be the 'less stable in character of foreign elements within London as well as the very poor in East and Southern London'. The people living in these areas were identified as 'foreign, Jewish and poor elements'. Speaking in support of the theory, a member of the committee, Major Tomlin of the Metropolitan Police, described people living in the East End of London during the First World War as having 'flocked out of their homes before the sirens were heard'. Major Tomlin claimed that this was the type of person who 'would be driven mad with fright'. (This statement was to prove, at the height of the bombing of Britain's cities in 1940, as far wrong as it was possible for it to be.) Other members of the committee agreed with the Major and decided that the best idea would be to get the population out of London before hostilities began, in order to prevent people from 'bolting and thereby causing panic in the streets that would undermine the morale of the country making it difficult to control'. As for the comments made about the various classes, it was felt that 'any discrimination against the foreign element or the poor was there for the sake of the whole'.

Looting was then discussed and once again Major Tomlin aired his comments regarding the poor who, he felt, in the event of the bombing of London 'would flock into the wealthier areas where they would find prizes worth having'.

It was decided to approach the London Transport Board with a request for the use of its buses and coaches which, in conjunction with trains – or, in the event of the destruction of a main-line railway terminus, instead of them – would move the population to the suburbs.

All agreed that the date of the evacuation should be selected rather than forced on the nation by enemy action. (It is interesting to note that this decision, made as early as 1931, was adhered to when the evacuation plan was finally put into practice two days before the declaration of war, on 1 September 1939.)

The problems that might occur at the receiving end were discussed at further meetings in 1932. Chairing the subcommittee was Wing Commander John Hodsoll, an RAF officer who brought with him valuable experience, having served in India in 1929 and been involved in the evacuation of the British from Kabul during the revolt of the Afghans.

The discussion centred on trying to ascertain the number of people that reception areas could tolerate. This was not easy, since summer and holiday fluctuations in population had to be tabulated before it was possible to arrive at a reasonably accurate figure.

In addition to considerations of the safety of civilians in the event of war, a major political dilemma had to be faced. If Britain's cities were evacuated before the onset of hostilities and then war did not materialize, the enormous unnecessary expenditure would certainly be looked on unfavourably by the electorate. If, on the other hand, war broke out and bombing began immediately, as was supposed would happen, and people began evacuating themselves, the authorities would completely lose control of the population. The possibility of main-line termini being put out of action further complicated the problems faced by those responsible for the future safety of

Britain's citizens.

In 1933 it was decided to make the news of the evacuation plans public knowledge for the first time. As one ARP committee member suggested, 'the surest guarantee of sane behaviour in time of emergency is to prepare public education'. There was good reason for this decision. Events in Germany were proving that Germany was being ever more tightly strangled by the tyrannical hold of Adolf Hitler. In May photographs of Nazis burning tens of thousands of books in Berlin shocked the world. Following a stock-taking conducted by the British Government, the Admiralty, the Air Ministry and the War Office reported on 'our grave shortage of war supplies'. In a letter to his wife, Clementine, Winston Churchill showed his concern. 'There is no doubt,' he wrote, 'that the Germans are already substantially stronger than us in the air and that they are manufacturing at such an alarming rate that we cannot catch them up.'

Throughout July the Nazis tightened their grip on Germany as they stepped up the terror tactics by outlawing trade unions and throwing those who were opposed to their ideas into prisons and concentration camps. Concerned at the growing danger in Europe, Baldwin's National Party decided to issue its first circular on air-raid precautions to Britain's local authorities. Meanwhile the subcommittee on evacuation had prepared its report and was ready to present it to the Government. The committee members felt that provided it was possible to maintain public morale, there was no reason why an evacuation on a large scale was not possible. The report held that those deemed essential should be left in London, but that women, children, the aged and the helpless should be encouraged to leave. Control of the transport would be necessary and, above all, the evacuation must be a voluntary action to save the Government the cost of any liability. It was suggested that the provinces be made responsible for reception, accommodation, bedding, food and education. As for the timing of the evacuation, it would take place before the commencement of war, with a fixed time-limit of 72 hours.

At this point it was decided to bring in the education authorities. After discussions with them it was decided that children should be evacuated with their schools. For the first time, concern was expressed about the reaction of the parents who would be sending their children to live with strangers.

A later survey, conducted by Margaret Cole in 1940 and presented to the Fabian Society, touched on the committee's lack of understanding on this matter. 'Surely only male calculations could have so confidently assumed that working-class wives would be content to leave their husbands indefinitely to look after themselves, and only middle-class parents, accustomed to shooing their children out of sight and reach at the earliest possible age, could have been so astonished to find that working-class parents were violently unwilling to part with theirs.' The concerns pointed out by Cole were certainly lost on this committee, as they suggested that all households of all classes were to be used as billeting homes, with one room per person an essential requirement.

More and more the news from abroad showed that Europe was heading for war. Benito Mussolini decided that 1936 would be a good year to launch his Italian army against a spear-carrying African nation called Abyssinia. For the first time since the First World War, poison gas was used to maim and kill natives who had even less protection than the thousands of troops who had fallen clutching their throats on the Western Front.

British military experts began to revise their thinking on the kind of war that their country would face. Bombs from massive fleets of planes would probably fall on Britain in an attack that would last for 60 days. Most of the bombs would land in the densely populated areas, killing some 600,000 people. Many of these estimates were based on news that was arriving from

Spain. The Civil War was taking a tremendous toll of civilian casualties as Franco stepped up his revolt against the Spanish Republic. Britain and France stayed out of the conflict, leaving the Fascist and Nazi movements the perfect location for testing out their weapons in support of Franco. Although reports of the bombing raids on Barcelona and other Spanish cities were vastly exaggerated, the alarm was understandable as Europe edged closer and closer to war.

The abbreviation of the words 'air-raid precautions' – ARP – became commonplace as both paid workers and part-time volunteers stepped forward to learn what should he done in the event of an air raid. Many people were unconvinced that a war was on its way, and thought that the members of any auxiliary service were wasting their time. A reserve fireman recalled the time his team was sent to the local golf club to put out an imaginary fire, only to be told by the members, 'Go and play somewhere else.' Even those attending anti-gas instruction found themselves the brunt of unkind remarks. One woman remembered that after taking one such class she was told by several friends, 'It's people like you who make wars.'

The House of Commons did not share this opinion, and on 27 May 1938 held their

47

first Committee on Evacuation meeting. The subject of panic dominated the meeting. Sir John Anderson suggested that they study foreign plans, such as those of the French, who he understood were preparing a scheme for the evacuation of Paris. Intelligence Branch notes reported that the attitude in Germany was generally opposed to evacuation, since the Government there felt that the effects of air-raid attacks on civilian populations were being overestimated. Before adjourning the meeting, the committee agreed that all its discussions should be kept confidential.

By the time the third meeting was held, on 21 July 1938, it appeared that war was inevitable. Following the successful annexation of Austria, Hitler had now turned his sights towards Czechoslovakia. The plans of the Committee on Evacuation took on a new sense of urgency. Danger zones were designated within London's Metropolitan Police District. These were split into three areas: one that was to be evacuated if possible; one where movement was to be restricted; and an outer ring for hospital patients. Astonishing as it may seem, it was decided that it would be possible to clear three to four million people out of the city, with Government help, in 72 hours. This plan relied entirely on rail transport and rested on the Government's giving the word to proceed when tension set in. In the committee's opinion, if the beginning was held over until bombs were falling, then all plans would become disorganized. Sir John saw the Government's role as one of giving 'guidance which would enable public-spirited persons to decide whether they should go or stay'. This brought up the subject of civilians' leaving an area of their own accord. All agreed that it would be impossible to prevent this but that the Government should exercise a degree of control over any movement of the population.

On 13 March 1938 Hitler entered Vienna and Austria fell. Within hours the Home Secretary, Sir Samuel Hoare, was appealing for 'at least a million men and women for work that in an emergency would be exciting and dangerous'. Less than half the number of people he needed showed up. It was decided that a woman's touch was needed. Lady Reading, Chairwoman of the newly formed Women's Voluntary Service, called upon women 'in every sphere of life ... to prepare patiently and thoroughly ... a protection ... for our loved ones and our homes'. Although this appeal met with more success than that of Sir Samuel Hoare, the response was disappointing.

Undaunted, the Government decided to mount a massive recruiting drive warning people of the dangers that lay ahead – but

Hitler saved them the bother. His actions in September made it quite obvious that he was obsessed with the idea of gobbling up Czechoslovakia. Churchill wrote to von Kleist, an emissary of the German General Staff, saying that Britain would fight rather than allow this to happen. He was wrong. On 15 September the Prime Minister, Neville Chamberlain, took his first flight and headed for Berchtesgaden to meet Hitler. The German leader assured Chamberlain that he did not wish to include the Czechs inside the German Reich. In a show of gratitude Chamberlain answered that he was not opposed to the separation of the Sudetenland from Czechoslovakia. On 18 September the Prime Minister of France flew to London and, after some resistance, agreed to an Anglo-French plan. Both countries then set about telling the Czechs what a good idea it would be to give up some of their land to Hitler. Chamberlain was so convinced that the Czechs would go along with this that on 22 September he headed back to Germany for another meeting with Hitler. Once again he arrived back in England with 'good news'. Hitler had no intention of taking over the rest of Czechoslovakia once he had annexed the Sudetenland and he, Chamberlain, was 'satisfied that Hitler was speaking the truth'. He added with some pride that he felt he had established 'some degree of personal influence over Herr Hitler' and was satisfied that the Führer would not go back on his word.

On 28 September the Prime Minister sent a telegram to Hitler asking for one more meeting, and then set off for the House of Commons. Almost 70 years of age, the straight-backed, wing-collared politician rose to face the House. As he was speaking, a note was handed to him. He read it, smiled and told the packed House that it was a reply from Hitler agreeing to his request for a further meeting. He announced that he would fly to Germany immediately, as an excited and appreciative audience rose to their feet. Even Churchill shook his hand and wished him Godspeed.

As the Prime Minister prepared for his flight, the British Government put pressure on the Czechs to accept the transfer of part of their country. President Beneš was forced to comply. On the following morning, Chamberlain arrived in Munich and gave Hitler the good news. As the British, French, German and Italian delegates set to work on planning the final details of the transfer of Czech territory they delivered the final degrading insult. Waiting outside were the Czech representatives. Only after the agreement had been signed were the doors opened for them to enter and be told their nation's fate.

Word of the agreement – the Munich Pact – hit the streets of London as newsboys rushed to tell a relieved country that war had been averted. Restaurants and pubs rang with the sounds of celebrating crowds. Leaving a hotel, Winston Churchill passed an open door leading to a dining-room packed with merrymakers. As he turned away he muttered to himself, 'Those poor people! Little do they know what they will have to face.'

The following afternoon, a jubilant Chamberlain arrived back in England to face a huge crowd at the airport. As he stepped from the plane he lifted an arm to wave the piece of paper he was carrying. 'I've got it!' he cried and then headed for Downing Street to be greeted by more cheering crowds. There, from an open window, he delivered words that were to haunt him for the rest of his life: 'This is the second time that there has come back from Germany to Downing Street peace with honour. I believe it is peace for our time.'

In a Foreign Office building nearby, a small group stood by the window in silence, looking down at the cheering crowds outside. One, Orme Sargent, spoke for them all as he muttered, 'One would have thought we were celebrating victory over a great enemy, rather than the betrayal of a minor ally.' He was not alone in his thinking. A short distance away, Clementine Churchill was suggesting to her husband that she be allowed to march to Downing Street and throw a brick through the window of number 10. Duff Cooper, a member of Chamberlain's Cabinet, signified his disgust by marching into the Prime Minister's office and handing in his resignation. His wife phoned Churchill to tell him the news. As he listened, his eyes filled with tears and he began to cry.

In fairness it should be said that those opposed to Chamberlain's actions were in the minority. Most of the press supported the Munich agreement, feeling that peace was certainly more attractive than war. Britain's dominions breathed a sigh of relief, since the agreement had released them from the necessity of making an embarrassing admission. Many of them had decided that in the event of war they would opt for neutrality, and even Australia and New Zealand, the closest of the family unit, would have entered only with the greatest reluctance.

Many have contended that the period of grace leading up to the war was the result of a deliberate delaying tactic planned to give Britain the opportunity to prepare for war. In my view this was not the case. Any increases in production, like the plans for evacuation, were the result of plans laid years before. Factories that in 1936 were turning out aircraft at a rate of 240 a month had, by the outbreak of war, increased their output to 660 a month.

Plans for the great ARP drive went ahead, with posters and leaflets appearing everywhere. A booklet entitled *The Protection of Your Home against Air Raids* urged the man of the house to take on the role of 'captain of the ship' and to conduct air-raid drills as he would a lifeboat drill on a ship. Other leaflets hitting the doormats were *Your Gas-Mask* and *Masking Your Windows*. Although millions of gas-masks had been distributed, as yet there were none for babies or small children. The BBC began to broadcast the sound of a siren for those who lived in an area without one.

As for the plans for evacuation, the Munich Pact did little to alter these, other than to emphasize how vital it was to be prepared. Some of the London schools needed little persuading. Lists of articles to be packed, including blankets, were given out to the pupils – though it is difficult to imagine how the students were expected to carry the suggested amount of supplies if they were forced to evacuate.

Those schools that did rehearse certainly did a thorough job. Edna Harding (now Jordan), who had just been appointed

Assistant Mistress to the Brondesbury and Kilburn High School in London, remembers how everyone was taught the correct way to cross the road when the time came:

We practised crossing the road by what I think was called the 'wave method'. A long crocodile of girls would be walking along the road, with the PE teacher in charge; at the first whistle they would halt, at a second whistle turn left, at the third walk across the road... In this way the minimum amount of time was spent on the carriageway as the thickness only consisted of two girls although we used up a great length of carriageway.

As many schools rehearsed for the evacuation, others found it was the real thing. For reasons known only to the Government, it was decided to send some schools to the countryside. Maybe this action was valuable for solving problems that would be faced on the day of the eventual mass evacuation. It certainly seemed that way to Sylvia Boughey (now Challinor). She lived in Essex and was a pupil at a tiny private school run by a couple of 'dear old souls'. Mere practice was not good enough, and before there was time to sneeze the pupils found themselves on a bus heading for Somerset – only to find that they were not expected:

We rode around in the coach for hours, and in the end it was decided that we would have to spend the night in the coach. I was 10 years old at the time and away from my family for the first time, none of my own immediate class had come away and I felt lonely and frightened. I recall one of the older prefects cradling me on her lap all night. The next night we were taken to a large, very deserted rectory in the middle of nowhere. There was little or no running water, we slept on our mattresses on filthy floors, food was very sparse and there were rat droppings everywhere. The whole thing was a nightmare.

Sylvia still has the postcards that she gave to a senior girl to post, written to tell her mother where she was. Eventually the children arrived back at their school, where their parents were waiting to pick them up. Sylvia was so exhausted, filthy and hungry that her father decided that when the time came to evacuate, 'come what may the family would all stay together'.

For teachers involved in these exercises it was even more difficult. And for someone like Laurie Lawler, who had decided to enter the teaching profession but had yet to experience the company of large numbers of children, it must have been devastating. He had registered for a four-year degree, but before he had even had time to start he found himself at Marylebone Station 'with literally thousands of children getting in special trains to go out to the West of London'. His mother was a schoolteacher and he had agreed to help her by taking a group of five-year-olds. After boarding the train he was astonished to find that there was no corridor:

Each of the children, apart from their pathetic bundles, had a large carrier-bag and in that was their iron rations. They included a tin of bully beef and a tin of pears. We were in the carriage for four and a half hours during which time the kids all ate their pears and were sick. I spent the four and a half hours with the window open (the train was jerking along very slowly) holding them out of the window one after the other, and the outside of the train was unspeakable.

It was a lovely day when we got to Thame and we all hauled ourselves up on to the road at the top. There was nowhere to sit except on the grass, so while the children sat on the grass, we, the teachers, walked up and down saying, 'What do we do now?'

An officious man, a sort of squire character, came along with a clipboard and said, 'Ah, now. I need a nice little family for a nice little house. About two or three.' So my mother said, 'Well, these are very nice children.' So he said, 'Right, off we go,' and he went off and for the next half-hour there was no sign of him and we had 200 children sitting there.

Then one of the women from one of the cottages nearby came out and went over to my mother and said, 'Would you like a cup of tea, dear?' My mother said of course and she came back with a tray of tea for the staff. The kids were given some water, I think, to drink and the woman said, 'You know, I could have put two of the children up but I didn't volunteer.' So my mother said, 'Oh would you take two? These are lovely kids.' So I found myself walking to one of the cottages with two of the children, and as we walked down the street, the woman said to one of her neighbours, 'Oh come on, Mrs Brown, you've got room in your front room for three of them.' Soon the women started coming out to my mother, who quickly got out her notebook and began writing down their names and addresses and handing them over families, and by the time the old squire chap came back nearly all of the children were billeted. Well, he just went off his rocker. He was furious. He wanted to get them all out again and my mother said, 'Now look here, dear, you can't do it tonight, it's now six o'clock. The children are dog tired. Leave it to tomorrow morning and sort it out.' Of course it never was sorted out. They remained with the families my mother put them with.

The New Year began with local authorities in the reception areas sending out volunteers to find out who had room to accommodate evacuees and who did not. Unlike those being encouraged to leave the danger areas, those on the receiving end had no choice.

The volunteers went from door to door and reported back that there was 'surplus accommodation' for 4,800,000 people. It appeared to be more than enough. Although at the time of the Munich Pact more than 80 per cent of London parents had said they wanted their children evacuated, now, just a few months later, only one-third of the mothers with children under the age of five were sufficiently concerned about their safety to want to send them away. Since their Prime Minister had declared that there would be 'peace in our time', what was the point?

Unfortunately, as Britain leaned back to enjoy the future, Hitler began slowly to tear the 'peace' pact into tiny pieces. Although he had agreed that Munich was the final settlement and that he, Germany's leader, wanted nothing more than the Czechoslovakian territory he had been given, he spent the night of 15 March in the palace in Prague and calmly declared that the rest of Czechoslovakia would henceforth enjoy the fruits of his occupation.

'Peace in our time' was rapidly becoming 'war in our time' as British civilians flocked to join the Territorial Army. In April, for the first time in British history, military conscription was announced.

In the November following the Munich meeting, Sir John Anderson had been brought into the Cabinet as Lord Privy Seal and put in charge of the ARP. The magnitude of the problem facing any committee meeting to discuss the safety of civilians in the event of air raids had increased with time. Experts had now updated their figures, and these were so disturbing that many MPs could only throw their arms up in alarm.

Estimates were thrown about with abandon. One estimate predicted that 100,000 tons of bombs would be dropped on London in the first 14 days, a figure that exceeded the total quantity of explosives that were in fact dropped on London throughout the war.

Even more frightening was the estimate that each ton of explosives would result in 50 casualties. Most experts took the attack on the Spanish town of Guernica as an example of what could happen, ignoring the fact that in that instance the bombers had attacked a defenceless village on a crowded market-day. But for Sir John and the ARP group, the figures only emphasized the urgent need for preparation.

Expenditure allocated to the ARP increased from £9,500,000 a year before Munich to £51,000,000 one year later. First it was agreed that all those who did not need to stay in the cities would be moved out and the country divided into three areas: evacuation, neutral and reception. All schoolchildren and mothers with children under the age of five would be moved from the cities believed to be most prone to attack and billeted in private homes in the reception areas. Trains would be used to transport them, and food would be provided for the journey. It was amazing how little had changed since the meetings held in 1924-25. Panic was still uppermost in the minds of everyone in the group, and at one point the thought of panic-stricken civilians running amok led them to discuss the possibility of using troops to control the mobs.

As the eyes of the German leaders began to wander towards Poland, Britain declared that it had run out of patience and would side with the Eastern country in the event of a German attack. The news that Britain had finally decided to take a stand against Hitler was greeted with more cheers for Chamberlain. The British lion had turned its head and was ready to bite whoever stood on its tail.

However, most Government officials felt that tough as Britain might be, it was going to need help. Hands were held out to Russia, and prolonged negotiations began in April, reaching a deadlock one month later. A second stage of talks, which ran from May to

July, also failed. Halfway through it was suggested that both sides switch to military talks, in the hope that indirect aggression would settle itself. The final talks were military and took place from 12 to 21 August. Midway through these talks Voroshilov, the Soviet leader, suddenly suggested that the Russian Army move across northern Poland in order to face Germany on her border. This suggestion was immediately rejected by the Poles, who had no wish to follow the Czechs in sacrificing part of their territory. The French thought otherwise. It was not, after all, French territory that was being discussed, and they appeared to be quite ready to allow Russia to occupy part of Poland, with or without the permission of the Polish Government.

The meetings finally ended on 21 August, with the statement from all that they had nothing to say Two days later von Ribbentrop, the German Foreign Minister, was invited to Moscow. On 23 August 1939 Germany and Russia signed the Nazi-Soviet pact. The BBC announcer Stuart Hibberd, who read the news to a shocked nation, probably summed it up best when he described it in his diary as 'a bombshell'.

Many travelling abroad saw the hotels emptying as volunteers hurried to answer the call to arms. Visitors to Holland became part of the crowds reading call-up notices on the walls of local town halls. Ferry-boats crossing the English Channel groaned under the shoulder-to-shoulder crowds returning from the Continent. L.A.M. Brech was a teacher who, together with her husband, had decided to take a holiday in Switzerland. They were in Geneva, a town full of students, many of whom were German:

They came in one day and were absolutely mad with joy and one of them called out to me and said, 'You can't do anything now. Russia is our ally,' and I just couldn't believe it. Someone might just as well have said to me that the devil and the Lord himself had formed an alliance. But it was true and I had the shock of my life when the British consul told me to pack up and get home quickly as I was to report for duty at the school on Monday.

L.A.M. Brech and her husband were not the only ones being advised to return. Telegrams recalling employees from their holidays were rushed around the country as companies prepared to move. The BBC made plans to establish its main centre in a country house in Worcester. The National Gallery hunted out a cave in a disused quarry in North Wales to store its treasures, while the Bank of England decided on the village of Overton in Hampshire as its new home.

For the first time in history MPs, along with tens of thousands of schoolteachers, all enjoying one of the hottest and driest summers for years, were called back by radio. Many of them were prepared for what was to follow, since the previous June had seen one of the largest civil-defence exercises ever, during which 5,000 children had been moved from 20 schools in the London area to the nearest railway station as part of a mass-evacuation practice run.

Many, feeling war was imminent, began to leave for areas of safety. The roads from the wealthier areas of London were crowded with streams of cars, piled high with luggage, hurrying to leave the city before the sound of the first air-raid siren.

By 26 August the exodus was under way. Two special trains carried 800 bank clerks and typists from London to their new offices in Stoke-on-Trent. The Prudential Assurance Company sent 450 employees to hotels in Torquay. Almost 2,000,000 people evacuated themselves to the countryside. Others felt that to be in the country at all was a mistake, and some 5,000 who could afford the trip set out for North America in a single 48-hour period. But for the majority it was the British countryside that would provide shelter – and the Government was willing to pay for it. All that was needed was a means of transport.

But how was such an incredible undertaking to be pulled off successfully? It had never been done before. There were no previous similar undertakings to study and benefit from. For Alan Stollery, who in August 1939 was a 23-year-old traffic trainee, it must have seemed that an impossible task had been dropped into his lap. While he was learning about express coach services out of Victoria Coach Station, he was recruited and sent off to Norfolk to make the travel arrangements for 16,000 children who were being transported from London to Norfolk over a four-day period:

I was provided with a list of train arrivals. Each train carried some 1,000 children and attendants. Taking as an example one train, the thousand or so children were to be dispersed to various villages throughout Norfolk, the actual number being taken to each village indicated. My job was to assess the number of coaches required to meet each train, then to check the receiving villages to which each coach should be routed. The task was not as simple as it may sound. Coaches in those days were of a smaller seating capacity than now, say an average of 35 seats. So for a train carrying 1,000 children, probably a minimum of 30 coaches was needed. This was the easy part. For each train there were probably 100 or more villages, each to receive a differing number of children.

Imagine perhaps 14 villages receiving in all about 150 children, the villages covering an area in the order of 20 square miles. I would probably assess four coaches and then I had to decide how best each of the four coaches would be routed whilst taking account of their seating capacity. I could not overload, whilst the converse, under-loading – if done consistently – would obviously lead to more coaches being required, more drivers needed, more fuel used etc.

Alan Stollery sat down to tackle his task on the afternoon of 31 August. He had until the next morning to come up with a complete operational plan. By that time the first trains packed with children would be leaving London:

I clearly remember filling in the last details somewhere between 3 a.m. and 4 a.m. on the morning of the first.

It was difficult to believe that a war was fast approaching, but the reminders were everywhere. The summer was a glorious one, and most of those living in the cities and able to afford it had found their way to the coast for a brief holiday.

Jean McIntosh (now Thompson) was 15 years of age in 1939 and lived in Leeds. Along with her parents, she stood on the Yorkshire coast and watched the sandbags

66

being placed around a local barracks:

I think it was on Wednesday 30 August that after hearing reports on the radio that children were to be evacuated, my parents decided to go home from holiday. The railway journey was unusual. Crowded carriages full of servicemen, dimmed blue lights – a long weary journey. Upon arrival home we found the letters from the school telling us to go there, packed and ready for evacuation. My mother must have stayed up all night washing and preparing my clothes.

Jean's father had been a Gordon Highlander in the First World War. He had a disabled left hand and dreadful memories of the war, and was determined to safeguard his children if another war began. Most other parents felt the same and were anxious to follow whatever orders the Government issued. Teachers were by now hurrying home to their schools to await further instructions. Since most of the time was taken up with packing and preparing to leave it seemed pointless to attempt any actual schooling.

Joan Murton (née Coleman) remembers:

…we just went to school every day and used to play snap.

Leslie Staples found that what he got in

place of learning was plenty of exercise:

Each day at school prior to our evacuation we walked round and round the playground in twos, armed with our little gas-masks in cardboard boxes, and each carrying a small case or bag. This was to get us used to walking along together, unless they intended us to walk to the countryside.

Some children found the war a useful excuse for missing out on regular appointments that they preferred to miss. Vera Tarn (now Bennett)'s mother used to take her for regular visits to a clinic:

I remember hoping that war would be declared so that I wouldn't have to go to get my teeth cleaned.

The radio constantly gave out the information that the time of the planned evacuation was near and that parents should be ready to send their children away the moment the school sent them home with their instructions. Many relied instead on the rumours that were passed around. Lilian Blewett (now Williams) heard the whispers and ignored them. She had a much more reliable means of knowing what was about to happen:

...my hat and coat and my brother's suit came out of the pawn shop and we knew something was up.

PART TWO

Time to Go

3

The Roots are Pulled

The children of Stowey House School were ready to move from the grounds to the street outside. Name-tags had been checked against bodies, and gas-mask boxes had been opened to see that the masks themselves were inside. The shouting and pushing by the teachers had finally established a semblance of order that would guarantee that the same number leaving the school would eventually arrive at the railway station. Ready at last, the three ranks left through an exit wide enough for one rank and tumbled on to the pavement in an even more disorganized group than had begun inside. Pulling of sleeves and grabbing of collars slotted the army of 300 back into position and, with a wave of the arm from the headmaster, the gallant troop moved off in the direction of the railway station, a 20-minute walk through dozens of puddles left after a steady evening's rain the night before. Dozens of parents trailed behind, making the most of the last minutes before the final goodbye.

As they wound their way through the narrow streets and out into the main thoroughfare, buses and cars packed with evacuees needing transport jostled for position. Posters screamed from the walls that the black-out was now in force and that by sunset, 7.47 p.m. British Summer Time, the slightest chink of light squeezing itself around a curtain would be the signal for a harsh warning cry from a patrolling warden.

For the children of Stowey House School these were posters that could be ignored. By sunset they would be miles away, lying in strange beds, thinking with teary eyes of the sooty homes they had left behind.

For most of the Stowey House group there was a feeling of safety in numbers as they giggled and laughed their way towards the station. It was all a great game and they'd soon be back home again after a free trip to a countryside that most of them had never seen. For me it was not the first time out of the city. Hop-picking in Kent had prepared me for grass and trees – though this time would be different, with no mother to rub a bruised knee and kiss it better.

As they passed through the iron gates and walked up the long hill, the Stowey House group joined those from other schools making their way to the same station, which seemed to have lifted above its roof a giant magnet that was slowly sweeping the area clean of children. Many without parents to see them off struggled to keep up as their tiny bundles of belongings scraped the dusty ground behind them.

This group was just one of hundreds that set out that September morning. Estimates would later register incredible figures. From the end of June to the morning of their march more than 3,500,000 people had moved from the areas that were felt most likely to be the targets of German bombs.

Before the month of September was over, an incredible quarter of the population had changed their address, including 825,000 schoolchildren, 624,000 mothers with children under school age, 13,000 expectant mothers, 7,000 blind people and 113,000 schoolteachers. The figures were mind-boggling.

The war was yet to start, and the strange spectacle of thousands of children leaving the unscathed cities for areas of safety made a deep impression on those who took part. Escort and teacher L. A. M. Brech was struck by the silence:

All you could hear was the feet of the children and a kind of murmur because the children were too afraid to talk. We had a big banner with our number in front. Ours was an 'H' something. Mothers weren't allowed with us but they came along behind. When we got to the station we

knew which platform to go to, the train was
ready, we hadn't the slightest idea where we were
going and we put the children on the train and
the gates closed behind us. The mothers pressed
against the iron gates calling, 'Goodbye darling.'

I never see those gates at Waterloo that I don't
get a lump in my throat.

If the memories bring a lump to the throat
today, at the time of the happening most
parents were unable to hold back the tears.
Alan Burrell, who was then about seven,
recalls:

I thought it was a Sunday-school outing down to
the seaside, sort of thing. And I looked out of the
bus window and I saw my mother crying outside
and I said to my brother, 'What's Mummy
crying for?' and my brother said, 'Shut up!'

Elizabeth Amy Ashley, now a jazz singer in
clubs around London, went to the station
and then came back again. It had turned out
to be a practice run. The next day it happened again. Her sister was crying, but she
herself thought it was a great adventure:

I turned to my sister and said, 'For goodness
sake, this is fun.' My mum had a shop opposite
the school and I ran over and said, 'Cheerio,
Mum, we're off.' She was crying her eyes out
and I couldn't make it out.

Alan Burrell thought he was being taken for a pleasure trip down the coast:

I couldn't understand it. I was full of beans and I thought this is marvellous, it's a lovely day out.

Gladys Crimmins (now Long) was four and her sister six. She was well prepared for any emergency:

I being the youngest led the line and carried a potty for use on the coaches.

Some mothers found it impossible to control their feelings. Their children were leaving for heaven only knew where to live with complete strangers. Little wonder that many parents changed their minds at the last minute. Betty Worley (now Window), aged nine, watched as a large bus stopped in their slum street:

Word went around the street (you know what little slum streets are like with little houses) that the children were being evacuated and all the mothers ran up to the school in their aprons and overalls. I recall already sitting on this bus with my two sisters and my mother screaming, 'Let Maureen off. Let my baby off. She's too young, she's too young,' and they said, 'It's too late now, it's too late now,' and I can see her running behind the bus screaming, 'Betty, don't let them go, don't let them be billeted with anyone else, you've got to look after them, you've got to have them.'

Betty's sister Maureen was only four and a half years old.

There were 10 children in Joan Postchild's family. All of them were evacuated with the exception of one sister, who was in hospital at the time and was left behind:

We lived in the East End. The coach we were to go on arrived at the local pub. I can see now all the children with their tags and the black boxes on their shoulders. Life was very poor. All our bits of clothing were in carrier-bags or paper parcels. We were told we were going to the country. Most of us had never had a ride in a vehicle before let alone been to the country.

My sister was in charge of us and she was told by my mother that we shouldn't be separated, if possible we were to be billeted together.

I couldn't understand why my mother stood outside the coach wiping her eyes with the end of her pinafore. I can see her now trying to make out she wasn't crying.

Dennis Galvin remembers the instruction he received the night before he left:

'Wash behind your ear-hole, you're off tomorrow.'

Gerald Moss wasn't sure when he was going:

We went to school every day with sandwiches, gas-masks and great big labels. And every day we came back from school again. We didn't know which day we were being evacuated. So when I went out to the toilet at the school I saw all these buses out on the street. So I knew that was going to be the day.

Nora Hogan (now Green)'s father had died in August 1937. There were five children in the family, ranging in age from nine to two. The evacuation was clearly going to be a great wrench for her mother:

I was seven at the time. My mother decided that we wouldn't be evacuated and suddenly on Saturday morning she changed her mind. I had been to the library and got myself a book and when I came home my mother said, 'You better put that book away because we are going to the station.'

For Kenneth Twine the leaving date could not have been worse:

My father's funeral was the same day that my

three sisters, my brother and I were evacuated. We all looked out of the bedroom window and watched the funeral cars depart, then we gathered up our bundles and went to our school.

It was bad enough that the destination was a secret. It was even worse if you thought the destination was a place you badly wanted to go to and then found out too late that you had made a mistake. Teresa Day was sure it would be somewhere nice:

When we left we thought we were going to Switzerland because someone mentioned Swindon and I took my bucket and spade.

She was not the only one to be mistaken that day. Beryl Heard (now Chew), aged 10, had been told the day when she would be leaving. The day came and went:

Then we were given another date, on which we never left London. My mother was fed up with packing and unpacking so when we were told to be ready on the third date given, Mum put a few clothes in a case. To her horror we were evacuated without half our belongings.

Doris Roker (now Ward), a 13-year-old evacuee, had marched along Hammersmith Road in London to the nearest underground station. Her friends and family were waving her off and everything was going fine – lots of smiles and no signs of sadness:

My mother told me many years later that immediately following our procession came the orphans from Nazareth House, shepherded by the nuns. This was the final straw for the mums – they just burst into tears.

It was just as sad for the fathers who witnessed the children's departure. In line with the traditional 'macho' male image, most fathers had always hidden any signs of weakness from their children. For them this day proved to be the most difficult of all. Jeanne Outred, who remembers it as the saddest day of her life, recalls:

I saw my father cry for the first time.

David Girr's father simply disappeared:

He suddenly vanished, he left us in the middle of the school yard. He couldn't bear to be in the hall of the school with us, so he just walked away so he wouldn't break down and cry in front of us.

For other children there were lots of last-minute instructions. Those with sisters and brothers were told that whatever happened they must stay together. Evelyn Rance (now

Game)'s mother gave her a little purse with sixpence in it, and then said:

'Don't lose your purse and don't look out of the train window. You'll get your head sliced off.'

In many cases the parents' pain at their children's leaving was compounded by their embarrassment at being unable to supply the clothes requested in a school list. Although these lists were sent home with the children weeks before the actual leaving date, it made little difference since the circumstances of some of the families hardly allowed them money to throw around the neighbourhood in a giant one-time spending spree. Some mothers, like the mother of Iris Bridges (now Collins), attempted to make the necessary garments themselves:

About a month before we finally set out we were given a list of clothing that we had to have. Well we were a very poor family and I can remember my mum sitting up all night sewing by hand my topcoat that I had to have. Well this was finished the night before I went.

There were, of course, other problems, not the least of which was to prepare the young girls, many of whom were about to experience their first menstrual period. Talks on this subject were given at some of the schools, and as the day of the mass evacuation drew nearer, the lessons on how the girls should conduct themselves were stepped up. Jean Hewitt (now Emmins) had several talks about what to take:

We were allowed one small suitcase. Sometimes we had a dummy run, taking our cases to school and having the contents vetted. I suppose some children might have packed a large teddy at the expense of night-clothes or undergarments.

The senior female teacher, who prided herself on being practical and down to earth, noticed that none of the girls had packed sanitary towels and asked what we intended to do about this. We said that naturally we'd buy the necessities from the local shops when required, and were informed that as our destination was unknown, it would be more likely that we would not have easy access to shops, so we had to find room in our cases for at least one dozen bulky terry towels.

Joan Chapman (now Harper), whose whole family was being evacuated, sorted out what she could squeeze into one small suitcase, and her thoughts turned to those she would be leaving behind:

Smut the cat, Joey the canary and a large tortoise we had had for 16 years ... what were we to do with them? There was only one thing left and that was to have them put to sleep.

I bravely put Smut into a box, the tortoise in a bag on my back and the cage in the other hand. I walked along the Hastings seafront to a vet's. I can tell you how much I hated Hitler.

Putting my sad cargo down to have a rest and have a cry, I was aware of a soldier staring at me. He asked what was wrong and when I told him he offered to help.

Only the tortoise never did get to the vet's – instead we put him into the local park flower beds. But sadly we joined a long queue at the vet's. People were all forced to do the same. Sorrowfully we walked back empty-handed.

Years later, Joan met the soldier again, and married him.

The plan for evacuation had itself long been kept secret, and one aspect of the secrecy was that no one should know where the children were going. John Aitchison felt that 'the planning of the evacuation was kept strictly secret to stop the Germans guessing where the children were going'. He was evacuated with the Kelvin Grove Boys' Senior School, a school run by a remarkable headmaster who seems to have been extremely efficient and determined that the children keep a 'stiff upper lip':

A list of basic clothing had been issued, haversacks sold at a shilling, envelopes had been stamped and home-addressed and rehearsals of the yard assembly held.

Mr Rollo, the headmaster, had instructed us to answer 'Are we downhearted?' with a resounding 'NO!' The fateful Friday arrived and we assembled in the school hall in a state of wild excitement for the great adventure, complete with haversacks, gas-masks and our sandwiches. We were issued with several tins of emergency rations and packets of biscuits to give to our hosts.

We formed into marching groups in the school yard, our gas-masks were again inspected and after the 'Are we downhearted?' question and the answer 'NO!' we were off.

One of the most important concerns was that the children should not get lost. It was decided that the simplest way of ensuring this was to tag each child, and although this may have given the appearance that the evacuees were being treated like parcels, it worked. The labels certainly made an impression on Beryl Coleman, and they are mentioned in a poem written at the time by her and a schoolfriend, Gabrielle Ray, entitled 'Evacuation':

> *What excitement, what a scurry,*
> *Tying labels in a hurry,*
> *Mother shouting from the stairs,*
> *'Have you got your socks in pairs?'*

85

Haversacks full to the brim,
Clothes all folded neat and trim,
Round each neck is tied a label,
To tell who's 'Joan' and who is 'Mabel'.

Lilian and her sister Rosemary watched as teachers came along the rows of children pinning the labels to them:

After the register was called we marched in twos to Cosham station and on to the waiting train which was to take us to Salisbury. There were crowds of mothers waiting to wave. I looked, searching for a glimpse of our mum and first saw her as we hurried into the carriages. I was bewildered. I felt empty and Mum's last words rang in my ears. 'Write soon and look after Rosemary.' Who's going to look after me, I thought.

Another item stands out in the memories of the ex-evacuees as a close runner-up to the label – the gas-mask, hung by a string around the neck of each evacuee. The children would never forget the feel of the small cardboard box bouncing against their legs as they struggled along the road with their belongings. Within days everyone would be carrying a gas-mask – farmers in the fields, workers heading for the factories, people on crowded trains – the boxes were everywhere. Overnight Britain had prepared itself for a gas attack as no country in the world before.

There was no law that obliged people to carry a gas-mask, but many places of entertainment refused admittance to those without one. The *Oxford Mail* was quick to print a letter from a reader warning the owners of such places of a 'deception practised by some patrons. In many cases people, especially those from the country, used their gas-masks to carry some of the articles they had collected in their shopping expeditions,' said the letter-writer.

Many had difficulty fitting the mask. First the chin was placed inside the rubber, and then the mask pulled over the face. It was an uncomfortable article to wear, though a story in the *Evening News* did suggest that one woman had found the answer: 'I found that by removing the glass the mask fitted much better and was much more comfortable.' She was reprimanded by a warden for taking the eyepieces out of her gas-mask.

Everyone – with the exception of children under five – had a gas-mask. This added up to an incredible 44,000,000 pieces of rubber with eyepieces, and for the first time in history the British population was ready to enter a war armed with an article of personal defence equipment.

As for babies, their war issue was still in the planning stages and the respirator known as the 'Mickey Mouse', for infants of two to four and a half years, had not yet been introduced. Aware that special arrangements had to be made for the protection of this age-group, the Government began working on a version of the gas-mask that would appeal to younger children. With large ears attached and painted red and blue, it did look like the famous Disney character and was a big hit with most of the young. In fact this kind of gas-mask became so popular that even those too old at the time to have been issued with one look back fondly on the small cardboard-box type of mask and speak erroneously of their 'Mickey Mouse'. Jean Carberry (née Birch) remembers that a man came to their house with gas-masks for all the family:

We all had the standard black ones except my little sister. She had a red one with a red nose on it that flapped up and down. The one my baby brother was issued with was something like a cradle with a window on top. When Mum put him in it he screamed and kicked up such a fuss, so Mum said, 'That's it! If we're going to die we'll all die together.' She then threw the gas-masks away.

The gas-mask box was not exactly a fashion-show item. However, the cheap cardboard box, complete with a piece of string for carrying, did its job, and for those who felt the need to decorate the outside there were many ways of doing so. Stores did a brisk business in outer covers, or, if you wished, you could make your own. One evacuee had a carrier with a red velvet lining and a zip pocket for ear-plugs:

I was told to memorize my identity number, NZKN 1384, and [remember] being told not to speak to strangers, unlike today, for no other reason than they may have been German spies asking directions, because of course all signposts had been removed.

The gas-mask itself was not comfortable to wear. Mae Collinson (née Walmsley) mentions it in a PS to her letter:

I almost forgot to mention the dreadful gas-mask we were made to carry everywhere. When made to practise wearing them we all felt as if we were being suffocated and the stench of rubber was overpowering.

William John Cambridge, now living in Australia, also remembers the gas-mask and the problems it caused:

We all hated putting on the gas-masks at school and many were taken off full of tears.

Patricia Ferman (née Silverman) has

forgotten everything about the preparations for the evacuation except the gas-mask practice that they had before they left:

...the awful choking sensation and sweating inside that rubber mask which had to be ripped off like one's own skin. Although I remember taking it on the train and being made aware that it was my most valuable possession, never to be out of sight, I don't recall ever using or seeing it again.

It was impossible to know how long the children would be travelling and how many meals would be missed. Many children were given small food packages by their parents, while others found that the schools in the reception areas had prepared food. Stella Single (now Isum) was given a carrier bag with iron rations to take to her landlady:

I can't remember what was in the bag except for the biscuits. Iron was right. We couldn't get our teeth into them and eventually the maid at one of the billets took them home to her dog, and he couldn't chew them either.

Some schools made their own arrangements. The headmaster of Sir Thomas Rich's Grammar School in Gloucester chose the last week of the summer holiday to send his prefects to the homes of senior boys to ask if they were willing to give up the remainder of their holiday to help with the expected influx of evacuees. Brian Wain was one of the recruits:

We soon discovered the roles to which we were to be assigned. Firstly we had to make up food parcels, one of which was to be given to each evacuee and secondly, escort the evacuees to their albeit temporary home.

There were only a few of us because most pupils lived on the outskirts of the city and were deemed to live too far away to be of direct use. Two masters were also in attendance as well as the headmaster and his secretary, a Miss Hale (disrespectfully known as 'Binnie'). The evacuees were coming from King Edward's Grammar School. Cardboard boxes were provided as was a mountain of various tinned foods and Cadbury's Dairy Milk chocolate. Each box was made under the watchful eye of the masters and contained something like corned beef, tinned fruit (pears, peaches, apricots), baked beans and half a pound of Cadbury's milk chocolate.

When Margaret Hunter (now MacDonald) left her house in Scotland she took her food with her:

We were all given a brown carrier-bag with one tin of corned beef, one tin of Carnation milk, one bar of plain milk chocolate and some biscuits …

there may have been more. In my case I don't remember ever getting any of the food to eat.

The various efforts being made to protect civilians against possible air attack were in evidence everywhere. Trenches were being dug in the parks, builders were reinforcing basements, brick surface shelters were going up on many streets and the Anderson shelter was making its appearance in many back gardens. Nearly 1,500,000 had been delivered to homes in the most threatened areas. But the construction of these shelters was far from easy. It involved the digging of foundations, the fixing of 14 or more steel sheets – weighing at least eight hundred-weight – and the protection of the sides and top with earth or sandbags. As a boy of nine, Alan Partington could not help but be excited at what was going on around him:

Manchester was all movement, air-raid shelters being built in our local streets, long brick and concrete things holding about 50 people in total, in two-tier wooden bunks. The very fortunate people at that time who had a garden had what was called an Anderson shelter built in the garden for them. This consisted of a square hole dug in the soil about four feet deep. This was then covered by sheets of curved corrugated iron. A small entrance was left at one end and the whole construction was then covered with soil and sods of earth.

The shelter was an unsightly monstrosity, sticking up as it did from the centre of tiny back gardens, and some people, such as Betty Williams's family, tried their best to do something about this:

The men dug as far as they could into the ground and after they had the iron in place they covered the shelter with earth...I remember we had a few plants growing over ours but on thinking about it we would not have had a chance if we had had a direct hit.

Direct hit or not there was no disputing the fact that in the fast-approaching war the cities were no place for children.

Many will find it hard to understand how parents could have allowed their children to be evacuated. Although there is little doubt that such an undertaking today would be met with overwhelming opposition, the horrifying pictures of bombing raids in China and Spain had both the population and the Government fearing the worst once war did arrive. The build-up in defences served only to emphasize the possibility of what many felt lay ahead. Yardly Jones, now one of Canada's leading political cartoonists, having emigrated to Edmonton after the war, remembers the concern of his mother. He never ever went into town with her, but the night before he was to be evacuated she felt so strongly about the dangers ahead that she made an exception:

We went down Wavertree Road and bought an enamel cup, a knife, fork and spoon from a list that we had. I guess we bought clothing as well, I don't remember, but I do know I was a little upset since I knew we weren't that well off and I knew my mother couldn't afford to go out and buy these things. I knew that I was going away for the evacuation but that seemed more of an adventure because we never had annual holidays. In fact I was more upset that night than I was next morning when it was time to leave.

The weather on the morning of Friday 1 September could not have been better. Led by 'markers' carrying boards with the name of the school and the reference number, the children made their way to the 72 transport stations involved. In retrospect it is hard to imagine how such a massive exercise was undertaken without dozens of mishaps. Over a four-day period 4,000 trains were used to transport more than 1,300,000 evacuees, yet not one casualty was reported. And it was not just trains that were being filled with children: London's famous red buses carried over 200,000 passengers to the railway stations or into the countryside.

Many of the drivers went without sleep in order to get the children to a place of safety.

The group from our school, Stowey House, eventually arrived at the railway station. The scene there was chaotic, as guards' whistles shrilled and escaping steam whirled above the heads of yelling teachers making their way through the swirling mass, struggling to reach those children who had already wandered from their designated lines. Parents dabbed at their eyes and re-assured laughing children that there was nothing to be unhappy about.

It was a scene being repeated throughout the country as major cities followed the instructions of the Government and began to empty their towns of children.

4

The Journey

It was not my first time on a train. A few years before the war my father had found regular work with wages that had given us the opportunity to take a trip to the cockney seaside resort of Southend, a short enough journey from London to make a day-excursion fare possible.

Stowey House School was lucky. The train we boarded was heading for the south of England, a three-hour journey over the Sussex Downs and on through the country to the coast. First one, then more tiny voices began to sing and, as the soot-covered buildings of London gave way to the green hills of England's countryside, chorus after chorus of 'Ten Green Bottles' could be heard throughout the train.

Other children were not as happy. Peggy Forster (now Kunzlik) had left her home in Newcastle and, along with the other children on her train, was already missing it:

After we'd been travelling for several hours, the train stopped for a considerable time. Rumours were rife. Nobody told us what was happening, but when the train started again in the direction from which we had just come, a loud cheer arose in the throat of every one of the children aboard and the noise must have resounded throughout the countryside. We thought we were going home. No such luck.

Many brothers and sisters found themselves together on the trains. All had been given strict instructions not to separate and the older ones various duties to perform. Doreen Outhwaite (now Davies), who was seven at the time, was evacuated with her elder sister, aged 11, and two brothers, aged

nine and five. Her mother had two other
children, both too young to leave:

*I remember my sister was told to make the sand-
wiches she gave us last until we got down to
Cornwall. It was a long journey there from West
Ham and I cried because we only had one
sandwich for dinner and my sister wouldn't give
us any more. We stopped somewhere en route
and had to queue to be given an injection. The
sun was very hot and I was terrified. After my
jab I fainted and to this day I still tend to pass
out after an injection.*

Christine Duggan (now Coutts) and her
two sisters stood at Central Station in Glasgow, crying bitterly, not knowing where they
were going and being packed on to the train
with no time to say goodbye:

*My little mind was really saying, 'Will I ever see
my parents again?'*

Pam Hobbs, now a travel writer with
Canada's national newspaper *The Globe and
Mail,* was nine years old at the outbreak of
the war. Her home was at Leigh-on-Sea, in
Essex. She had been off school for a year,
because of diphtheria followed by compli-
cations, so she was petrified when told she
had to report to her classroom. She had
none. She and her 11-year-old sister set off

for the station, each holding her clothes in a sandbag. Their father was a labourer and had been stacking sandbags on the sea-front:

My mother couldn't come to the school, she was too upset. My father came. We had never been close so it didn't seem too bad saying goodbye. I went to my sister's class and we were all put on the buses to Southend station. There we boarded trains. My sister and her friend immediately brought out lipstick and rouge. I was afraid we would be thought of as adults because of their make-up. I remember asking Lila, my sister's friend, why all the people were standing in their gardens waving to us, and she said, 'They feel sorry for us. Try to cry, to make it worth while.'

It was a strange coming-together of all types. Some children came from better-off families who could provide a few extras for the train journey, while others, like Tommy McSorley, were content with the little they did have and, like children everywhere, were anxious to get a good seat – one near the window if possible, for they were about to travel through a new world and the more they saw of it the better:

Except for any little bits and pieces of our personal knickknacks, usually tied in a hand-kerchief, most of us [were] with hardly a decent pair of boots. Certainly with no extra luggage. A great deal of the usual jostling amongst ourselves so as to be near the windows or next to our pals started. (In my case I managed to get a seat beside my mother so I was quite happy.)

As the train started moving forward there was a mighty roar from every compartment which could be heard for miles as the whole train was so full it was bursting at the seams. After about half an hour though, the whole train went dead quiet, for on looking out of the window everything had suddenly turned to green, and I was passing through some place called Stirling, a place I had only heard of in geography class, and though now I know it is only 30 miles away from Glasgow, then it was to me as if I were going into another country with as much mystery about it as there is today about Darkest Africa.

How much further? I thought, could it go before the train fell off the coast of Scotland into the sea, for even at this young age I knew Scotland ended at water's edge somewhere or other.

On and on we went, seemingly for ever, until at last after six long weary troublesome hours the train came to a halt. I don't know much about the journey past Stirling, for I think for the remainder of the journey I sat with my eyes tightly closed in fear, and it seemed every time I opened them I was surrounded by nothing but mountains and very strange animals I had never seen before. There were so many of these strange creatures I felt they would at any time gang together to attack the train and devour all the passengers. It was a good while later I discovered they were sheep.

June Evans (now Addison) was just six when she set off from London's St Pancras Station on 1 September. She was hungry and bored and missing home:

…then a miracle occurred. Mr Reid, our headmaster, asked the boy sitting opposite to move so that Miss Ireland could sit there. Miss Ireland my teacher was going to sit opposite me! To me she was the most beautiful person I had ever seen, with silver-blonde hair, lovely clothes and painted nails. I just gazed in wonderment.

Although in many cases the journey was a short one, to the children who had never ventured far from their homes it seemed that they were going to the ends of the earth. Margaret Scicluna (now Done) little realized that it would be many years before she would be home again and that her formative years would be spent growing up with someone else as a parent. The night before she had hardly slept for excitement and she had been unable to eat most of her breakfast. At the station she had clung to her best friend for fear that they would be split, and now she found herself in a compartment with most of her school chums:

The journey seemed to take for ever, it can't have done though, because as I found out later we were only about 85 miles from home. It's funny but I can remember that journey so well. We got tired of counting fields as we passed them – for many it was the first time they had seen fields. I was just a little more fortunate. I was once taken out into the country. I can remember though how we had to cross a viaduct, how frightened we all were in case the train should come off the rails and we would all fall into the water underneath. You should have heard the sighs of relief when we crossed safely.

Some of the trains' occupants were rougher than others. On 1 September Olly Burns travelled from Newcastle upon Tyne to Carlisle. He was nine, his brother Robert 11 and his sister Marjorie 13:

We were packed aboard a train with no corridors and no adults. Various fights broke out but soon my brother, nicknamed 'Bonzo', who was a bit of a tough nut, was in charge. On the journey to Carlisle there was lots of singing and the boys peed out of the window.

Monica Buckley (née Dray) recalls:

I was seven years old and, prior to the declaration of war, had constantly asked my mother to buy me a knickerbocker glory in Lyons Teashop on Kilburn High Road. I was denied this pleasure on the grounds that it would make me sick, but also, I suspect, on financial grounds too! Anyway, when the dreadful day came for me to be shipped off out of London and away from my parents, my mother decided that the time was ripe for me to get my wish. I had my knicker-bocker glory and it was so big I couldn't even finish it...

We boarded the train amid much confusion and emotion and I remember being very fright-ened and not understanding at all what was happening to me ...What with the fright and the motion of the train, the obvious happened – up came the knickerbocker glory – to add to my distress.

Some children, like Walter Leeds, were sur-prised when they eventually discovered where they were going:

After what seemed like hours of stopping then starting we arrived at our final destination. We had expected green fields and trees. What we got was Luton.

Not all the evacuees found themselves boarding trains that September morning. Every means of transport was brought into service to carry the children from the cities. Donald Jackson left by a boat that made its way down the coast:

We were going eastwards close to the coastline. Someone said that they saw a periscope on the starboard side and everyone crowded to this side of the boat. An announcement was made to get back sharply because the boat would turn turtle. A destroyer or corvette, I don't know which, raced to the area. It had been in close contact all the way, continually circling the heavily laden boats, but presumably nothing was found. No depth charges were dropped, although we may have scared off the U-boat. I remember feeling very proud that the Royal Navy had saved us all.

Julia Davis was a stewardess on the pleasure steamer *Crested Eagle* and asked to be a volunteer on the ship to evacuate the children from London. Her daughter, Maureen Mancha, writes:

We discovered years later that my husband was on that boat as a small child.

Elsa Van Boogaard recalls boarding a boat for a short trip:

On the morning of September 1st 1939 we arrived at our school complete with a change of clothing and as much squashed into our knapsacks as was comfortable. There were many tearful mums and dads at the school gates as we boarded the buses to take us to the ferry. Some mothers came along with their families, also a number of teachers. We sang as we made our way to the ferry and it was just like a family picnic. The teachers were warm and friendly to us, they seemed to have lost their sternness.

On arriving at the ferry there were more tearful scenes as some parents waved goodbye. There were simply hundreds of children, some looking tearful and others quiet and full of wonder. Many schools were assembled at the pier waiting to be shipped away. We stood quietly in line waiting our turn to board the ferry.

It took us about 20 minutes to sail across the river and at the other end we were again grouped into our classes and boarded buses. I remember the sun was shining and we were very happy.

Eileen Pulsford (now Sandwell) rose very early that Friday morning. There was lots to do and the orders were that they were to assemble at the school at 5.00 a.m. Her mother had thought of everything:

I carried my new pencil-case and had a change purse on the side with my going-away money, sixpence, inside.

We arrived at Charlecote Road School to form up a column with the other evacuees, and started to walk to Dagenham docks accom-

panied by our parents and other relations, who, like my sisters, had to drop off on their way to school or work. I am not sure how many miles it is from Charlecote Road to Dagenham docks, but on a rainy September morning it seemed to take for ever.

Fortunately, about half-way there – on Heath-way Bridge to be exact – we were given lifts in vans and lorries the rest of the way.

After arriving at the docks I bid a tearful fare-well to mother. (Only years later, as a mother myself, did I reach any understanding of the fears and pain she must have suffered, not even knowing at the time where I was going.)

I went aboard the Queen *of the* Channel, *one of the last of the old day-trip steamers. This particular boat was later sunk in the evacuation of Dunkirk.*

As we pulled away on that rainy morning, leaving my mother on the dock, I think the sense of adventure was replaced by the loneliest feeling in the world, and the wondering of what I was doing there instead of being safe at home with my mum.

Although the distance to the ferry was not great, to many of the children it seemed like miles. Donald Jackson remembers:

I was woken in the early hours to be taken by my mother with my four-month-old brother to our local senior school. I was then transported by

*charabanc to the Princess Cinema in Dagen-
ham, and then [there was] the long walk down
Kent Road. It's about one mile long but to my
eight-year-old legs it was miles. My mum could
not help, she was carrying my brother.*

*We were four or six abreast across the pave-
ment to Ford's private jetty where there were
three paddle steamers, the* Royal Daffodil *being
one of them. We were loaded aboard.*

Whatever the means of transport, once on
board everyone had the same thoughts.
'Where am I going and what did Mum pack
in my bag for me to eat?' Beryl Hewitson
remembers she was dressed in a navy-blue
coat and felt hat and began to feel quite
uncomfortable in the crowded train. She
decided to do something about it:

*I remember opening my suitcase on the long
journey and changing my warm fleecy knickers
and putting on a thin pair because it was so hot.*

Another evacuee recalls:

*Early morning at the station ... subdued parents
watching from the opposite platform. We children
were excited to be wearing Sunday-best clothes
on a weekday, with a label through the coat
buttonhole, and to be carrying our belongings in
a brown paper carrier-bag with string handles.
One other detail: I had a half-pound of choco-*

late wheaten biscuits in a paper bag (no packets in those days) all to myself.

As I said, I never remember the train journey. I can recall being in Oundle Public School, eating jam sandwiches and drinking lemonade. Next, a red bus dumped 32 kids outside the church at Thurning.

5

'I'll take that one'

Thousands of children found themselves on trains that travelled for most of the day. Since there were no toilets or corridors, inevitable accidents for some children turned the journey into a nightmare. It was dark before many of them, hungry, tired and in soiled pants, finally tumbled from trains into the arms of horrified villagers.

Our train eventually puffed its way into Eastbourne, a quaint seaside town on the south coast of England. As we spilled out on to the station platform, teachers and billeting officers worked together to herd us aboard buses, which then headed for a local school – a school that in a few months would be bursting at the seams as it attempted to cope with the extra students from London.

Inside a large hall, a group of would-be billeters stood and stared at us new arrivals as we slouched our way into the room and stood in line for inspection. We were not an impressive group. We were all tired and far from home, and for most of the children the glamour and adventure had faded hours before. After a short welcoming speech, the locals stepped forward to choose the children they wanted and gave the names to the billeting officers standing by with clipboards and pencils.

Although I was not the first to be picked, I was not the last. It is something I have often thought about over the years. What would it have felt like to be the one left standing alone, overlooked by dozens of prospective parents, and how must this have affected that child in years to come?

For L. A. M. Brech, a teacher and escort, that first day was an awful start to a 'new' life. When she and her group reached Wareham, it was pouring with rain. Then, on arriving in Weymouth, the whole school found themselves split owing to a mix-up with the coaches at the station. Her two coachloads were 'dumped into an empty church hall':

They treated us as runaway refugees, they picked the children as though they were picking I don't know what, and the children were extremely well brought up. One little girl was in tears because no one would have her and she came to me and said, 'Doesn't anyone want me?' It was a very ugly situation. Eventually they all went. Nobody wanted the teachers. Somebody gave us permission to sleep on the floor, which we did.

Joan Mary Hay (now Barrett), who was nine, had left her home in Wimbledon to arrive at Arundel:

We were marched up to a table where the Duchess of Norfolk gave out the largest bars of Cadbury's milk chocolate I have ever seen (possibly other things as well but that is all I remember). We were then marched off to the High Street (I assume), where the locals stood and selected one or two children at random. The pretty and attractive ones went first and I thought I would never belong.

As one of those who suffered the humiliation of waiting to be picked, I know that it is something I will never ever forget. Every one of the thousands of letters we received mentions the moment as if it had been seared into the writer's mind with a branding iron. Yet it was not the fault of those who came to choose the children they wanted. Most of them had gone to the selection spots with kindness in their hearts and an eagerness to help shelter the children and give them a new home for as long as was necessary. Once again it was the system that was at fault. On paper, no doubt, the idea looked worthy of a Nobel prize. A booby prize would have been more appropriate. Beryl Hewitson might agree:

We were told to sit quietly on the floor while the villagers and farmers' wives came to choose which children they wanted. I noticed boys of about 12 went very quickly – perhaps to help on the farm? Eventually only my friend Nancy and myself were left – two plain, straight-haired little girls wearing glasses, now rather tearful.

A large, happy-looking, middle-aged lady rushed in asking, 'Is that all you have left?' A sad, slow nod of the head from our teacher. 'I'll take the poor bairns.' We were led out of the hall with this stranger and taken to a farm where we spent two years.

Diana Coleman (now Burton) wore her Belle View High School uniform, which was brown and gold. She has forgotten the exact arrangement whereby each child was allocated to the lady who was destined to stand in as 'mother', but does remember that when all the other girls had departed with their hostesses, she and her sister were the last two left:

We felt like cattle at an auction when one of the remaining ladies, who looked rather forbidding, was spoken to by an official and later declared, 'All right, I'll take these two.'

We were ushered out, gathering up our satchels and carrier-bags, and stepped out at a fairly smart pace from the hall back over the bridge and along the main road to Caldene Avenue, which was quite a long road and seemed to get longer instead of shorter. I remember looking at each house along the way and hoping that each nice-looking one was where we were going, but it turned out to be the very last house along Caldene. The string handles of the carrier-bag dug into the palms of my hands and the carrier contents seemed to get heavier with every step, and while we were walking along I remember trying to protect my hands by pulling down my blazer sleeve, but unsuccessfully. To add insult to injury our hostess complained that she had her name down for two little boys, but she'd have to make do with my sister and me.

Harry Wright was taken to a school where they had biscuits, sweets and chocolates:

…and I thought, 'This is a nice holiday.' So then the welfare officer said, 'Come on, you're coming with me.' And I said, 'Well, where are we going then?' So she said, 'Home.' And I was a seven-year-old kid and I thought, 'Home? You mean I've come all this way and now I am going to

111

*turn around and go home?' She then took us to
our billet.*

Towards the end of the day, Greta Herring
(now Reid) found that just she herself and a
'rather plump little girl' were left:

*They put us into the back of a car (in my
memory it looks like a Volkswagen but I think it
was probably a little Morris), and drove us
around from door to door asking if they would
take us in.*

With many of the children who were left
unchosen it seemed there was nothing to do
but gather them up and begin a walk from
door to door. The strange, sad lines making
their way through the village streets were a
common sight as the billeting officers or
teachers tried their best to find someone
willing to take them in, if just for the night.

Everything had started out so well for
Irene Brownhill (now Smith). Together with
her sister she had left Salford for the seaside
town of Fleetwood, in Lancashire. She was
eight and her sister six; they came from a
family of 10 children. To go to the seaside
was wonderful since they had never been
before. They found themselves sitting on the
floor in the Marine Hall as local people
circled and decided who to take:

We noticed next to us a little thin girl sobbing and very upset and wanting her mother. I put her in the middle of my sister and me and she stopped crying. The people coming around to choose kept saying they would take my sister and me, but they did not want three girls, only two. We could not leave this little girl as she got upset so we had to all stay together. By 10 o'clock that night all the children had gone and only we were left. They took us round all the houses in town. I remember it was dark and we were all crying by then. Then we came to this big house with lovely Auntie Betty in it, who was going away next day on holiday, but cancelled it to take us in.

Things ended happily for Irene. She still keeps in regular contact with her foster mother in Fleetwood, and calls her 'Auntie Betty' to this day.

(As this book goes to press, Irene Smith has written to us again: *'An ending to our story,'* she writes. *'…Auntie Betty, who we were staying with during the war, died aged 96 on April 13th [1988]. My sister and I met the third evacuee we were with at Victoria Station to travel to Fleetwood for the funeral. We had not met since she was six, so it was a big reunion. We talked all day and are keeping in touch now.'*)

In cases where there were brothers and sisters it could be particularly hard to find a home willing to take more than one of them. Many of the evacuees had promised their parents that they would stick together and this they were determined to do. Albert Edward Stanley Gardener came from a family of eight:

Three of us were evacuated, ages five, six and I was 12. We went to a little mining village in Derbyshire. We were taken to a little school and we sat on the floor cross-legged. There were literally hundreds of us there, and there were mostly families of one or two. I promised my mother and father that I would keep my brothers with me at all times. Up until eight or nine o'clock at night people were coming in and saying, 'I'll take that little boy or that little girl.' We were still waiting because there were three of us. So we spent the night with the school caretaker. Nobody told us that we weren't going to be there permanently.

The next morning someone came running across the park to tell us we were going home. Of course, we were very upset anyway and wanted to go home. We hadn't wanted to go away in the first place. But we were taken in the Lord Mayor's car, possibly only 200 yards away. The car stopped and the chauffeur said, 'Mr Stanley Gardener,' (that was my little brother) 'will you step out here, please.' And I wouldn't let him go and there was a bit of a kerfuffle. But they took him and placed him in a home.

The car started up again and we were in tears,

and it went to number 16 which was on the other side of the road and the chauffeur got out and said, 'Mr Albert Gardener,' which was myself, 'you step out here. Robert Gardener, you with him.' So I got out with my little brother. We stayed in this place for one night and we thought that was going to be our regular place and I could still go and see my other brother. But the next day the chauffeur arrived again and I was taken to a house 17 miles away which was run by an American missionary, who we called Master, and a matron. It was a massive place, a castle, with its own moat, and I was billeted there with 76 other children.

Lilian Blewett (now Williams)'s mother had told her son not to let go of his sister. They got to a little room in the Town Hall and didn't know what to do. It seemed everyone wanted a little girl. Lilian's brother refused to let go of her hand and by the end of the day there were just six children left. Her 12-year-old brother decided that the six should stick together. 'We all go together or we're all walking back to London,' he threatened. Off they went with a billeting officer and finally ended up at the local pub:

The publican came out of the pub and they said, 'Will you take these children from London, they're evacuees?' And he said, 'No, no, I can't take all of them, I've got a business to run. I only said I'd take two.' Just then his wife came out of the pub and she saw us all and we were all poor with labels on us and she said, 'Oh God, poor little things,' and she said, 'Come on in,' and she took the six of us.

Betty Worley (now Window) found herself walking around Chelmsford, being one of the last three. After knocking on a number of doors, the billeting officer left her and her sister with a woman who, she remembers, had curlers in her hair:

I was praying and praying that she wouldn't take us. As we approached the door this great Alsatian rushed up to us and my sister screamed, and the lady got my sister by the hand and she said, 'Follow me,' and she ran us all the way back up the street, saying, 'They don't like dogs, I can't have these evacuees.' They spoke to her and persuaded her, and back we went.

Betty recalls that the woman was very strict, but that her husband would sometimes give the children a sweet from behind his newspaper. They were eventually moved to another billet.

Some who had previously agreed to take evacuees changed their minds or were on holiday on the very day the children arrived. Having arrived in Oxford, Sheila Desmond (now Baily) found herself with her two brothers and younger sister sitting on the kerb, waiting for someone to take them:

Being September, it started to get dark early and there we were with torches being shone on us. I know in my case it was difficult to place four children as we obviously wanted to stay together, but there were also single children waiting there.

Teresa Day was one of the lucky ones. A chance happening meant that she and her two sisters were billeted to the same home:

What happened was that my two sisters went to the toilet and they thought I was on my own, and this lady came up to me and said would I like to come and live with her. But I never told her I had two sisters so she took me, and about an hour later my two sisters were at the door, crying, with a lady who said these two children want to be with their sister. Anyway, we all ended up together ... but we were soon split again.

Lilian and her sister Rosemary went to Salisbury together. They were marched from the station on to waiting buses and taken to a hall where soft drinks, sandwiches and cake were waiting:

I didn't feel hungry owing to a lump in my throat, wishing to be home in Cosham. We all had to file past a nurse who quickly looked in our

117

hair. Then it was back on the buses again and to yet another hall. There we had to stand in rows for absolutely ages while posh-talking women armed with notebooks and pens walked along the lines of us evacuees and selected ones and twos. I looked around after about an hour or more and out of the few hundred there were about 11 of us left. I thought, 'What's wrong with us, will anyone want us? ... perhaps it's because we haven't expensive coats and shoes on.' I tried to make myself smaller, Rosemary was crying and I had to fight back my tears for her sake and pretend it would be like a holiday. Little did I realize it would be just the opposite. Suddenly a lady said, 'You two, follow me!' and we got into a car with two other evacuees who were dropped off first, then Rosemary was taken into a house screaming. Until now we hadn't given it a thought that we might be separated. I could hear her screams and was helpless waiting in this car. After about half an hour they still couldn't calm her down and the 'lady' appeared and said, 'Mrs Harrison really wanted a girl your age and as you are sisters she has decided to have both of you.' I was relieved and couldn't get into the house quick enough to cuddle Rosemary.

To the older children who had the responsibility of taking care of younger brothers and sisters, it must have seemed like the longest day of their lives. All Alan Burrell's brother wanted was a little peace and quiet:

We went (my brother and I) to this place in Essex and we sat in this church hall all day long. 'Why can't we go home? Why can't we go home?' I kept asking my brother and he said, 'Shut up!'

One man, who wishes to remain anonymous, was an only child who was in a group of evacuees that included a brother and sister whom he knew. Local people were about to take them, and he became very upset. The family saw this and came back:

They told the people in charge that they really intended to take only two children but as I was so upset they would take me too. They were wonderful people and I have never forgotten their kindness and understanding.

There is no question that appearance often played an important part. Some boys were picked because they looked as if they would be useful workers around the house or on farms. Other children were chosen because they were attractive. Joan Topp (née Whiddett) remembers the cries of 'I'll have that one!':

If you were a child with glasses or with spots, they were always left till the end.

In some areas, those who had applied for children had their minds set on just the kind of child they wanted. Oliver Went remembers how set the locals were on having someone like himself, his brother and his sisters:

My sisters were crying because women were pulling them this way and that. My brother and I were dragged by one woman up against a wall, and another woman was fighting her for my brother. We were torn from our homes, shipped all over the country and ended up seemingly on an auction block... In the end my eldest sister got the four of us together and as we were trying to get out of that screaming, clawing school, two very nice ladies were just entering the area and seeing us all crying, took us to one side.

But there would always be children whom no one seemed to want. John Wills was sent from Battersea and found himself in a local school in a small town in Devon:

The local ladies would walk through the mob and make a selection. If you were similar to Shirley Temple you were grabbed right away. The little angelic girls all went first into the homes of who knows what or where. Perhaps some were chosen by the local child-molester. But most girls went into the best homes. In the event, if you were like me or my friend Alfie, who always looked filthier than I did, your chances were pretty bleak.

When they finally arrived at a home, the biggest shock to John and his friend Alfie was the fresh air: 'Nearly knocked us off our feet.' It took a long while for their 'little London lungs to adjust'. Adjust or not the pair decided that the countryside was not for them:

We walked home on the thumb with the odd lift. I much preferred to take my chances in the air raids.

By the end of that first long day, once the teachers had done their best to make sure that each child had a home, they began to look for shelter for themselves. Eileen Farrell (now Saunders) and a colleague finally settled in the home of two maiden sisters:

I shall never forget that night, heavy vehicles driving through the town all night, and we had invaders in our bedroom: we had to share a bed, and the scrabbling of cockroaches went on all night ... we killed lots and threw them out of the window.

It is difficult to know for sure why certain children were picked in preference to others. It seems that, in many cases, chance had a lot to do with it. Edith Salmon (now Secretan), who was 15 at the time, found herself and a busful of other children making a tour of the town. By the time they had finished 'delivering' the various evacuees, there were five left:

It was getting quite late. I think the bus-driver must have been tired too, because he said, 'I'll take you lot,' so the five of us were driven to our new home.

Edward Paine remembers that his youngest brother, Brian, who was four and a half, took matters into his own hands:

He finally offered the billeting officer a three-penny bit to keep him.
  He ended up with the best house in the village.

Eileen Monaghan (now Savedra) had recently come out of hospital and had a plaster cast on both legs. She was in a wheelchair when a woman approached her:

I remember she asked my name and when I replied, 'Eileen,' she said, 'I have a daughter Eileen.' She then took me home although it was only the name that swayed her. They were very kind to me, and we were called Eileen 1 and Eileen 2.

For Margaret Gluck (now Gawthrop), who stood in the hall looking lonely and frightened, it was her initials that did the trick:

They wanted a little girl with M.G. initials because their sports car had M.G. on the bumper.

One couple, who had recently lost a little girl, were overjoyed to accept another one into their home. Marion Berry, then a teacher, remembers the incident:

She was the same age and exactly like the daughter they had lost, and they took her back to their house and even the dog went mad with happiness.

On arriving in Hollingworth, Noreen Smith (now Holland) found that the local school-children had been invited to choose an evacuee to take home with them:

Margaret picked me. Her father and mother, who were both at work when I arrived at her house, had no idea they were getting an evacuee until about 8.30 that night, when they told Margaret to take her little friend home because her mummy would be worried about her. It was only then that Margaret told them I was an evacuee. I was fed, bathed and put to bed and they couldn't have treated me better if I'd been their own child. In return I gave them all scabies.

Noreen will never forget Fred and Lily Webb:

They were wonderful people... I never lost touch with them while they were alive.

And why did a lady who had not even troubled to put her name down for an evacuee take Laura Welford (now Norris)?

She chose me because I patted her dog whilst she was enquiring why we were still on the street so late at night.

The dog apparently hated strangers, and it had surprised the woman that the dog had not bitten Laura.

Ronald Larby had got smut in his eye from the railway engine during the journey. The endless attempts to remove the dirt had left his eye looking red and raw:

None of the villagers wanted me as they thought I had some dreadful disease. Meanwhile I had befriended an old English sheepdog that one of the helpers had brought with her. I refused to be parted from this dog, with the upshot that the helper had to take me home with her for a few days. I stayed three years.

After picking me, my own foster mother started for home. She was slim and probably in her early thirties. I followed her to the car outside. It was the first car I had ever ridden in and I was sure that at the end of the journey there would be a palace on a hill. Not quite. Actually we arrived at a grocer's shop, but it was a big grocer's shop, in a turning just off the high street.

The woman was kind and pleasant and, taking me by the hand, headed for a side-door that took us to a flat above the shop. The first surprise was that the house had electricity and no matches would be needed to light a gas-mantle. A very old man stood as we entered the room and shook my hand. He was the grandfather, and in the coming weeks would be the closest friend I had in the house. An only son was introduced and was told to take me to a small but comfortable bedroom at the top of the house.

It was at dinner that I met the man of the house. He had been busy in the shop below and had had little opportunity to show himself. A self-made man, he was proud of the small shop that had grown as a result of his hard work.

As I began my first meal in my new home, evacuees across the country were trying to adjust to their new surroundings. Joan

Quinn remembers she was given a meal in a school building before facing the group of strangers who were there to take the children to their new homes:

I remember crying because I thought a strange-looking man with watery eyes was going to take us home. My sister told me to look the other way. We were very relieved when he didn't pick us. The number of children dwindled and my sister and I thought we would be put into a home because no one wanted us. However, we were collected by Mr and Mrs Owens, a middle-aged couple, and they were to be our foster parents for the next six months.

Two other little evacuees were taken to a house with a 'kind of a ladder' to the upper floors. They were met by a woman dressed in strange clothes:

Out came a lady wearing corduroy trousers! This was a shock because I had never seen a female in trousers before. She was followed by an elderly man with a big white beard who immediately terrified the two of us mites. They took us both. We clung together in the big bed and cried ourselves to sleep. I found out later that 'Auntie Edna', who was housekeeper to Mr Walters, actually went outside the house and banged on the wall with a broomstick and told us it was the local policeman who wanted us to go to sleep.

After filing through a room that reminded him of a polling-station, Geoffrey West found that by the time his turn came to face those sitting behind the trestle-tables, they'd run out of families willing to take evacuees. He was put in the care of an elderly man and off they went from door to door. He recalls what happened at one:

It was opened by a middle-aged spinster named Miss Hunt. She lived there with her father and when asked if they would be able to billet me she answered, 'Which school will he be going to?' I told her I'd be going to the council school. Her reply to my escort was, 'Oh, I want someone who will be going to grammar school.'

Geoffrey eventually arrived at the home of a Mrs Knight, where he stayed along with a boy named George. He remembers their foster mother as an attractive woman:

She had, as she often said, a nice figure. Hemlines were just above the knee, with no material to spare around the seat, which was the fashion.
She would sit by the fire on one of those low padded boxes used to stock coal or wood. Her legs had that mottled appearance that toasting them by the fire can give.
Sometimes she would sit with her back to the

fire facing the room with her knees apart. George, who had reached puberty, would make the most of the situation, as the male of the species is apt to. I clearly recall her saying, 'There's nothing to interest you up there, George.'

For some, the wonder and excitement of the journey was equalled only by the curiosity as to who would be their new foster parents. Lilian Mary Sheldon (now Langlands) had left Newcastle upon Tyne with her school and found herself in Carlisle, where the children made fun of being placed in 'animal pens' to wait for their new billets. Along with her nine-year-old sister, she was taken by car to a country farm:

On our arrival at the farm I saw this lady shooing chickens away. When I got out of the car I spoke to the lady but she ignored me. I then said to my sister, 'I won't be liking it here because that lady didn't want to talk to us.' Then the farmer came to us and told us the lady was deaf and dumb. I then said to my sister, 'I still don't think I'll like it.' But how wrong I was. We could not have been with a more loving and caring couple. He taught me to speak in the deaf-and-dumb language, which has been useful in my lifetime.

Once in their new-found homes, the children settled down to sleep. It was not easy. Rita Friede (now Symons), who was with a young sister, was lying in bed, in a room lit by a candle since there was no electricity:

I had the candle beside my bed and my sister said, 'Something is under the bed,' and I said, 'Don't be silly. Go to sleep,' and she said, 'No, Mummy said you've got to look after me. Look under the bed.' Now, my hair was so long that I could sit on it. I put the candle on the floor and leaned over the bed to have a look under the bed. My hair caught alight, the counterpane caught alight, I was sitting up in the bed and I didn't know which to put out first, the bed or my hair and I was saying to my sister, 'Call Mr Hendry, call Mr Hendry!' And she jumped out of bed, stood at the foot of my bed and said, 'I don't like to.' She wouldn't call them but they heard the commotion and came up and put the fire out and after that we went to bed with a cyclone lamp.

Gladys Long (née Crimmins) remembers Teddy Cook, a plump boy with little steel-rimmed glasses. He had left his home on the back of a lorry, and when his group finally arrived at their destination he stood quietly with the others as potential foster parents inspected the contents of the truck:

One lady chose Teddy and as he started to climb

down clutching his little cardboard case she saw a set of twins and said, 'Oh, no. I've changed my mind, I'd sooner have them.' Poor Teddy had to climb back up and ended up being the last one left.

In the end Teddy went to a lovely lady, who treated him well and always delighted in telling him how the twins were real monsters and gave the woman a hell of a time setting fire to her haystacks amongst other things.

Jean Oldland (now Warner) was nine when she set off from Brentford with her five-year-old brother, leaving a crying mother and a father who 'stood white-faced and silent, then held us tight before turning aside to blow his nose noisily'. After a few stops their coach arrived in Amersham. At this point, her brother, who had been playing happily, decided that he did not like the look of the place. Jean told him that they'd soon be in a nice house with lovely people and that he must not cry or he'd get his blouse wet. Finally a kindly-looking man with spectacles that kept slipping on his nose took them to a Mr and Mrs Barker, who lived in a big white timbered house set back a little from the road:

Suddenly I wanted to be sick. I managed to get my head out of the car window in time to avoid a mess in the car but couldn't avoid the garden gatepost. The poor man mopped up as best he could with his hanky and we walked up the garden path to the front door. He knocked on the door which was soon opened by a tall woman with dark hair in a bun and wearing glasses. Our 'nice little man' – I was holding his hand so tightly I was getting pins and needles in my fingers – said, 'I've got your evacuees here, Mrs Barker.' Imagine the sight we made. Two tired bedraggled children who had been up since the crack of dawn and had seen no soap and water since leaving home. Mrs B. looked down at us and said, rather crossly, 'But I only asked for one.' As if it were the baker calling round with two loaves of bread.

Our friend, who knew there was not much chance of finding any other place for us so late in the day, became rather flustered and wiped his face with the back of his hand. He told her that we had never been away from home before and because we were so young he didn't want us to be separated. She looked at us again and then said, 'Well, all right then. I'll take them. She can help me and the boy can give my husband a hand in the garden.' There was silence and my little brother peered at me around the legs of our friend. I thought he was going to cry and I swallowed hard and took a deep breath. 'Please Miss, my brother's only five years old and he doesn't know how to garden.' She gave me a cold look which dripped off the end of her nose and said to our friend, 'These London children are cheeky. If I take them in I won't have any rudeness.' He smiled apologetically and patted my head, explaining to her that it had been a long tiring day for everyone and he was sure that I was a nice, good-mannered little girl. Without more ado he plonked my brother into rather unwilling arms and with another pat on my head and a push of encouragement, he was gone.

We found ourselves in a large, cool and rather dark hall with polished wood floors. There was a long hall table with a brass tray and ornaments as well as a round china bowl of flowers which were very pretty. On one end of the table was a big brass dinner gong which I recognized as being like the one our seaside landlady had. Mrs B. took us upstairs to a bathroom where we washed our hands and faces and I combed my brother's hair and tried to flatten the front bit that always stood up. Having done that we stood undecided holding on to each other at the top of the stairs, unsure what we were expected to do next. After a few minutes Mrs Barker appeared and called us to hurry downstairs for supper. She showed us into a large kitchen and told us to sit at the table and eat quietly. There was an open door leading to a dining-room with a long table and steaming dishes on it and a man, Mr Barker, sitting eating.

My heart sank as I took my seat at the kitchen table where there were two plates containing one slice of corned beef each and an enormous pile of spinach. My brother peered at his plate and wanted to know what all the green stuff was. I was able to tell him because the year before when we were on holiday in Margate our landlady had served it one day. None of us liked it but my mother manfully struggled to eat her portion so as not to offend. She also told us that it was good for us. I remembered too, that it worked wonders for Popeye and told my brother this, but he refused to touch the stuff. He quickly polished off his slice of corned beef and some bread and butter while I tried to shut my eyes and munch my way through most of my spinach and then eat some of his so that Mrs B. would not be upset. He then said in a loud voice that he was still hungry and wanted to know where his big chocolate bar was that he had brought from London. (We never did discover what happened to those lovely bars!) By this time I was feeling sick again and wanted my mummy and daddy and to be back in that little terraced house all together again.

Later, in a strange cold bed at the end of that long weary day, I hid under the bedclothes and cried. Then I remembered that we hadn't said our prayers and with this as an excuse I climbed into my brother's bed while he said, 'Gentle Jesus...'

At the end of our prayers we curled up together and my little five-year-old brother said, 'Don't cry, Jean, I'll look after you.'

As the last of the trains carrying the evacuees pulled away on that Friday, the Government gave orders for the general mobilization of Britain's armed services. Hospital beds were cleared and extensive mortuary services made ready. The sun went down and the black-out of the cities was brought into force. The heads of hundreds of thousands of children rested on new pillows damp with tears as their thoughts wandered back to their homes and the loved ones they had left behind.

PART THREE

Behind Closed Doors

6

Far from Home

As many evacuees sat down to their first breakfast in their new homes in the countryside, Britain's Cabinet was about to make a decision that would affect them all. By the Saturday afternoon, their patience gone, they decided to contact Hitler and insist that he order his advancing army in Poland to withdraw.

The crisis was coming to a head. At 7.30 p.m. the Prime Minister appeared in the House of Commons. As MPs sat back to listen to the wording of the ultimatum, they were surprised to hear Chamberlain describing how the opportunity was still at hand to hold another conference, provided that the Germans agree to withdraw from Poland. When he sat, no one cheered.

Clement Attlee, the leader of the Opposition, was not in the House that day, since he was convalescing after an operation. All eyes turned to the deputy leader, Arthur Greenwood. As he got to his feet there was a shout from a member of the Prime Minister's party, 'Speak for England, Arthur.'

Greenwood answered by explaining that 'every minute delay now means a loss of life imperilling the very foundations of our national honour'. There was an uproar and, at the end of the sitting, Ministers were demanding that Chamberlain send an ultimatum to Hitler. At 9.00 a.m. on Sunday 3 September 1939 it was delivered. Most evacuees and their new parents sat in silence as British people everywhere glued themselves to the radio for news of the impending war.

The Germans did not reply to the ultimatum, and at 11.00 a.m. the Prime Minister told the nation via the radio that the country was at war with Germany.

Evacuees sat with their new families, far from home, listening to the historic message. What had once been seen as a short trip to the country had now taken on a different aspect.

Those who had agreed to take the children into their homes now had the likelihood of a long stay staring them in the face.

To those about to be evacuated with the final wave on 3 September, it no longer felt like going away on holiday. Beryl Murray (née Holmes) vividly remembers walking along a street of small terraced houses in Liverpool with her mother, on their way to the school from which she was about to be evacuated:

As we passed one house there was a woman standing weeping at the open door, and inside we could hear the voice of the Prime Minister on the wireless. My mother asked the woman if war had been declared and she nodded. My stomach turned over and I looked up at my mother and saw her lip tremble, but she squeezed my hand and tried to reassure me by telling me, 'It won't last long.'

Alfred Norris and his brother, who had gone to Hastings from the East End of London, were so disgusted with the house they were first sent to that they took a tram back to the school and complained. A shoe-repair man took them back to his house with him:

The first day we went to this house we were sent out for a walk and it was in fact the day that war was declared and we had our gas-masks with us. The air-raid siren sounded. We immediately put our gas-masks on and my brother started crying his eyes out and I didn't know what to do, but I saw a lorry coming along and he stopped and we jumped on board and there were six or seven other people on board in the same situation. The lorry driver took us back to the house that we had been allocated to and dropped us off there and, of course, it was a false alert.

On the Sunday morning Edith Salmon (now Secretan) was in church with her teachers when the parson suddenly informed them that the country was at war:

Although this came in the middle of the service, a group of soldiers who were there were immediately marched out.

Gilbert Charlie Gustave Sillence was halted by armed sentries at an ack-ack battery. He was a bus-driver and was delivering evacuees:

They were searching for 5th Columnists. They informed us that Hitler's troops had invaded Poland, whereupon one of the escorting nurses swooned and fainted at the news. We arrived in the evening safely and after discharging our young passengers and having a meal we were called to a meeting of the union delegate.

The authorities requested drivers and vehicles to return the same night in the dark because of the seriousness of the situation. The union delegate rang the depot superintendent and requested to know if any driver involved in an accident driving on a strange road and in the dark would be absolved from all blame. This assurance was not forthcoming so the union delegate advised all drivers to wait for daylight. This we did and travelled back to London the next day.

When war was declared, there were still plenty of children waiting to be evacuated. Reg Castle was 13 at the time:

My mum cried, Dad didn't say much. I guess I was too young to take it all in. I remember a policeman riding by on a bike shouting, 'Take cover, take cover.' I don't know why, nothing happened.

The overriding feeling for most people was one of puzzlement. 'Now what?' they asked themselves. For Sheila Smith (now Rimmer) it was one of anger:

My eighth birthday fell on September 3rd, 1939. I felt personally insulted that Hitler started a war that day and ruined my birthday! I remember my father, who was a chemist, coming home for lunch on Friday, September 1st, with a friend of his, Sam Cantor, who was a Jewish doctor. I listened to their conversation and saw my mother's expression when Sam said, 'Liverpool will be bombed flat by Monday morning.' They decided that my sister and I would be evacuated right away, along with my grandmother and one of my aunts who had a bad heart. On Saturday morning we set off for Aberystwyth, where my mother's second cousin lived. We were all jammed into Dad's Morris 8. It was very hot and the traffic was terrible. We ran over a dog just outside Ruthin, I think, and it was very badly injured, so Dad had to kill it with a tyre wrench or something. It was a ghastly journey.

For this correspondent, 3 September 1939 began just like any other day:

Belvedere, a sprawling suburb in South London, held few surprises and little glamour for the residents of the terraced houses and corner shops of the time. Certainly, that day I was not cognizant nor caring that we sat happily on the bull's-eye of Hitler's dart-board, surrounded as we were by factories. I rose and attended early Mass as usual and on returning Mother pushed me through the front door to do my usual Sunday errand. I had one and sixpence wrapped in a piece of newspaper. I had to call at a cottage three streets away for the sweepstake tickets. Some months earlier Mum had won the incredible sum of 30 pounds so of course it was a matter of supreme importance that I brought the tickets back safely.

Sunday always seemed different from the rest of the week; a more relaxed air, a changed note in people's voices. But this Sunday the atmosphere appeared to have an expectancy on every corner, and a wireless was on in every house. Returning with the tickets wrapped in the same piece of newspaper, I passed some children, my cousins, playing with a skipping-rope on the pavement outside my aunt's house. They were chanting the obligatory rhymes as they leapt over the rope. I made for home.

It was exactly 11.15 a.m. when the air-raid siren sounded and tolled the knell of passing peace. In terror I threw the tickets away and ran up the three hilly streets to home. I fell in the front door to find mother demanding her sweepstake tickets. Not even the threat of impending doom was mitigation for the loss of the one and sixpence of hard-earned money, which resulted in the inevitable good hiding for losing the tickets and being frightened.

Although disappointed at the news of the war, my new family appeared resigned to the fact that their new lodger was going to be around for quite some time. Their only son appeared to enjoy my company, so they probably felt that things could be worse. Soon after the siren had finished announcing that there was, after all, nothing to be alarmed about, I set off to explore my new surroundings.

Since Eastbourne was a noted holiday resort, most of the newcomers from London had made a beeline for the beach. Coils of barbed wire wound themselves back and forth across what had, just weeks before, been a pebble beach full of holidaymakers. Everywhere there were reminders of the dangers of invasion and, although the war was just minutes old, in the minds of the evacuees thousands of Germans could be seen rushing up the beaches only to be entangled in the defensive wire.

Like me, other evacuees throughout the safety areas spent their time adjusting to their new surroundings. For children like Frederick Partridge who had come from areas devoid of animals other than a mangy cat or dog, the sight of colourful country beasts was just too much:

We didn't know anything about nature and we ran after the peacocks and tore the tail feathers from them to send home to our mum. We were 48 children and they only had billets for 46. The rich man of the village said he didn't want any evacuees and his son lived next door. When the vicar explained they had two boys he agreed to take one and the son took the other boy.

So I spent two and a half years living in his big house. We were driven up by the vicar the next day and I'd never been in a car before. On the gear-lever was a diagram that I thought was a swastika. So when we got to the house we told him that the man who drove us had a swastika in his car. So the local bobby was alerted and went round to interrogate the vicar.

The local children in many areas looked on the evacuees as some kind of invading army. And who could blame them? Patricia Barton (née Sinfield) still remembers how tough it seemed to be for them to accept the new arrivals:

The village didn't know what hit them when we first arrived, it was gang warfare between us and the local kids. There wasn't a fruit tree within miles around with a single item of fruit left on it. After a while things settled down to an uneasy truce.

My friend Eileen and I were always planning to run away back to our parents in London. I used to have a sixpenny postal order every week from my family. Our plan was to walk to St Neots [in Cambridgeshire], then catch the train using the sixpenny piece for the fare, but by the weekend there was always something more interesting to do.

For the little brother of Gwen Leahy, the countryside creatures were strange and frightening. It was one thing to have seen pigeons and sparrows, but bantam cocks were something else:

They used to fly up and land on his head. He used to cry his heart out. The snakes that used to curl up on the sandy soil in Dorset used to scare me to death and the flying ants used to smother a bike I had borrowed.

The first thing Alan Pickstone did after unpacking his things was go to the local shop and buy postcards. He had been given strict instructions to let his family know where he was the moment he arrived:

On the way to the post-box I fell in a stream, which fascinated me, and got soaked, requiring an immediate change. The postcards all arrived in Manchester on the Monday morning, and the postman was going round shouting, 'There's rain in Derbyshire!'

Some children found that their foster parents were vastly different from the ones they had left. Estella Spergel (née Halfin) remembers:

Reg was a nice man, kind man. He did imitations of George Formby, whom he resembled.

At first, Gloria Needler (now McNeill) was paired off with another girl. After a few days their hosts decided that one was enough, and Gloria found herself on the move once more. She was rebilleted with a couple who had just lost a child of their own, and was welcomed with love and affection. After the thickly populated streets at home, where the usual playing surface was hard, the fields and valleys proved to be an absolute joy:

I learned to pick blueberries and treat nettle stings with dock leaves, to recognize mulberries

146

and wild strawberries ... to consider cakes with condensed milk spread on them as the ultimate teatime treat. At the town library I took out the maximum number of books per day and, to fill in the loneliness, read every book by Angela Brazil, and because I was still very young, The Blue Fairy Book, The Green Fairy Book, *and all the colours I could find.*

To us the country town of Lancaster was as exotic as the Far East.

The countryside of Britain had never seen so many enthusiastic visitors. For many it was a first time, and like John Feltis they were going to make the most of it:

During the dark nights we filled cans with small pieces of wood, punched holes in the can, set it alight with paraffin and, having attached wire to the can, whirled it round and round to keep it alight. In front of the rows of cottages where I lived was a brook and I was taught to tickle trout. Illegal, but fun. The autumn saw us collecting conkers and acorns and I remember wandering for hours in the countryside.

Once settled in their new homes, many children found new things to enjoy. For Amba Mary James (now Dalton), it was the food:

Soup. It was a first. I'd never had it before. And

we had three-course meals and even at such a young age we loved the variety of meals, but they hardly ever spoke to us. They were a young French couple and of course they spoke to each other, mostly in French so it all seemed very weird to us.

We grew to dread Sunday. There were never any visitors for this couple except, with frightening regularity, on Sundays. What frightened us about this one visitor was that the poor lady had one side of her face eaten away and covered in some form of white powder, probably medicinal.

We felt sorry for her but we didn't like having to sit opposite her at the table.

Joan Coleman (now Murton) was the youngest of a large family of seven brothers and two sisters. She decided to make friends with another little girl. They found themselves in the home of an undertaker and his 28-year-old wife who, as a devout Baptist, insisted that nothing hot be served on Sunday:

I felt very homesick. Very spoiled I was for love and affection because I came from a large family. She thought anybody coming from London had fleas so she had paraffin ready to wash our heads with. Her husband was just an ordinary chap. He used to let us do things when she was out. Soon after we got there the rector of the parish died and it was going to be a very

148

pomp and circumstance funeral and he had to have a coffin lined with mauve and a mauve cushion. We had to make these cushions. And the cushion I was making, well I could only think of the head lying on it. I couldn't think what a lovely cushion it was. We always had to come through his workshop where all the coffins were to come into the house and I was terrified because these coffins used to stand up and you had to walk past them.

Given the circumstances of his new family, there could not have been a better time to have moved in with them, thought Peter Latchford as he lifted his tiny bundle of belongings into the house that was to be his home for the coming months. Yet for some reason his foster parents did not seem happy:

The wife had just won a knitting competition and with the winnings had bought a house. And I don't know what had happened in the past between the man and woman but they never spoke to each other direct. It was always through one of the children. It was most extraordinary. We would be in the kitchen and she'd lock the rest of the house off, so you could never go up into your bedroom. It was rumoured that she had once run off to Taunton and he went and brought her back again. I think she used to go meeting Canadian soldiers in the evenings.

149

He was a tailor who used to sit there and do his sewing. I was supposed to do homework and he would sit smoking cigarettes, with ash dropping down the suits he was making.

Music is often the fastest way back into the past. The songs and melodies that have been part of an important event snatch the event from the air the moment we hear the tune again. Derek O'Brien's father ran a pub just 200 yards from the Liverpool docks and the entrance to the Mersey Tunnel, so it's no surprise that Derek and his brother were evacuated:

Five of us boys were placed with a Mr Castell, a widower who owned a shoe store in Newton. It was a lovely house half-way up the hillside, there was a piano in the parlour and the sheet music on the stand was 'Deep Purple'. I used to pick out the tune and I always connect Newton with the tune. 'As the deep purple falls over sleepy garden walls' – to a city boy the long twilight and the garden walls made those words ring true.

There is no one to equal children in the speed with which they make friends. Within weeks most of the evacuees were settling down with their new-found local buddies, who were also experiencing a new happening in their lives. John Aitchison found that

150

the sounds he made attracted new friends:

We made friends immediately with the local boys, who were captivated by our accents. Two mixed gangs were formed of Geordies and Yorkies and the latter acted as guides to the completely new world. We visited Castleside Aerodrome, sat on the fence and talked to the Spitfire pilots who then took off to practise dogfights. The River Swale was pure and fast with jumping fish, quite different from the coaly Tyne. Rabbits abounded and old boots were pulled from Colburn Beck for the crayfish inside.

Patricia Silverman (now Ferman) felt she had really struck gold when she found herself being delivered to a manor house. However, the children were quickly shown to the servants' quarters. Even her parents, on rare visits, were given sandwiches to eat outside the house. Eventually Patricia went on to stay with a kind elderly couple who had a spare room:

Unfortunately it was filled with stuffed animals and birds in glass cages. It was terrifying going to bed with a candle, lying frozen in bed, an owl with outstretched wings keeping watch above.

For Sheila Price (now Price Bourne), a whole new world opened up:

The year was 1939. As I sat and sought solace in St Peters, Hammersmith, London, I prayed for my father. War had just broken out and news of Dad's call-up for the Territorial Army had just reached me.

The second of eight children, I was devoted to this poor family and my dad. Within the week three of us from our family were sent to be evacuated to Farnham, Buckinghamshire. Some 20 miles away, it seemed like a thousand to this 12-year-old.

As we left our tiny school, our belongings in white linen pillowcases and a tearful mother clutching tiny brothers and baby, we sombrely left London. My mother's strange orange hat set over a tragic face stays with me always.

As our transport delivered us to our prospective houses, it was with great awe that I encountered my fairy-tale house. A distinguished, white-haired gentleman met us at Foston House. His warmth and genial hospitality afforded such comfort. This I never forgot.

Colonel Drew was a widower and had lost a daughter aged 20. He was also Magistrate of Stoke Poges. There were six of us from my school.

The orchard bore fruit, we had a car to take us to school, a piano, a beautiful home, servants, typing lessons, mini-golf and a fine lawn. Most of all we had met warmth and understanding, for us poor children, cast into the country by the fate of war.

Such a happy life I had found, though Mother

never strayed from my thoughts nor indeed my whole family. My father came on leave and I was very proud of him in his uniform. However, he could be a 'know-it-all' and I must confess I felt a little ashamed at his first meeting with Colonel Drew. For in my eyes 'mine host' was far superior. Years later as I write, I can now see — perhaps my father was right. He was a good man.

The education, kindness and the insight to a 'better' life brought with it a change in me. I became a snob ... but still caring for those at home. Each weekend I'd board the bus home. The street looked dingy – poor, and I hated it.

I remember seeing my father cooking a pigeon on our kitchen fire and the repulsion I felt stayed with me. I could never eat fowl or meat ... now or then.

I have many memories of my evacuation days until Mother called me home to help care for the others. Then my lovely world crumbled.

Barbara Yeomans (now Hutton) did not come from a loving home and felt she had landed in heaven when she arrived in Nutley. A Mrs Harding took her and her sister into her home and taught them all manner of things:

She used to say, 'If you want a helping hand there's one on the end of your arm.' She also told me I'd marry a man whose name began with an

'H' because I always called her 'Arding'. And I did!

The occupation of the man in the new home of a young girl called Carol caused a bit of a shock:

I was introduced to this black-faced man eating a cold lunch left for him. He gave me a sandwich and a cup of tea and after I'd got over the problem of the local dialect I spent the late afternoon back at the station while he 'bagged up' the coal delivery. Auntie came home in the evening and it turned out that the coalman and his wife were a young married couple expecting their first baby.

Making room for the incoming evacuees was difficult. Rooms had to be changed around and depending on how many children a family was expecting, new beds and more chairs had to be found from somewhere. For Mr and Mrs Reeves living at their old farm it must have been like a Charlie Chaplin movie. They had only 24 hours' notice that they were about to receive 10 children. Jean Kircher (now Pash) was one of them:

They were elderly with three grown-up sons. The farmhouse was old with a sloping garden going down to the lake. There was a white and liver spaniel called Suds who was a gun dog. That night we slept on mattresses on the floor. But by the end of the week the attic had been raided and we were all in beds. Four of us in one very old brass bedstead. These were soon replaced by wooden and canvas camp-beds supplied by the Government.

The first week on the farm we all went hop-picking because Mrs Cronish, wife of one of the farm men, was cooking in the farmhouse for us instead of her usual hop-picking, so we all pitched in to help her out. We were not restricted on the farm except for our own safety, and were encouraged to help where we could.

We watched literally open-mouthed when we saw a cow milked for the first time – I mean milk came in bottles in London – and the amused cowman squirted milk into one of the girls' open mouths. On another occasion I was unhappy when I found a dead kitten in the hay.

In the mornings a fire was lit in our playroom and the Reeves family joined us for breakfast, and when we came in from school in the afternoons the fire was lit in the dining-room and we spent the evening there, darning stockings while the father read to us, mostly boys' books – Peter the Whaler *was one I remember.*

Those on the receiving end have their own stories. H. Johnson was seven years old and was living with his parents in one of the reception areas. He remembers the afternoon when, after a short conversation at the front door, some unknown people 'deposited' a strange boy at the house:

Our visitor, rather bewildered and a little wary, clutching his cases and the inevitable gas-mask, was introduced as Kenneth Upjohn, and it was explained that he was from London and was going to live with us until a return home should be possible. Kenneth was around my age although rather taller and came from Tooting. His two sisters – one older, one younger – were billeted together at another house.

Kenneth and I 'got on', because there was little option, although it could not be stated that we became good friends. There was a gentle rivalry never far from the surface. For instance we both drew at about the same level of competence. However, when it came to drawing trees Kenneth drew a form of elongated club with long bristles on top. I expostulated with him about this and pointed to real trees outside (there was a large oak near the bottom of the garden), saying, 'Yours aren't trees, that's a tree and yours are not a bit like it.' Kenneth insisted that he did draw real trees and nothing could convince him otherwise. Many many years later I paid my first visit to London and there, along the roadsides, were Kenneth's trees, exactly as he drew them. I wished so much I could see him again and apologize.

When a group of 34 boys arrived with three

male teachers and four girls, Jean McIntosh (now Chartrand)'s mother and father agreed to take the four girls. When Jean arrived home that evening, she realized something was wrong:

Mum said one of the girls needed massaging, another one could not walk up the stairs, another needed special medication and the other was full of aches and pains. Next morning I talked to the headmaster and sure enough, later that morning, the matron came looking for her lost 'patients'.

The added responsibility for a stranger's child was not lost on those who agreed to accept the evacuees. What happened if a child became seriously ill, or worse? Hilda Williams's experiences were dreadful:

I had one little boy who died while he was with me and I had a family that were lousy. They gave the whole school lice. We had one dreadful child who called my lovely farmhouse 'a hole' and that's as far as I could go, I couldn't take any more, so I said, 'Well if it's a hole, darling, you'll have to go back and face the bombs.'

Ceta Cherry and her husband had a holiday bungalow near Great Yarmouth. At the outset of the war they left immediately. Soon afterwards, their bungalow was taken over

by the local 'organizer' responsible for housing evacuees:

*I do know that there was nowhere to go and
nothing to do so after a few months the evacuees
returned to London. By this time they had
ruined the bedding, and broken most of the
household articles. The only thing intact was an
electric fitting of a Cupid, which at this moment
is hanging in my hall.*

Mabel Johnson was living in a small village
named Barnby Dan, near Doncaster, South
Yorkshire:

*Evacuees came early to this place. Before they
left I was a nervous wreck, or would have been
if I had been of a weak nature.*

One woman who was a foster mother, and
who now describes herself as very old and
very slow, remembers a six-year-old girl
from London:

*Her first words were, 'Who's boss here, Auntie?'
and being a bit taken aback, I did not really
know what to say so I said, 'I am the boss of the
house and Uncle (my husband) is boss of the
garden,' to which she replied, 'Well God and me
are boss of the lot.'*

Ruth Hill (now Askew) was a Girl Guide

and took two children to the local rectory to ask the local rector to take them as evacuees. She explained that a Mr Underhill had requested that she leave them there, and met with a flat refusal:

I took them away and Mr Underhill was furious. He said, 'Right, come with me,' and off we went up the hill again, to the front door this time. A heated conversation ended with the children staying there, but not for long.

If it was not easy for evacuees who had never been to the country before, it could be just as difficult for those who took them in. Although not all the children were seeing a cow for the first time, some had come from homes that did not find it necessary to observe various rules. Along with her mum, dad and sister of 19, Joan Tyson (now Lowe), who was 21 at the time, found herself sharing her home with two boys aged six and nine. It was a far cry from the poor area of Manchester they had left behind:

Each night was spent in de-lousing these two little boys, as they were infested with lice. With newspapers spread out on the table, a small toothcomb and a good light, it was a case of who could collect the most lice between my sister and me. They did not appear to know the use for a knife and fork as they never sat down to a meal at the table and lived on sandwiches. When [they were] out playing, their mother lowered their food down on a rope as they lived in a flat. It seemed to us one long battle to get them to stay put at the table when eating a meal, as they seemed to prefer eating under the table and would disappear at the slightest chance. When their parents came from Manchester to see them, arriving by train after lunch, their first call was the public house, so they were always merry when they reached us late in the afternoon.

Their father would always sing for us, standing before the fireplace. He was usually in good voice and this 'entertainment' would go on for some time. My mother found this embarrassing but my sister and I would be stifling our laughter till we ached with the effort.

There were also children who had been accustomed to a better way of life than they encountered in their new billets. Jerry Pam was the only child in the home of an elderly couple and will never forget the first meal he received:

We came down and it was just boiled potatoes with vinegar poured on them, but when you're hungry you'll eat anything. Then they said, 'Now, up to your room.' Not 'Sit down and listen to the radio with us.' Just 'Up to your room!'

Jerry Pam finds life a lot easier today as a

160

Hollywood press agent for some of the biggest movie stars in the world.

Josie Weston remembers she had not only her sister to take care of but also someone else's child. She was 12 years of age, and as she was leaving to go to the station in Leeds, a hysterical woman thrust a four-year-old girl into her arms and left. When they arrived in Crofton, she and her sister Phyllis insisted that they all stay together. They were taken home by a woman who agreed to look after the three of them:

The lady, Mrs Stephenson, was then 59 years old, her husband a little older, they had never had any children. Anyway, by virtue of having a spare bedroom they had a ready-made family.

When Uncle Joe came home from the pits I'm not sure who was more shocked. He looked us over and said, 'They'll do.' Some time after we were all in bed on Saturday night there was a banging on the door – the little girl's mother – again hysterical – she wanted her baby! The Stephensons didn't want to get her up in the middle of the night and said they'd take her to her mother on Sunday afternoon. On Sunday afternoon we went to this huge mansion which was full of [evacuated] mothers and babies. The mother was hanging out of the window in a state of undress. Uncle Joe was always worried that he had to leave that child there. We never heard a word from them after that afternoon.

Those who were involved in an official capacity in coordinating the evacuation also had their work cut out for them. The task of the billeting officer was not an enviable one. Human nature, being what it is, threw many a spanner into the best-laid plans. First someone would claim they had really wanted a boy, others a girl, while still others would exclaim, 'Evacuees? This is the first I've heard about it. You'd best speak to my husband [or wife], he [or she] runs things around here.' Muriel Viney was an assistant billeting officer and was told to expect about 3,000 children. After she had organized the welcoming committee, no evacuees showed up. She was informed after the scheduled arrival time had passed that the arrival had been cancelled. Exactly the same happened the day after. Finally 5,500 showed up. Incredible as it may seem, all were accommodated, with the exception of one family:

By the end of the day we were left with one very harassed billeting officer. She [still] had one complete family, consisting of a retarded mother and six children, the eldest being a boy of about 10, with no hope of billeting them. Then someone remembered a cottage recently left empty; this was hastily requisitioned, and several volunteers went with the family, lit fires, took food and made sure that everything essential had been provided.

They reported back throughout their efforts, the mother had just sat and watched, whilst the boy of 10 helped to light the fires, looked after the other five children and organized them for the evening. A receiving officer from their area, together with Miss Wall, a welfare officer from the LCC who had travelled with them, told us that on the following day the mother had demanded, and got, seven pairs of wellington boots because the country was 'muddy'.

Amba Mary Dalton (née James) and her sister have good reason to remember their billeting officer. Each time they were moved from one home to another, which was often, he drove them in his car:

I can remember exactly what he looked like after all this time and I know his name. This is not because we grew to like him but because he sexually abused my sister each time he took us anywhere. I wonder how many ex-evacuees remember him for the same reason.

Since the evacuees were largely from the poorer areas of the cities, a preconceived notion that they would be lacking in manners and discipline built up a hostility that was reinforced with their appearance in the reception areas. A poorly dressed army of scruffy waifs, they arrived tired, hungry, dirty and smelly after their long train journey. In addition, for some it was difficult to speak without the use of a swear-word, making them somewhat unattractive potential family members. Yet it would be a mistake to generalize. Not all the children were seeing the countryside for the first time and, although poor, most had come from families who prided themselves on the cleanliness and good behaviour of their children. Joyce Galloway (now French) was living in a reception area. Her dad had moved to a new job, leaving his family a three-bedroomed house. They took in four evacuees:

When I came home from school my mother lectured me that I mustn't copy these deprived children who had undesirable habits like 'going behind the door'.

Sometimes, however, the country hosts saw their worst fears confirmed. Bryan Coleman's parents took the Bates family (not their real name) into their home in Dunstable:

The children would make wild animals' behaviour look like angels. Their toilet training – they were 10, seven and five – was non-existent, absolutely appalling. Mrs Bates, their mother, went out every night to the local with her friend Mrs Davies [not her real name], who was taken in by my grandmother. Mrs Bates brewed tansy tea the following morning which she took as a 'get rid' potion. Mr Bates appeared suddenly one weekend, he had apparently just been released from a long prison sentence. Mrs Davies disappeared, taking my grandmother's best fur coat with her.

Joan Newton (now Downes) decided to take matters into her own hands at the very beginning:

My mother took in two evacuees. A girl, 13, and her brother, four. The four-year-old bit me when I was trying to put his clean clothes on, but he only did it once. I bit him back.

A police sergeant went to visit Mary Jay, who had recently been married and was willing to take evacuees:

When he saw we had brand-new furniture he said, 'Forget it!'

Mabel Louvain Manning was a young mother with a six-month-old son. Her husband worked on the railway. She took in two little boys:

The first morning I was awoken about 6 a.m. by such a noise, it was the boys fighting in bed! One had a bloody nose which had splattered all over the wall. I cleaned them up and got them ready for breakfast. They had no idea how to use a knife and fork and picked up a fried egg in their fingers.

They didn't like stew or pies, only beans in tomato, which they wanted to eat out of the tin, and chips. Of course, we had no shops, except for a butcher's and the village shop, they had nowhere to go except for the fields and they didn't like those.

One day I asked if they would like a picnic, it was a lovely summer's day, and packed them up lots of sandwiches, cake and lemonade, thinking they would be out for an hour or two. They were back within half an hour asking when tea would be ready.

When they came to me, one was wearing wellingtons, the other plimsolls, and no coats or extra shirts or underclothes. I cadged what I could from friends, then decided to write to the parents for more. The mother wrote back saying she would have to get their suits and shoes out of pawn, which she did, and sent down.

The parents came down once or twice, but neither the boys nor the mum and dad seemed particularly pleased to meet. In fact, as soon as the pub was opened they were in there, with the youngsters outside clamouring for chips and drinks.

A boy who appeared to be a real angel turned up at Celia Haywood (now Johnson)'s home. Her family occupied a fairly large three-storey house, and since there were only three of them they were an obvious choice when possible billets were being hunted out prior to the arrival of a grammar school from Manchester:

I'll call the angel Val, his first name. In fact a real Michelangelo cherub in his choir robes, that is until the vicar caught him pinching grapes from the harvest display. How wrong you can be. It appeared he also borrowed two shillings and sixpence from the same vicar. All in all we were not sorry when he had to pack his bags and we could put it down to 'Experience No. 1'.

Another little girl was part of a fostering family, and when trainloads of London children arrived, her father was part of the ARP reception party. By 6.00 p.m. on the day of the arrival most of the children had been placed, but there were three sisters who clung together and did not want to be parted, so her dad brought them home. Her mother took them in and in country fashion made them welcome:

They arrived in only cardigans, frocks and plimsolls with a shoe-bag or carrier-bag each, with just a dirty towel and a change of pants each. No other clothes at all. When we requested more clothes be sent we were told we were being paid to look after the children so we should provide them. The only clothes ever sent were satin party frocks of the wrong size at Christmas, no pocket-money or sweets or cards were sent by 'loving' parents. Once a month the family arrived on Sunday by car (where the petrol came from I don't know), usually in fur coats and wellies and the men in caps with white scarves. We had never seen the like and seriously learned how the other half lived.

Helen Burgess (now Johnson), who lived in the tiny village of Arthingon, took in four evacuees from the centre of Leeds, who were very poor. Their mother had 16 children and her husband was an unemployed hand presser for a tailor:

The two boys were aged 12 and 13 and the girls five and 10. Their natures were lovely, but their habits appalled me.

They all grew to be fine adults, and one of the boys continues to visit Helen every two or three weeks.

Jean Chartrand (née McIntosh) remembers two boys who were billeted with her mother's cousin. They were anxious to help on the farm and went off to the barn to milk the cows:

When my mother's cousin went out to see how they were making out he almost died laughing.

One boy had put the pail under the cow's udders and was holding it there whilst the other boy was using the cow's tail like a pump-handle. They were both very disgusted when there was no milk forthcoming.

When the first trainload of evacuees arrived in Exeter, Dorothy Grimes took a five-year-old boy. He soon made friends with her sons, despite some difficulties with his cockney accent and vocabulary:

The boys were playing outside and I overheard this: Victor (the evacuee): 'Does your old woman go to the boozer?' I am sure my eldest son did not know what a boozer was. His reply was: 'No, but my mother belongs to the Women's Institute.'

Unlike the evacuees' parents, who were given the choice of whether to send their children away or not, the foster parents were made to take the number of children that the billeting officers felt appropriate to the size of their house. Frances Guy (now Driscoll), was ordered to take four children. The eldest was obviously the boss:

She had a face like granite. The younger ones never took their eyes off her. We fed, washed and decked them out in what clothes we could rake up. We prepared a room with two double beds, gave them sweets and water and left them to sort out their own sleeping places. When we thought they must be asleep, our friend, staying at the house, went up to check and came down the stairs three at a time, white-faced as there was no sign of them. We looked in every other room, with no results. We rang the billeting people and the police. They looked in the room, and searched the house. Finally they went back to the room. They found them when they saw a movement under the beds. We were all heartbroken, and had a hard job getting them into the beds. The police gave them some tablets and we watched them until they went to sleep.

Our friend put a mattress on the floor for himself. No amount of coaxing would make them settle, so finally they had to be sent home as all they wanted was Mum and Dad and the 'safety' of the slum, but home, they knew.

Some foster families found themselves saying goodbye to one group of evacuees and then quickly preparing the beds to take in the next lot. Elizabeth Few (now Hill)'s mother had an old Victorian house and at various times took in seven families:

The first was an Irish mother with four children and a baby. The baby arrived with no clothes. My mother, bless her, loaned her all the clothes from my baby doll. She left two weeks after with all of them. Then there were the Harrisons and then the Donahues. Man, woman and child. He died in my bed of TB. It was quite a shock to a 12-year-old to walk into her room and find a dead man in it.

Ellen Campbell (not her real name) had lost her two-year-old son in a horrific accident five months before the evacuees arrived in her village in Dorset. At the time she and her husband felt that maybe their child had been spared from 'something worse' and wanted to do their best for other children. A mother, a baby and two or three other children arrived. Ellen gave the baby her own deceased baby's cot to sleep in:

By the time she went home the mattress was absolutely soaking from the baby's urine. It was very hot weather when war broke out, but those older children went all round my house urinating against the walls.

Although we had two toilets, one being outside with very easy access for them, they never used them. Although my husband and I told the children and the mother off about this filthy habit they took absolutely no notice and our house stank to high heaven.

However, these occurrences were not all one-sided, as Jean McCulloch (née Cross) points out:

How I wish the prevalent view of the evacuees

171

could be changed. We were not all raised on a diet of fish and chips eaten from newspaper, and many of us were quite familiar with the origins of milk! It was just as traumatic for a clean and fairly well educated child to find itself in a grubby semi-slum as vice versa.

Eleanor Stoddart (née Smith) agrees:

We went under the Government scheme and came from very respectable homes. Some of the girls ended up in tiny cottages, three to a single bed, with bedbugs which they had never seen in their lives. I wasn't allowed to wash my hair for four months since we had to bring the water up a hill from the village pump.

The fear and anxiety of children who had been separated from their parents for the first time resulted in the most common complaint – bed-wetting. From country windows everywhere the newly washed sheets were often to be seen hanging out to dry. It was the biggest headache for many billeting officers. Apparently it was something the organizers had not anticipated. According to one officer:

It proved to be devastating for some of the host families. Although rubber sheets were provided later, the damage had been done.

Damage was right. But it was the children who suffered the embarrassment and discomfort. Joan Gordge (now Porter) listened to visiting adults as they discussed the 'naughty, dirty child' they had living with them:

I became enuretic, and my punishment was to be shut in a cupboard under the stairs. I got used to this and was able to lose myself in my imagination. I was more scared of the woman's rages when my bed was found to be wet. I would do my best to hide the evidence and I can remember being angry with myself and bewildered. At night I would try and stay awake, but the first thing on my mind when I woke was, 'Have I done it again?'

If I was dry I had sugar on my oats, if wet, salt.

Joan grew up to become a social worker.

Margaret Dockray (now Tomlinson) was put in a household that consisted of three females. One, the middle-aged daughter, was deaf. She turned out the lights:

My bed-mates were strangers to me and I did not know the geography of the house, besides, it was dark. I decided to hang on. I failed. My crime was discovered next morning when the lady with the nautical hair-style came to rouse me. The disapproving stare that she laid upon me caused something inside me to shrivel and die. My self-confidence stayed dead for many a year, through adolescence and into adulthood.

Although bed-wetting was traumatic, there were other common complaints from both the foster parents and the evacuees that indicated deeper psychological problems. James O'Connell found himself being turned out of his foster home at eight o'clock in the morning and told not to come back till half-past four:

We ganged up and turned into ruffians, really. We were stealing things out of shops and we got into a lot of trouble. When we'd come home from school at four thirty our foster mother would be very drunk and she'd think it was nine o'clock and make us go to bed without any food. So we used to get up later and break into the larder and we were caught. This woman considered my young brother was the culprit and he got the hammering. He was only five years old. My mother came down and saw my young brother. She threw a fit because he was alive with fleas and had running sores. We were both re-evacuated.

It was being separated from her family and from the love of her parents that Geraldine Stirrat (née Gardner) remembers. She was seven when she said goodbye to her mother and father:

He said, 'You mustn't cry. You must be very brave.' And of course that stayed with me, so I just didn't allow myself to cry. You wanted to throw your arms around somebody's neck and tell them how you felt but you couldn't because you weren't to be weak.

Teresa Day also remembers how she hated being separated from her parents:

We used to go to the coaches on a Sunday to see if our mother got off the coach and when she wasn't there we used to walk home sadly. The postman became an obsession for me. I used to see him and want to rush up to him and ask if there were any letters.

Joan Dean (now Evans)'s foster mother did her best to help allay her fears away from home:

I had a huge bedroom but there was a photograph on the wall and the eyes of the photo seemed to follow you. I mentioned this and she took the photo down.

Religion played a major part in the lives of many evacuees and those who took them into their homes. Catholic children found themselves in Protestant homes and vice versa. Children who had never been inside a church found themselves attending a regular service, some as many as three a day. For children of the Jewish faith it was particularly difficult. A recent study of the period has shown that three-quarters of the British population had a degree of anti-Semitic feeling. Many of the Jewish children who arrived in the countryside were looked on as foreigners, especially in areas that were seeing Jews for the first time. Once successfully billeted, they then faced the problem of adapting to an entirely different way of life. The Chief Rabbi, aware of the problem, relaxed the strict religious orders associated with the faith and gave instructions that it was not necessary to eat kosher food and that they should 'worship where you can'. These liberal suggestions would in time eat away at the religious culture of the children and steer many of them away from their more orthodox beginnings for ever.

For Allan Sanders, a small Jewish boy of six at the time, being separated from his mother was 'the most traumatic time of my life'. Leaving his home in the East End of London, he was bundled off on a train to the safety of Norfolk. He waited in a reception hall and eventually a large lady came over to him and instructed him to follow her:

She led me to a nearby country lane and pointed to the rear red light of a bicycle. I can remember running behind her bicycle with only the rear red cycle-lamp being visible as it was pitch dark. She cycled for what seemed like ages through fields until we arrived at a little cottage in a place called Barton-on-the-Turf. I was sobbing and she told me to stop snivelling. My foster parents were firm but fair, but ways and culture were totally different from my previous upbringing. I had to go to church services and being of the Jewish religion it was totally alien to me and I was made to sing hymns and so forth, but I suppose they looked after me the best they could.

Allan Sanders went back five years ago to 'exorcise' himself. The whole experience, he explains, has had a lasting effect on him.

Catherine Osborne lived with her husband and three-year-old son in Cambridgeshire. The evacuees arrived and they had no option but to take two little Roman Catholic schoolboys:

One of the boys was Albert Cazzani whose parents were both Italian. Albert firmly declared, 'Mussolini will never go to war against Britain.' So sadly he was proved wrong. His father was interned for the duration.

Grace Saragoussi (now Brooks) spent her

time with a spinster lady in Wiltshire:

There were three of us Jewish children there and they kept telling us that it was our fault that Jesus had died on the cross. The war was also our fault – it was a direct retribution and the world was going to end. There was a thunderstorm going on as they were telling us this and we were quaking in our boots.

Some evacuees saw a different side of the coin. One girl and her sister found themselves with a Jewish family who were kind enough actually to insist that they go to church each Sunday:

She would say to her son, 'Phillip, take the little Gentiles to church.' And this in fact was my first introduction to church. This led to my becoming a preacher myself in the Methodist Church in Wales.

Freda Risley (now Costa) came from a strict Roman Catholic home and found herself in the home of strict Methodists. Her hosts had never met a Roman Catholic but had heard plenty, 'none of it good'. Before the month was out she was writing to her parents, asking them to come and take her home. By the end of three months her foster parents were refusing to talk to her, and spoke only to preach about the iniquities of her religion:

It may seem trivial but I began to think, 'Maybe they're right and I will go to hell.' I used to lie awake at night worrying that my whole family and I would end up in hell. It all seemed very real to a seven-year-old, and it was definitely mental anguish. Eventually 'Auntie', as I was made to call her, had a fit of vapours and said the worry of having a sinner like me (yes, truly) in the house was making her ill. I would have to go. A new hostess was found for me and 'Auntie' whiled away the time when I was waiting for the transfer by telling me horror stories about my future home – I would be beaten and starved etc. By the time Mrs S. came for me I was in a right state.

Never was so kind a person slandered. I cried the first night so I was put on a camp-bed beside her. I told her, with a lot of trepidation, that I was a Catholic and had to go to Mass. 'That's fine, dear,' she said. 'My last little girl was Jewish but she couldn't go to service because we haven't got a synagogue. But it is interesting meeting you children with different religions.' If I could have stayed with Mrs S. I think I would have been happy for the rest of the war.

One Jewish boy, Jack Levy, who came from a poor family of nine, found himself in the home of a car-owner. He had been living in appalling slum conditions, so for him the house was one of 'outrageous luxury'. He was introduced to a life he had never known existed. His brother sometimes proved to be a bit of a problem:

He managed to swing on an antlered head on the wall and bring it down. We'd come back when Mr and Mrs Davies weren't there and play with their car and ruin the battery and they were terrific considering. They had never known Jews and were interested in our religion but that was all. We had bacon for the first time and though it was wrong we loved it.

When Rita Friede (now Symons), a Jewish girl, arrived in her foster home the woman began to look in her hair:

I said to her, 'We've got clean heads, what are you looking for?' And she said, 'I'm looking for your horns.'

For Romain Bettel, who went to Cornwall, being evacuated was a bad experience. She and her brother were treated like cattle and 'being Jewish they naturally thought we had horns':

There was this farmer who took us in and he had daughters and they all thought we were born with horns. They couldn't believe it when we said we didn't have horns.

It was pleasant sometimes but we had to work

very hard on that farm. We'd be up at five in the morning making nets for camouflage and they supplied the school with milk and we had to wash all the bottles.

Mrs Harvey was actually a pretty nice woman but the daughter and Mr Harvey were very hard. There were bedbugs in the straw mattresses and I caught impetigo and I was isolated on the Lizard (an island off the coast of Cornwall) for six months. I had all my hair removed. My brother got beaten a couple of times so eventually I scribbled a note to my mother, who said, 'Well, if we've got to die, we'll all die together,' and she brought us home.

It was not the first time that Monty Mazin had been away from home. He had had polio before the war and so had already experienced life outside the East End of London when staying in a convalescent home. This had introduced him to the outside world to some extent but, as he found out later, there was still a lot that, as a Jew, he was not aware of. He was evacuated to Totnes, in Devon and, as he told us, 'It changed my life':

I will always remember Mr and Mrs Pratt. They were so kind. He took me to catch rabbits and they encouraged me to catch up on my education which I had lost through having polio as well as the evacuation. I went to night school there. Later my family were the first Jewish family

181

that ever settled in Totnes, which is the second oldest town in England. When my five-year-old brother went into the Catholic school he went into a tantrum and said no way was he going there because he had seen Jesus on the cross and said, 'My baba (grandmother) will kill me.'

Monty Mazin later emigrated to Canada, where he is now one of the leading members of the Jewish community.

The first evening spent by one Jewish evacuee boy in the home of Olwen Dunets caused the latter's mother some concern:

My distraught mother came to me and said he would not go to bed because he had not brought his cap with him. It was his yamulka and he could not say his prayers without it. Well I talked him to sleep and someone found a head covering for the next night.

The reaction of some of the billeters was astonishing and, for the brother of Noreen Smith (now Holland), differed wildly from one home to another:

The boy next door took my brother home but his mother threw him out as soon as she knew he was a Roman Catholic. A childless couple took him off the street and were wonderful to him. When he wanted to go home they offered him everything to stay. A pony, clothes, a bike. They wanted to adopt him but he missed his own family so much he returned home.

Betty Wilson, a foster mother who took in three little girls from Edinburgh, remembers that *she* was the one who was reprimanded:

They were Roman Catholic children, and I am Protestant. One night they called me to their bedroom to ask if I would draw the black-out curtains to let them see the stars, which I did. In a few minutes they called me again to say they had seen an angel, and could I see one. When I said, 'No,' they said, 'You see, Mrs Wilson, that is because you are not a Roman Catholic.'

John Jasper is black and a Roman Catholic. Five of the children in his family were evacuated to Darwen, in Lancashire. Few foster parents were prepared to take five children, but his eldest brother insisted that they stay together and stay together they did. Off they went to the vicarage, which seemed to them 'like Buckingham Palace'. It was, John remembers, a story of rags to riches:

We were taken on holiday with them to Blackpool, to Wales – to three- and four-star hotels. The vicar was transferred to Preston and took us with him. We had a younger child at home who was also eventually sent to the vicarage, so there were six of us then. We lived in a lovely house just outside Preston with a farm and we were given a pony and a donkey. There were very few black people in Darwen and none at all outside Preston.

Olwen Dunets, a teacher, found herself caring for two tiny black children in the local school yard. Everyone seemed to ignore the children, but finally a kind couple decided to give them a home:

Imagine the surprise to the neighbourhood when their well-dressed parents turned up in a week's time with a carload of food and presents for the foster parents.

Once the evacuation was complete the Government sat back to assess the success or failure of the scheme. What they found was that fewer evacuees had left the cities than had been expected. Furthermore, a significant number were drifting back. Estimates suggested that as many as 6,000 a week were returning to London alone.

In the 'safe' areas, children were being bounced from billet to billet as foster parents found themselves unable to cope. Many of the latter were elderly and, although they were willing to help, their days of being able to care for children had long since passed. In fairness to all who agreed to accept evacuees,

184

it must be admitted that their doors were opened to a variety of children few of them had expected.

Within days of the start of the mass evacuation the Government was facing major problems. Opposition to the scheme crossed even party lines as member after member leapt to his feet during parliamentary debates. Sir Henry Fildes, the National Liberal MP for Dumfriesshire, spoke for the reception areas and attacked the Government for forcing British citizens to take into their homes 'persons suffering from venereal disease, scabies and all sorts of infectious complaints'. Major Owen, the Liberal MP for Caernarfonshire, declared that it was 'ludicrous' to send working classes to the beautiful Welsh countryside. He then read from a report that had been sent to him by billeting officers in his area, criticizing the health and hygiene of the evacuees and referring to their having 'different habits and different thoughts'.

Naturally, MPs for the urban areas were quick to get to their feet and attack those in the reception areas. Campbell Steven, MP for Glasgow-Camlachie, shouted out that 150 evacuees in Inverary had been put into a 'miserable cold hall' with only two lavatories, while the Duke of Argyll's home, with its dozens of bedrooms, had scarcely been used. The Duke, he added, had taken in just a few evacuees and had put them in the basement.

This feeling of resentment soon showed itself in the reception areas, as the poor made it known that many of them were carrying the burden of billeting while the wealthy avoided opening their homes to the newcomers. This resulted in overcrowding in the poorer homes and prompted many of the poor to ask, 'Why us and not them?'

It annoys Alma Deaves to this day. He was born in 1909 in an old thatched house beside a wood full of rabbits. With the start of the war he immediately joined the Home Guard, and remembers when an evacuee was supposed to be placed in every house in the village with a spare bedroom. Some members of the community had it easier than others:

There was half a dozen farms in the parish, several private houses – not one had evacuees and all had two or three spare bedrooms. I doubt if war broke out today evacuation would work. Country people are too smart.

My own memories of life in the home of the Eastbourne grocer during the first few weeks of the war are now hazy, but what I do remember vividly is the last day. It started with the son, myself and a large electric train set and ended in a fight, the reason for which I have long since forgotten. We were separated by a shocked mother, who immediately sent us to our respective rooms, and we then waited for a tired father to climb the stairs from the grocery shop below.

After a meeting of the family members, with only the grandfather showing any support for me, it was decided that the happy home of the grocer was no longer happy with a stranger in it.

It was back to the billeting officer and a desperate search for someone with an extra room. This proved particularly difficult since the room in question was needed by someone who had been found unsuitable by a previous home.

The house that took me was half-way up a hill, as I remember, and attached to a string of homes that had seen better days and older boarders than the one about to drop in. The 'Bed and Breakfast' signs that had hung in the windows of the parlours had been removed and were now safely stored away for the duration of the war.

A roly-poly woman with a ruddy face and kind smile led us to the kitchen in the back. She had taken two London children into her home and yes, she'd be happy to take a third if no one else wanted him.

The woman was without children of her own and welcomed the opportunity to be a mother to three strange boys from London.

It seemed I'd struck lucky. She was jolly and extremely kind, and as she bustled around the kitchen preparing the evening meal, I became acquainted with the two evacuees she had taken in some weeks before.

It was supper-time before I met her husband – a fat, seafaring slob who staggered into the house from the local pub and promptly threw his and everyone else's meal across the kitchen. His wife did her best to stop him but was thrown to one side as he turned and made his way to the parlour to lie down on the settee and sleep. The rest of our meal was eaten in silence.

By bedtime the sleeping giant had woken and emerged a different person. Now sober, he began to entertain us, and by the time we were ready for bed, we children and his wife appeared to have forgotten what had occurred earlier.

Unfortunately, once we were in our beds a new man appeared – a sickening, cuddling brute who revelled in long hugs and kisses for each of us. The months that followed were not happy ones, despite the kindness of our foster mother. The slob continued to drink and be obnoxious to the point where we evacuees began to dread the end of a school day, which would find us once again back in the house occupied by the oaf.

On the war front so little was happening that even Chamberlain was heard to remark on 'this strangest of wars'. The Allies had taken up their positions facing the German Army along the frontier between Germany and France.

The war at sea was a different story. A passenger liner, the *Athenia*, was torpedoed and sunk by a U-boat as it left Britain, and another U-boat slipped into Britain's great naval base at Scapa Flow in the Orkneys and sank the battleship *Royal Oak*. In the air the RAF had flown over enemy territory to drop not bombs but propaganda leaflets.

By the time the first Christmas arrived for the evacuees, most of them had documented these happenings in their own way as, in crowded classrooms around the country, they bent over their pieces of paper and drew British ships sinking U-boats. For most of the children, as was to be expected, it was a sad time. Christmas was a reminder of home and happier times. Many foster parents tried their best to make their charges happy. Elsie Neville (now Hill) and her sister, who had been sharing the home of an older couple, were moved when the woman of the house was hospitalized. At 2.30 p.m. on Christmas Eve they were told to go and pack their things as the billeting officer was taking them to a new set of foster parents:

On Christmas morning I awoke, stretched out my legs and my foot touched something. I awoke my sister with the words, 'Wake up, Santa Christmas has been.' She replied, 'I wish you meant it.' However, she was convinced when we opened our socks to find an apple, hair ribbon, clips, perfume, handkerchiefs and one or two other items of delight to two teenaged girls.

When Nan Chalmers woke up on Christmas morning in her new home in Maybole, she hurried to the large pillowslips hung by the fireplace. But it was the common-room that held the surprise:

We found strings tied across the room with a present hung from them for each child.

Although there was a hall full of children dancing and prancing around, Joan Johnson (now Hellyer) knew no one. She had been sent to the party by her foster parents and was absolutely choked up. A woman was playing 'Waltzing Matilda' on the piano:

I was missing my family so much that I just couldn't sing it but every time I hear 'Waltzing Matilda' today I'm looking into a picture of me standing by that grand piano. I remember standing there and hurting like mad, but no tears.

Shirley Gibson (now Shine) had never had a visit from Father Christmas. Her mother was so poor that she did not remember toys being handed to her from anyone before now:

I remember waking up on Christmas morning and feeling something heavy on my feet at the bottom of the bed and there were all these presents. It was lovely.

As the first months of the war came to a close, the question on the lips of most civilians was, 'What war?' The British Army seemed to be spending most of its time involved in a waiting game as those at home spent their leisure hours singing songs about hanging out the washing on a Siegfried line. They were bored with looking towards the sky and had given up believing they would ever experience danger from the air.

Those who had sent their children to the countryside for safety began to have second thoughts. If nothing was happening, why were they being cared for by someone else? So the trickle back began. Soon the numbers of returning evacuees grew so large that many in the cities became concerned.

Those who did return found little to do, since all the schools had been closed and compulsory education abandoned on the day they had left. The schools had been commandeered by the military, for civil-defence purposes, by the Auxiliary Fire Service and to be used as warden posts and mortuaries. To reconvert them would take time. In the meantime, amusement arcades and cinemas were seeing growing numbers of bored children crossing their thresholds.

For teachers back in the cities it was particularly trying. Margaret Smith (now Birnie) remembers going from house to house to teach the children in their own homes until the schools could be reopened:

Our school was finally opened after being used as a food storage for emergencies, and also my classroom was going to be used as a mortuary.

Eileen Farrell (now Saunders) was another teacher hunting for children in London after most of them had left and some had returned:

We walked around the streets to find some of our own pupils and it was heartbreaking to see them run away when they saw us, because in those days 'Teacher' was part of the family as we had often taught three or four children from the same family. Anyway, we managed to speak to a few and by the end of the day we had 72 children on our list.

Then next day we sorted them into groups. The idea was that Miss F. (the colleague I'd chummed with during the evacuation) take the younger children while I had the older ones. They were put into groups of 10, she in a staffroom at

one end of the building, and my groups in an-
other at the opposite side. This would avoid a
heavy death toll in case!

Soon the Government was being bom-
barded on all sides. With the evacuees now
pouring back to the cities, they had to decide
whether they were serious about evacuation
or not. In effect, they were trapped. Either
they had to open the schools for the returning evacuees and admit that the original plan
had been a disaster, or they had to do something to stop the mass exodus back.

The decision was made to encourage those
who had left to stay where they were. This
would not be easy, since the billeting officers, having borne the brunt of the attacks
from both sides, had now begun to rebel.
Ways had to be found of encouraging more
foster families to take children in and of
persuading those who already had evacuees
to keep them.

Throughout the opening months of 1940
the whole evacuation programme began to
edge towards disaster. Lack of co-operation
from the foster parents and the horrendous
problems being faced by billeting officers in
the field had begun to take their toll.
Attempting to find new billets had become
virtually impossible as door after door was
slammed in the faces of those looking for
homes for the children. Recommendations

were made to the Government by head-masters and headmistresses to exert more pressure on those in a position to take in evacuees.

The Civil Defence Committee decided on a plan that would go into effect the moment the bombing began in earnest. It was decided that the new evacuees would be limited to schoolchildren and expectant mothers. Original evacuation areas would find some relief since a number of their evacuees would be redirected to areas in South Wales. This caused renewed protests of unfairness as the weight of responsibility would once more be on the poor, since it was the depressed mining areas that would be providing homes while the wealthier areas would be left virtually untouched.

A major problem for the Government was posed by the stories pouring into the letter-boxes of local MPs. Reading these gave the impression that the countryside had been flooded with problem children. Those not wetting the beds were stealing and using language hitherto unheard in the green fields of England. Although these things were true in some cases, what was not taken into account was the fact that many of these children were suffering as a result of being constantly shifted from one home to another. Orphans who had come from institutions now found themselves in homes and a part of a family. Some came from workhouses, Victorian shelters for the desperately poor. Some went to workhouses. But such was the outcry that the Government was forced to take action and decided to build camps for children who for one reason or another were deemed unmanageable. Thomas Barclay Anderson was a medical student and spent some time helping to staff hostels for unbilletable evacuees:

They were London children and were unbilletable because they were socially unacceptable – bed-wetters, potential criminals or medical liabilities – severe eczema, severe asthma.

Sarah Williams 'processed' 300 children from Liverpool and 200 from London between 1941 and 1946:

They were all medical cases. My job was to get them well and clean, ready for billets.

Some worked in several hostels. Denis Bollen was a house father in the West Country. The children in his care had originally been placed in private billets but, for whatever reason, these had not worked out. Some, from London's East End, used a rough street language which the foster parents feared would rub off on their own children. Others had been involved in petty thieving:

A respected children's social worker at the time wrote a book titled They Steal for Love, *and perhaps a little patience and affection would have resulted in a great reduction of this problem. We certainly found this to be the case in our hostel families. Head-lice too were another problem that we found easily curable...*

My first hostel was in a small village a few miles from Bristol. A large manor house had been taken over for the purpose. We had about 30 children in all, divided into four family groups of eight. The youngest group contained a few little girls, but the other groups were all boys.

There was a psychiatric social worker in charge of the hostel. A state registered nurse was matron, responsible for health matters, baths, hair-washing etc. There was a gardener, a cook, a part-time washerwoman and a night-watch-man. Each group had house fathers and these also had other duties, myself being responsible for the children's footwear and maintenance of the building.

But what was it like for a youngster who had been sent from at least two homes as 'un-desirable' and now found that the hostel was the end of the road? Kenneth John Webster had never settled and was always in trouble. He had been moved from billet to billet and now found himself in what was known in the area as an 'awkward evacuees' home':

It was outside the village of Bradford on Avon. At Conigar House there were 30 to 40 of us and it was run by a dear old lady called Miss Murray. She had a sister, Dr Jean Murray, who was very well known in the district mainly because of her work with the evacuees. The home was strict but fair and, more important, we all felt secure and loved.

A book should be written about these two lovely ladies. I still treasure my time at Conigar House and in fact I was heartbroken when I had to leave.

Maureen Harris (née Baggott) doesn't remember too much about her time in an 'awkward evacuees' home':

I was housed at Speedwell House with quite a few other children, including my brother. A lady who lived opposite used to throw sweets to us once a week and we all seemed to wear odd socks.

Jean Talbot (now Chapman) was an orphan in a children's home in Leeds when war broke out. She and her sisters were evacuated to Greenboro and, after walking from street to street with a billeting officer, pleading with people to take them in, they finally found a lady who agreed to take in her other sisters, but not her and her sister Agnes:

I was eventually taken in by a woman who decided that one night was enough and it was back to the billeting officer and I went to where my sisters were. Then I was moved again and my sister Agnes and I were separated. I never saw her again from that day to this.

7

The Phoney War Ends

The 'phoney' war finally ended with the invasion of Denmark and Norway by Germany in April 1940. For the British civilian at home the war had once again come to life. Disaster followed disaster as the Allied forces began to fall back against the fast advancing German Army. Chamberlain stepped aside and, in May, Winston Churchill became Prime Minister. On 13 May he stood in the House of Commons and declared, 'We are in the preliminary stage of one of the greatest battles in history,' and continued, 'I have nothing to offer but blood, toil, tears and sweat.'

Parents who had decided to bring their

children back home during the unexpected quiet began to think again, as Rotterdam was obliterated by the German Air Force and more than 1,000 civilians lost their lives. German pilots were seen machine-gunning civilians who were fleeing the cities by road. This only strengthened the Dutch Government's determination to pursue the policy of evacuation that had been formulated before the declaration of war. Meanwhile, with the continuing retreat of the Army in France, Britain was now facing the problem of trying to keep the roads clear for military traffic racing to the coast.

With the growing crisis in France, a new situation was emerging. Civilians were about to face the possibility of being in the same danger as the troops at the front. Many of the children who had been tugged from their homes in order to be protected from the horrors of war were soon to be at risk of finding themselves in the front line, closer to the enemy than anyone else on the island.

A 10-mile zone was designated inland along the coast from Norfolk to Sussex, and all citizens deemed non-essential were urged to move inland. All London children who had been evacuated to the areas within the zone in 1939 were re-evacuated to South Wales and the Midlands.

In a broadcast to the nation, Churchill

warned the people of the danger: 'There will be many men, and many women, in this island who when the ordeal comes upon them, as come it will, will feel comfort, and even pride, that they are sharing the perils of our lads at the front.'

A week later the Chiefs of Staff met to review the prospects of victory if France collapsed. The major problem was Britain's air defence. If France fell, Germany would be in a position to send the whole of its Air Force into battle. Long-range aircraft would be able to reach any part of the British Isles they chose.

As the British Army fell back on the small French coastal port of Dunkirk, I was being told to prepare to leave the drunken slob who had made my life so miserable.

In France, British soldiers scrambled aboard tugs, fishing-boats and anything else that could carry them back across the Channel to the safety of England.

The evacuees were also preparing to retreat. Before long, on board the familiar trains, they would be shunted away from Britain's new front line of defence. Jeane Outred was in Pagham, Sussex, when the first troops from Dunkirk arrived:

There were these two soldiers, all he'd got on, this one, were his little shorts and I said to him, 'Do you think the Germans will come here?' He said, 'No, they'll never get here. There is our first line of defence out there.' That was three big warships. Then he said, 'We are the second line,' and I said, 'What, you? Your mate is fast asleep.'

Marjorie McDonagh remembers trainloads of wounded soldiers passing through Marden in Kent:

They would write letters for us to post to their families, just give them to us through the train windows.

Some evacuees were billeted in the homes of those who had a member of the family involved in the retreat from Dunkirk. Irene Marrison (now Brough) was with a 'very nice lady' whose husband was fortunate enough to make it back from the Dunkirk beaches:

The men were landed at Dover, and as soon as our hostess heard this news she took off to meet her husband, leaving us behind in the care of an 80-year-old lodger. The first night she was away we were awakened about midnight by the air-raid siren. Now although it would have been rare for any bombs to be dropped in the vicinity (after all, wasn't this the safe place we'd fled to?) we were all well versed in what to do 'just in case', so we hurriedly flung our topcoats over our nighties and hastened along the hallway to awaken the old lady and get ourselves to a safe *place under the stairs. By this time we'd already noticed a most odious smell everywhere and were quite convinced the Germans had dropped gas on us, when I noticed a light under the bathroom door. The poor old dear had gone in to take a bath and the gas pilot on the water-heater had gone out and gas was escaping – hence the odour. The old dear was pretty deaf and no amount of hammering on her door could wake her so I sent to raise a neighbour or someone who could help. Luckily there was an air-raid warden up the street. He forced the bathroom door open in time to revive the old lady.*

Brian Tooley's father was a chief engineer on the cross-Channel boats and was soon heading for the beaches of Dunkirk and the thousands of soldiers who were waiting to be rescued. He was away for days at a time. Brian and his mother hurried to Dover from their home in Brighton in the hope of seeing him. They watched the columns of black smoke lifting into the sky on the other side and heard the muffled explosions:

When my father did eventually return home he fell on the bed in his clothes and slept for 15 hours. Then came a notice that all non-essential personnel were to leave, and Folkestone entered upon its four-year existence as a ghost town. For us, it was back to our home in Brighton, but this time travelling was no easy matter. All the trains had been requisitioned for the servicemen, and we waited for hour after hour as the trains rumbled through Folkestone Central, the soldiers showering the platform with their now useless francs.

On 10 May a lone German aircraft crossed the English coastline and made the first attack on British soil, near the villages of Petham and Chilham near Canterbury, in Kent. There were no casualties and no damage. This attack was followed by a period during which German aircraft frequently crossed the coastline on reconnoitring flights.

Between early June and early July, the number of enemy aircraft increased and air raids became more frequent and more widely spread. Attacks on airfields in East Anglia, industrial areas and Aberdeen were soon followed by air raids on Cambridge. On the day Cambridge experienced its first air raid, the people of Croydon, in South London, heard the sound of German aircraft overhead. The capital was about to receive its first German bombs of the war.

With the Germans now occupying France, an invasion appeared to be imminent. The Government once again decided to move the children who had been sent to the coast for safety.

The pupils of Stowey House School

boarded a train that headed west and slowly made its way across the Welsh border and into the town of Llanelly. We had arrived in a land of Joneses, Evanses, double 'I's and wonderful, hard-working people.

The familiar buses were there to meet us, and once again 'the mob' from south of the Thames were bundled on board. After an hour of driving through the green hills of our new home, we came to a tiny village that hugged the foot of a giant slag-heap of discarded coal.

Cross Hands (I never did find out why it had been given such a strange name) boasted a working-men's club and dozens of tiny miners' cottages, glistening with freshly whitened window sills and doorsteps in evidence of the inhabitants' fight against the black dust that drifted across from the nearby mine.

Once again we assembled for inspection in the local school and once again I set off with a stranger, hoping that my new home would be better than my last.

Mr and Mrs Jones were in their early thirties and had been married for a number of years. They had no children of their own, and taking in an evacuee was the perfect way to try out life with a child in their home. They would be paid for doing it and, if things didn't work out, an evacuee – unlike a child of their own – could always be handed back.

Their home was small and clean. The Joneses tried their best to make me happy. On my first Sunday with them, I was taken on a trip to the mine where Mr Jones worked.

The small cage dropped down the shaft and came to rest at the entrance to one of the main tunnels. The lamps on our protective helmets threw shadows against the dark, damp walls as we began the mile-long walk through the long, silent cavern. A small wooden ladder stood on one side, leaning against a four-foot hole in the side of the wall. I followed as Mr Jones climbed the ladder and vanished into the hole, bending to crawl along the stony surface as the roof got lower. The passage led to an area four feet square and three feet high, a damp burrow that was home for Mr Jones for eight hours a day, six days a week.

Mr Jones smiled and, leaning on one elbow, handed me a pick that had lain half-buried in the dirt. 'Take a piece of souvenir coal,' he grinned. I gave the side of the wall a gentle tap and began to place the little piece of loosened coal in my pocket. He took a pick. 'I said a piece of coal,' he said, laughing, and hit the side of the wall. I don't remember the size of the piece of coal that was dislodged, but I do remember that Mr Jones disappeared in a cloud of coal dust that whirled around the light on his helmet. In a few short years Mr Jones would die a horrible coughing death, another son of Wales who had lived like an animal underground in order to provide comforts for others.

Work in the mine was done in eight-hour shifts. The one I remember best is the afternoon shift, which finished at four o'clock, when Mr Jones would crawl back out of his burrow and make his way slowly down the long tunnel to the cage that would carry him to the surface. There he would join others as they set off home, the thick black dirt from another age and another world clinging to their clothes. Pit-head baths had yet to arrive, so each miner had to carry the filth home with him. There, in the bath, Mr Jones would sit and scrub, battling to remove the coal dust that had ingrained itself into every crevice of his gnarled and bruised skin.

After dinner at the Joneses' house it was jigsaw time. For hours the miner would sit, pushing pieces into place to form the country scenes he no doubt dreamed about when he was underground. I once made the mistake of trying to help, and received a slap on the hand and a long lecture on how it was bad manners to interfere in someone else's enjoyment.

It was the toilet that forced me out and into another home. I was terrified of it – not of the toilet itself, but of where it was situated. It was down at the bottom of the garden, a garden that after dark was filled with shadows and monsters just waiting to pounce on anyone heading for the small wooden hut. Most times I measured my stomach calls and was able to make my visits before it was dark outside, but one night I was caught short.

I was in the bath when I became aware that not only was it dark outside but my stomach was giving me a message. Rather than face the monsters of the night, I used the emptying bath, hoping that the fast vanishing water would carry away the evidence. It did not, and by dawn's early light I was on my way back to the billeting officer. I was about to enter my fourth billet and join yet another family.

Betty Hill (now Sheahan) had also boarded a train for Wales, which, unlike our train, had been pulled on to the siding to allow the trains carrying soldiers from Dunkirk to go through:

I will never forget how weary they looked and the pitiful condition of some of them – or the emotion I felt when I observed the people on the station, who were waiting there to greet them, all rush forward to shake their hands and to serve them with refreshments of tea and sandwiches, etc.

Many other children had, like me, been forced by the latest mass move into new homes. To some it seemed they had no sooner unpacked than they were getting packed again and shunted off somewhere else. Beryl Turner (now Gutsell) went to five billets, and although she missed her home, she had a chance to see another kind of life, both in wealthy homes and, finally, in the care of a wonderful elderly couple. Nevertheless, before she had time to settle down in their home she tried to run away:

We ran away over the River Dart, to Kingswear Station, because we heard that Brixton was only a little distance away – we came from Streatham – we thought they said 'Brixton' but they meant 'Brixham', a seaside resort. After many hours of waiting for our train home we were returned by the police to our foster homes in disgrace.

Beryl remembers another, earlier home, where she had been forced to sleep with an old lady:

She would comfort me by telling me she was often visited by her long-dead mother all dressed in a 'bootiful white nightie'. I was terrified, especially as her husband was making plans to skin their ginger cat to make a tobacco pouch. I went back to the hostel to wait for another billet. This one was a lovely old empty house with trestles and camp-beds and lots of empty rooms. We had no sheets, but when we were visited by 'the authorities' we were issued with strips of sheeting to put in front of the pillows to make them look like real sheets. I remember that place well as we all had to bath together – and I caught chicken-pox ... we all did!

Betty Gant (now Wells) also suffered when she found that one of her many billets was the home of a very old lady:

Her stories and her behaviour so frightened me I insisted on coming back home.

Monica Eveling remembers she shared three homes with her schoolfriend Christine Browne who lived, as she did, in Kentish Town, North London. Their first home was with a young couple:

I had hiccups and had been accused of taking money from the mantelpiece. I was very frightened and after a while the man said, 'Have your hiccups gone?' That was the fright remedy – in fact I seem to remember it working. The second home was with warm-hearted people, but a dirty house and very, very poor. We cried most of the night. Our mothers had quite a 'to-do' with the school staff about putting us into such a shocking home and we were transferred to a wonderful young bubbly couple.

Joe Duggan found himself in an abbey:

I was hugely homesick and each night dreaded my first vision of a long-dead abbot. I never saw one. Then, with another boy, I was told that I had been found a billet in Buckfastleigh.

One of the homes that Alun Roberts entered was a run-down café, owned by a rather strange bachelor of 50, who was kind enough, but apparently hoped to make money from the eight shillings a week allowance for taking in an evacuee:

The breakfast menu of a two-inch cube of porridge sticks in my mind as it did in my gullet then. His café was running with damp and my model aeroplane came unstuck so we complained again to the 'authorities' and got to live with a gypsy and his wife.

Betty Gant (now Wells) had been evacuated with an infants' school, since her own school had left the day before. It seemed she had been waiting in the car for hours when finally an elderly lady poked her head in and said, 'Yes, I will take her.' She had expected someone between five and seven, but when she saw Betty she decided that maybe someone older was a better idea after all:

She was a lady who had been comfortably off and I had a delightful bedroom. I do believe she enjoyed my company. She had an old uncle who was blind and when he came to stay I read the newspaper to him. He had a Rolls-Royce and a chauffeur and I used to go out with them.

Back in the village of Cross Hands, I said goodbye to an obviously relieved Mr and Mrs Jones and made my way back to the school with the local billeting officer.

The villagers had by now taken in the evacuees they wanted, and few were ready to receive any more. It was not easy finding someone who was willing to take a small boy who had already been tried out and found 'not suitable'. But wherever you go in the world, there is nearly always someone who will offer help to those who need it, and in Cross Hands it was a Mr and Mrs Roberts, with a daughter my own age, who agreed to share their home. They had already accepted one evacuee but were willing to take another if no one else offered. No one did, so off I went.

It was Mr Roberts who came to the school to get me. A short stocky man in his mid-forties, he was everything a village smithy should be – strong yet gentle, with arms that were capable of holding the strongest horse in place as he hammered home a shoe. He had a limp – the result, I believe, of having been kicked by an irate horse many years before.

The village was small, and so was the Robertses' cottage. It was situated close to the school, and its doorstep and window sills gleamed as a result of Mrs Roberts' handiwork with the whitening block that seemed to be standard equipment in all Welsh homes. It had low wooden beams inside, so it was fortunate that Mr Roberts and his wife were relatively short people.

The home of the smithy was the centre of my world. Next door was the working-men's club with its snooker tables, where hours of spare time were spent hitting balls around the green baize.

Perhaps my life in the village and work on the tiny farm at the back of the Robertses' home should have given me a love of the land. It didn't. Maybe it was the morning when Mr Roberts and a handful of neighbours woke me so I could help them slaughter a pig that killed my enthusiasm. Since to kill anything other than humans during wartime was against the law, it was decided that 4.30 a.m. would be the ideal time.

Before sunrise we sneaked out of the back and approached the sty. Long before we reached the pig, it got wind of the fact that this was to be its final hour, and began a series of squeals that got louder the closer we got. After a good deal of pushing, shoving and slipping in the sty, the five of us finally succeeded in manoeuvring the poor animal into the shed close by. With Mr Roberts limping and shouting orders, we lifted the animal on to a wooden bench and rolled it on to its side. As we lay across the pig's body, Mr Roberts grabbed an empty bucket and placed it close to its head.

The squealing had now reached such a pitch that it was difficult to hear even Mr Roberts as he screamed for someone to hold back the pig's neck. He then took a long, thin skewer and with a swift jab buried it in the unfortunate animal's throat. With the action of an Errol Flynn withdrawing a sword from the body of a villain, he swept his arm back, pulling out the skewer, and in the same action grabbed the bucket. A long spurt of blood shot out, forming an arc, and hit the inside of the bucket, while we lay across the body until the last squeal had faded.

Just 50 yards from the house, the entrance to the school led down a lane to a long, low, one-storey building, where the teachers were undistinguished enough to have long ago erased themselves from my memory. What I do remember is a plot of land that was set aside for lessons in gardening and to this day I can recall how to 'double-trench' a weed-covered patch and make it suitable for growing potatoes – a skill I have never had the opportunity to put into practice.

With the fall of France and safety areas now few and far between, schools in the evacuation areas were having to cope with vast numbers of pupils unheard of then or since. Jill Fisher (now West) felt that, for her, the situation was 'catastrophic':

The fact was that I was more advanced scholastically, and to go to a two-roomed school (divided by partitions) and go back to lessons, threw me completely, and I really didn't (at that age) know how to cope. Did I show off? Or pretend I was learning? I chose the latter, and pretended I was stupid and coasted along every day, dreaming, with no stimulation from very apathetic 'wartime' teachers in a village school.

Amba Mary James (now Dalton)'s sister learned there were some things you could do at school, and some things you couldn't:

My sister was found out after drawing a rude picture. She was really in disgrace and not allowed out. I was not allowed to see the drawing and could not imagine what could be so bad. The Salvation Army Captain was called for and shown the picture. His advice was, 'She will grow up to be a bad girl. Lo, she has the eyes of a Delilah.' I was really worried for her – she was about 10 years of age at the time.

Geoffrey West realized that there appeared to be two sets of rules at school – one for evacuees and one for locals:

We had two lady teachers who came with us from Chingford, Miss Bristow and Mrs Weatherspoon. Mrs Weatherspoon wore plus-fours and smoked a pipe. I don't know why or how the evacuees got into so much trouble, unless it was because a very biased eye was kept on us... We weren't all villains. One afternoon Mrs Weatherspoon assembled all the boy evacuees in the staffroom. I can remember Mrs Weatherspoon saying, 'You know I have to be tougher with you evacuees otherwise the local people will think I'm favouring you.' We may have been dim but we would have had to be stupid not to realize there was nobody going to stick up for us.

When Barbara Partridge (now Alder) arrived in Sutton Courtenay she was sent for lessons in the village hall:

It was divided into four classes by curtains. Those teachers deserved a medal, trying to teach in such circumstances.

Patricia Perriman (now Taylor) went to school only for half-days:

Other times we met the group leader (a wonderful teacher called Mr Toms) on the common and went for rambles.

There weren't any schools for Michael Clark, so he was taught in a church hall:

There were several rooms and us boys were in the billiard room and our desks were set around it.

The schooling arrangements for Dulcie Lilley (now Rollingson) must have been less than adequate:

There was 100% failure when we sat for the scholarship exam.

Pam Hobbs was staying in the same village as two of her own teachers, one of whom gave her extra encouragement:

We were in Mapperley for several months. During that time the schoolteacher, in the one-roomed school, coached me after school and urged me to sit for a scholarship. He beat the boys mercilessly, but never the girls. I think my sister went to another school, probably for older girls, because she wasn't with me and I was one of the oldest at my school. Anyway, with the 'gaffer', as they called him, helping me I walked to a town some miles away and sat for this scholarship. It took several hours each day. Luckily a boy from the village was also taking the scholarship and he knew the way.

In Mapperley that spring and summer, one of the boys' uncles, a naval officer, used to come home from the sea with chocolate bars and oranges. He would get us girls to do cartwheels and play wheelbarrows so he could see our underwear (I suppose). We knew the reason, thought it harmless, and wanted the goodies. Then my sister's friend told her she would go to bed with her pyjamas on and, funny thing, she always woke up without them. One time she saw him leaving the room. (She lived at his house, but he was away most of the time.) My sister told her teacher.

I knew nothing more till she and the girl in question were taken to court. What the man was found guilty of I don't know. All I knew was that a frantic teacher came banging on our door and said we had to be packed within an hour. All the evacuees had to leave, because the villagers were out to get us. They thought we were troublemakers and the naval man unjustly accused. He was sentenced to a prison term if I heard it correctly. I was so worried about my bike. My mother had promised to send me one once the rag-and-bone man had one she could afford. It had arrived two weeks earlier. My foster mother was furious, said she would give the bike away and we were practically thrown on the bus.

We arrived in Kirk Langley in the early morning. My sister and I, billeted together, were

217

sent to a beautiful house with ivy on the walls and baby chicks running around the grounds. The woman was arthritic, in a wheelchair most of the time. The man worked with horses at the co-op in Derby, he had a car (I had never been in one) and kept pigs, one of which we trained to roll over on its back to be tickled when it saw me. We called it Mardi. They were super people, took us on outings at weekends and we all had a lovely time. I loved the countryside, and the big old house, and the home-made bread and pies made by a housekeeper who came each day to take care of things.

We were there only six weeks or so when a post-card arrived saying I had passed my scholarship.

Patricia Silverman (now Ferman) found she had problems just getting to school:

I don't know which I dreaded more, meeting a herd of cows in the lane home, or being cornered by a bunch of local boys.

At least the teachers were often familiar, since many of them had travelled with the children and knew them and something of their background. Eugene McCoach was enrolled in the local primary school and was fortunate enough to have his own teacher from Clydebank:

Mrs Hindson encouraged us in our homework

and I must confess that to a great extent she was responsible for my success at being first in what we termed the qualifying class.

Estella Halfin (now Spergel) was not so fortunate in her time spent at school in the evacuation area. Someone reported that she had been seen with a young man in the evening when she should have been in her foster home. She denied the charge but was brought up in front of her headmistress:

I remember being smiled at pityingly. 'You were seen by a teacher.' That meant of course that I was lying. A teacher could not be wrong. I wasn't even told the details of this awful crime. I know I burst into tears, worried about what my mum would say and worried sick that now I would be labelled 'fast'.

A couple of weeks later a teacher visited my foster home – this was routine to check on the conditions, I believe, etc. and the next day the teacher apologized to me for the above accusation. The man I was seen with was my foster father, Reg Scott. He was teaching me to ride his wife's bike in the evening after work.

Eileen Adams remembers the words of her headmistress after a girl called Rita, who was German, had arrived at the school:

'Now we all know Rita is German,' said the

headmistress from the school stage, 'and that Germans are our enemy. But we must be kind to Rita because she is our friend.' After that it didn't occur to anyone that Rita wasn't our enemy.

Pam Hobbs remembers interrupted days at school:

A teacher at Kirk Langley put me on a train and gave me the postcard with Chapel-en-le-Frith written on it. At every stop I checked the station name to see if it was my destination. I didn't think I was crying but tears kept flowing. Nobody on the train talked to me...

At Chapel-en-le-Frith I left the train. A little woman, completely round, with a gym tunic above her knees, came bouncing up and asked if I was Pamela. She ignored my tears, and said, 'We don't wear our hats like that old thing,' and promptly turned down the brim of my panama. She had a pony and trap, and when she put her leg up on the side to steady herself I kept looking at her long navy bloomers. She took us to the most beautiful mansion and I cheered up thinking I had really clicked this time. It turned out to be a hostel. She was not my foster mother, but the gym mistress, and the mansion was a sort of holding station for kids not yet assigned billets. It was very crowded. I had a cot in the corridor, and a prefect told me we had bangers for tea. I had always read a lot of girls' books, and this was heaven – just like boarding school in the books. We went, in a crocodile line, to another mansion which served as our school. Whenever a teacher came into the dorm I was later assigned to, I said I was unwell, so somebody else got taken to a billet. Finally she said she was sorry, but I couldn't stay any longer. I had made friends with a girl called Betty, who lived in town, and the teacher said I could go and live with her...

My new foster home was very modest. There was a toddler called Arthur, so I guess the parents were quite young. We didn't see much of the man because he worked on the night-shift... We slept in his room at night, and he had it in the daytime. His wife had a boxroom with a single bed, in which Betty had slept before I arrived. Betty's mother visited us. I still hadn't seen my mother since I had left home with the junior school. Betty's mother told our head-mistress she wanted us moved. It just wasn't nice our sleeping in the same sheets the man was using, and his filled chamber pot was under the bed when she was there. I can't say I ever noticed anything amiss. I didn't particularly like the little child, probably because I was the youngest in my family and had no experience with toddlers. The headmistress was very disgruntled, saying good billets were hard to find, and put us in another home, which was something of a nightmare.

The couple were quite old – maybe around 50, which seemed old then. She had greasy hair in a *plait and used to ask me to braid it for her. I hated doing it. I don't know where the old man worked. If we were sick we had to wait until money arrived from our parents before she would get medicine. We weren't allowed in the house till about 5 p.m. and in the evenings had to sit in the scullery with its stone floor. She said the alternative to us was a couple of Irish labourers, otherwise she would never have consented to our living there. I think she was trying to save money on the allowance given her. We became very thin. At 7 p.m. to 9 p.m. at night we met with two other girls, similarly treated, and would sit in the bushes, around a fire if we could steal matches, talking about when we get home...*

We used to be so hungry we volunteered to wash the teachers' dishes at lunch-time. The staff lived at the school, and had lovely raspberry bushes in the kitchen garden. Sometimes we stole the berries. When we washed their cups, we found bits of Marmite at the bottom, added water and drank it. Our own lunch was half a sandwich each. My foster mother said she couldn't feed us on the allowance. We used to drool at the sweet-shop. Rationing was in, so we could get a few now and then. We used to dread going home so much, we went into the library after school if it was cold or wet. Our feet used to tingle because our water-boots were so tight. Later my mother told us she had sent money for new boots.

Our teachers didn't want to listen to our woes. They used to go home to Leigh regularly, so did some of the girls. I felt then, and now, that it was because we were scholarship kids from working-class families and this was one very posh school. With 'free' stamped on my atlas and dictionary, and my working-class accent, there was no hiding that I wasn't one of them...

Before leaving, Betty and I agreed to let out the foster mother's budgie. Very unkind I know. She loved that bird. She didn't come to the station.

With the classrooms in the reception areas so crowded, many children found themselves wondering what to do with their time. Margaret Cable (now Rowe) was billeted with a woman who felt it important that she plan their spare time for them and keep them busy:

She sent us miles away to buy one item of shopping at a time, thinking that the walk would keep us occupied. Each evening she would be away from home she encouraged us to go out after tea and she would leave three bowls of cornflakes on the step made soggy with milk to ease our pangs of hunger until she returned home.

My sister and I devised a plan. We knew that Mrs Hudson read our letters from home before she gave them to us to read, and she insisted on reading the letters we sent to our parents before she would give us a stamp to post them. We

223

therefore wrote to our parents telling them how unhappy we were and left the unsealed letter in our bedroom. We didn't have to wait long before our plan showed results. The same day we returned from afternoon school to find our belongings in the front garden and we had no reply to our banging on the front door.

We went to tell our story to the headmaster who lived a short distance away. He returned with us and knocked on Mrs Hudson's front door but found no response. He picked up our bags and he took us to the sea-front where he deposited my sister and me with the bags and told us he would try and get us accommodated for the night.

We must have looked an unhappy pair. A lady came along with a dog and she asked us what was wrong. We told her our tale and she sat beside us and promised that we could go home with her and stay with her as long as wanted to. When the headmaster returned he was overjoyed as he had found it impossible to find accommodation.

Some who were homesick were too young to write home and tell their parents. Peter Anthony Whyman found this was another job he was saddled with:

My brother became homesick, yet the little bugger wouldn't write home – he left it to me to do. I had unwittingly accepted responsibility for

Children on their way to the railway station during an
evacuation rehearsal, June 1939

Three brothers and a sister arrive at school for another rehearsal, August 1939

The rehearsals over, this is the real thing

Walking to Blackhorse Road station, North East London

Evacuees from Silver Street School, Edmonton,
North London, 1939

2 September 1939

Evacuation of London schoolchildren, June 1940

Waiting at the station

Evacuees at Paddington Station, 1940

23 May 1942

Children leaving, mothers weeping

The billeting officer says goodbye to her callers

Evacuees having dinner, October 1939

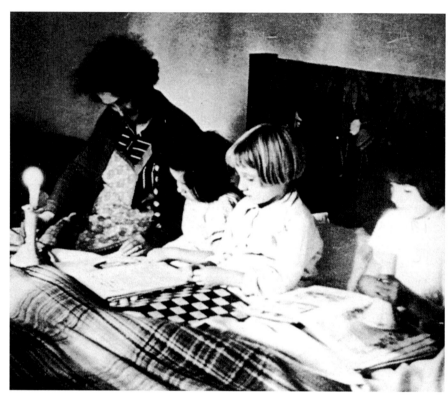

Bedtime in a foster home, November 1939

Evacuees at bathtime

11.3.41   7 Park Rd
          chard,
          Somerset.

Dear mummy and daddy
we recieved your letter safely
thank you for the ~~st~~ five
Shillings each Betty the
dog is dead it died last
friday, Auntie came down
stairs friday morning
and thout betty was going
to be sick and **pickt** her
up and she died in Aunties
arms have you had eny
raids latly we had a
warning on friday afternoon
and one on sunday morning
in chapel and it terned in
nicely with the music today
I went in a field and saw
a spitfire on the field ~~a~~ a

One of evacuee Joyce Wright's letters home

spitfire is not very big is it
ask daddy if he could get
me eny comics if not it
does not matter I have two
milks a day at school
some girls and boys in
jeans class are going
in for the scholarship
tomorrow, tomorrow Jean
has to run messages for Miss
Sheffield and Mr wall
I got all my English
Write today and all my sums
I love arithmetic because
My teacher gives us easy
sums how is rene tell
her I am going to Write
to her soon will you tell
Mrs fitch that I will write
to bruce and send it with
renes letter well darlings
I must lose now with
love from your loving
x x daughter x x joyce x x x x x x
x x x x x x x x

DEAR MUM
I hope YOU ARE WELL
AND THANK YOU FOR THE
SHILLING AND THE

LOVELY PAINTS. I hoPE THE
WAR WILL BE OWER
SOON, DO YOU? I hoPE
YOU WILL COME DOWN
AGAIN SOON. IGIVE MY
LOVE TO AUNTIE ELSIE.
LOVE FROM Betty Sacre

X X X X X X X X X X X X X X X X X
X X X X X X X X X X X X X X X X X

Betty Sacre writes to her mother

him. I cannot remember feeling homesick myself, but I did miss our Saturday tea treat of a pint of winkles.

Both evacuees and their hosts encountered a similar problem: 'What kind of language is that they're speaking?' With local customs and accents brought up against various city dialects, it was often difficult for people to understand one another. For some children, evacuation was an introduction to a Britain that for all intents and purposes could have been China. The first thing Renée Selvage (née Bickerdike) remembers about village life is that she had to be measured for some local footwear:

It was bleak and cold and we had to go into Ramsbottom and be measured for clogs. It was quite a novelty running along the road making sparks as they struck the surface.

After telling him that she would feed him, do his washing and so on, Edward Harvey's foster mother gave him a task:

She said, 'The only thing I want you to do is mend your own bed.' I didn't recall seeing it broken, but went upstairs to take a second look, nothing wrong with it. When I remarked on this fact, she said, 'Funny lad, I mean straighten the sheets and blankets when you get up.'

While Edward Harvey struggled with the peculiarities of a 'foreign' language, his sister mastered it:

I learned that a bowl was a 'panshine', pork was pork, lamb was lamb but beef was meat. The man's boss was 'owd gaffer', and if I said something that he thought was silly, I became a 'silly wapyead'. My sister started using the local dialect, which grew stronger and stronger, so by the time she returned to my parents two years later, I don't think they could understand what she was saying.

Ken Lake also remembers the local customs:

Every village child swore like a trooper and [I have a] recollection of a stupid game called 'crowns' which entailed the loser being beaten over the head with the clenched fists of the winners.

Peter Gallagher decided that 'in the interests of survival' he'd better learn to speak Geordie:

So if one of the local lads suggested, 'Let's ha'way oop the bank t'gaff,' I knew that he was suggesting that we go to the pictures at the local cinema.

Evacuation certainly widened many children's horizons, sending them into a dream world that at any other time would have been impossible. From a world of Saturday-morning movies, fish and chips and washing dripping on a clothesline, many were transported into the kind of home that other people crave. Just outside Penzance, in a large house, lived a woman who was a millionaire, and it was with her that Charles Foster found his third home:

She had a big Rolls-Royce, a Buick and lots of servants and big grounds. The woman, Mrs Buchanan, was bedridden. She was about 80 and we saw her just once when we first got there. One of the servants used to take us round the garden each day and the one who could name the most flowers got sixpence.

Barbara Partridge (now Alder) saw how the 'other half' lived when she went to stay in a large house with three bathrooms. She came from an extremely poor home:

...partially because of the depression in the thirties, but also because my father was a very difficult man so that even when jobs were available he couldn't keep one. (He was the only man I knew who got sacked from 20 munitions factories in wartime, quite an achievement.) We lived in a series of unsavoury flats in Catford

and Finsbury Park, bathrooms were unheard of, bedbugs not unknown. Then suddenly I am in a large house with three bathrooms, electric lights, a huge garden, plentiful food – seems I'm in heaven.

Culturally I gained enormously. Mr and Mrs Porter were world travellers before the war. She was a New Zealander and they went back and forth many times, in those days by ship, and they would tell me of the places they had visited during their travels, so I developed an interest in the rest of the world which I might not have done otherwise. I was always an avid reader and their house was full of books, of which I could take my pick, another plus. I also came in contact with what's known as the 'landed gentry', Sutton Courtenay being a very snobby place. (They didn't impress me.)

Then suddenly my parents left London to escape the bombing and wanted me to join them. I did. They had no money for furniture, so for the next three years I slept in the sitting-room on a canvas and wood camp-bed with grey blankets and a straw-filled pillow supplied by the local council. Some contrast.

Nellie Bly came from a family of 15 children, who used to sleep at least three to a bed. Her father had died when she was six and things at home were tough. Being evacuated to Sussex opened up a new life for her:

I learned how to pluck geese and to live like a farm child. I was taken to the Squire's house where there were maids and you had to curtsy to the lady of the village, Lady Beaumont. I really got my education there. I learned about flowers and wildlife generally. My own family were proud people but rather ignorant. Even though my mother had 15 children she was not happy to see any of them go. With the experience of the evacuation I am able to appreciate the good things of life.

Laurie was sent to Howdon Dene with her pillowcase and a tin of corned beef. She was one of 10 evacuees taken in by Lady Straker-Smith:

I saw a part of living I had never seen before. Kindness and lovely clean things. Lord and Lady Straker-Smith were not snobs. They had servants. We stayed in the servants' quarters.

The manor house that Iris Key (now Macleod) moved into when she was eight remained her home for four years:

We were looked after by the head housekeeper. Meals were silent, with Miss Foster at one end of the table and the butler at the other end. We were not allowed in the orchard or the front of the house. They had twelve black retriever dogs; their names all began with 'D'- Dick, Don,

Darky, Deirdre, Dolly, Dumpy etc.

Iris Thrussell (now Davis) must have been the envy of the school:

If the weather was bad the chauffeur would pick us up from school in the Rolls-Royce. I shall never forget his spats and gloves.

Another young girl, on the other hand, was made to earn her keep:

One of my chores was to empty the chamber-pots each morning into a bucket upstairs and carry it down to the toilet. This particular morning I fell down the stairs and the bucket of – yes! – completely covered me, so you can well imagine, I got smelling quite sweet, and soaked through.

For mothers expecting babies it was particularly difficult. Many of the hospitals in the cities were being prepared for air-raid casualties, while the last person anyone in an official position wanted to see in the evacuation areas was a pregnant woman. Joan England was 18 and expecting her first child. She had no alternative but to agree to be evacuated and was soon on board a train crowded with young children. On arriving at her destination, she had to wait a long time before finding a home to go to:

230

Of course, 'Pregnant Penelope' sat there right to the very last. A wealthy lady who had just come back from abroad approached me and said, 'I'll have you. I've got a house and I haven't any staff and I can't cook. If you are willing to come with me and help out I'll give you shelter.' It was Pamela Brown (the actress)'s mother. I lived in luxury. I was only 18 but I managed to cook something. Between us we survived.

I was about to go into hospital to have my baby but I had high blood pressure, so they took me to this lovely country home that had been taken over for use as a maternity hospital. There I met hundreds of East London pregnant mums. They'd all had six or seven kids each and been deserted by their husbands. It seemed the War Office had taken over the building of all Army huts. Fabulous salaries were being offered and their husbands had just upped and taken off. They had no option but to be evacuated. My husband was about the only husband who ever came to visit.

It was quite awful at times but also fun. We had no doctors and lost several babies a month because of that fact. One baby's mother died and was adopted by the Lord and Lady. One crowd of London mothers were put in [a building] like a giant cow shed. They were a happy little crowd. One of the mothers had been in labour about 24 hours and was in difficulty. They needed oxygen and had difficulty with the machine. They needed a wrench. Someone said, 'What we need is a man.' I said, 'Well, there is only one I know. The butler.' So we rang for James and he went racing off and came back with the biggest spanner you've ever seen. By the time he got back the baby had been born. 'It's all right,' I said. 'It's too late, James, the baby has been born.' To this day I think he felt that we needed the spanner to get the baby out.

Anne Bradman believes she was the last pregnant woman in London at the beginning of the war to be taken by car with a VAD nurse to St Albans:

The place was called 'The Pregnant Town' as almost every woman in it was pregnant.

Pat Senior (now Smith) was evacuated with her mother, brother and baby sister to Blackpool, where they were all given a tiny room at the top of a very large house. By the day after their arrival, the landlady had still not offered any milk for the baby, and the family set off around the town to look for something better. Finally, exhausted, the children's mother collapsed beside the window sill of a closed café and began crying. Pat remembers:

The next thing that happened was the owner of the café came out to see what was the matter. The next thing we know is a chauffeur's car is picking up our luggage and we are whisked off to this big beautiful house in Hornsby Road. The man who owned the café turned out to be the local councillor. Life then became fantastic. Mr Jenkins used to sing to us, 'Down the road away went Polly'. I can still picture him singing it.

When Joyce Eileen Hanson (now Steen) was 11, she was evacuated for a second time, along with her pregnant mother. They found themselves in Chesham in a small condemned cottage. At the same time another woman laid claim to the cottage, so both families moved in together:

The funny thing was that my mother's name was Day and her name was Knight. She had one little boy and he had Down's syndrome. When we went into this cottage we didn't have anything, so I went out with a pram and went round to the houses and asked people if they had things they didn't want. The bloody pram was bigger than I was. I couldn't see over the top of it. I would go up past Billy Butlin's farm and I would knock on the houses and when the woman opened the door I'd say, 'We are evacuees. We've just got our empty cottage and nothing to put in it. Have you got anything you can give us?' One day I came back with a double bed and went back to get the mattress. Someone else gave me blankets and bedspreads. You name it, we had it. We didn't have

233

to buy anything.

During my first two years away from London, my mother came to visit me once, while I was staying in Eastbourne. The cost of the train fare was almost prohibitive for her, but somehow she managed to find the money. On the day of her visit I was wearing shoes that someone had given me after the ones I'd had when I was first evacuated had worn out. These shoes, although almost new, did not fit, and I was later told by an elder sister that Mum arrived back in London extremely upset, since most of the day had been spent with me limping around with my heels hanging over the backs of the shoes as I gave her a guided tour of the town.

When I was moved to Wales it became impossible for my mother to visit, as the cost of travel was far beyond the family's means. Many evacuees' relatives, however, still managed to go and see them. Concerned about the welfare of their children, parents hurried to board trains at the first opportunity or packed into cars and used up their meagre petrol rations. Eugene McCoach was evacuated to Helensburgh:

It was invaded by parents, uncles, grannies etc. It was just like sheep searching out their lambs.

Sheila Saunders recalls that when her father went to see her, he got quite a shock:

I was three and my father came down to visit and knocked on the door. I opened it and left him standing there. I went back into the house to the lady I called Auntie and said a Mr Lindsay was at the door.

Doris O'Donnell (née Griffiths) remembers when Ronnie, the first evacuee her mother took in, was visited by his parents:

His mother and father drove over to visit him one Sunday. Mother was only too happy to provide tea, which they greatly appreciated. In return, they took my stepfather down to the local hostelry for the evening and treated him to all the drink he wanted. A good time was had by all, and the next time they came they brought an aunt and uncle with them, because they said, four could travel just as cheaply as two, and again a meal was provided for them, with a repeat visit to the pub.

Over a period it went from one to two cars and so on, until one Sunday, what must have been the whole family – uncles, aunts, cousins, etc. – turned up in a minibus, again because they said it was cheaper and they all so enjoyed the peace and hospitality provided. By this time, of course, it had become custom and practice that Mother provided the meal and they in turn took the old man down to the pub. Now, please don't get me wrong, they weren't scroungers by any means. I remember they always brought presents for Mother, and I'm sure they really did enjoy the day out. However, as far as I was concerned it was just blooming hard work.

When Rosemary Richman (now Johnson)'s mother came to visit, the day started off beautifully:

She took the four of us, who were all billeted in different homes, on a picnic across some fields where we all took off our shoes and socks and Mum took off her stockings and set out the food. There were lovely home-made meat pies. What we didn't notice till too late was a herd of bullocks slowly coming our way. Suddenly they were on top of us and we all ran like mad and climbed over the fence. They devoured everything, and I do mean everything. We found not a trace of our socks or our mum's stockings.

Irene Brownhill (now Smith)'s father had been at Dunkirk:

He had been made a Sergeant, so had extra money to come and see us when on leave. It was near Christmas so he took my sister and me and my mother around the shops. He bought us presents, and then we went to this little café where the lady found us some boiled-ham sandwiches

– which were scarce with rationing – and some cream cakes, she said because my dad was a soldier. She gave us a lovely tea. After a lovely day we went back to our foster lady. I remember I cried after my dad because he was going. I always had a fear he would get killed in the war. I can feel the rough khaki now of his uniform as he held me to say goodbye. He used to call me Bubbles and my sister Squeak.

Jeanette Cox (née Sines) recalls that it was a few minutes after the all-clear that there was a knock on her billet door:

It was my dear mum. She had walked all the way from Brighton through the deserted streets, and when challenged by a policeman who told her to take cover, she told him she would do no such thing until she had located her daughter and niece.

Ruth Whitehorn (now Glaister) was three and a half years old when she was evacuated from London:

I was made welcome by George and Flo Hardy, a childless couple. Flo was a Jamaican, married to an Englishman, and as both loved children it was a good and happy home. I started school at four and a half for the first time while I was there. One thing sticks in my mind: it was Flo's custom to put a little rum in tea whenever she brewed up, and naturally some went into my tea. This went on for some months, until one day, on a visit, my mother discovered what was going on and sparks flew in every direction. My mother was strictly teetotal and any suggestion of alcohol was decidedly frowned upon. Needless to say the rum ration stopped after this.

James Moseley remembers the remark he made to his father during one visit:

'We only get real butter when you are here.'

Shortly after that visit, James developed impetigo and left for home immediately.

On the first Sunday after they had been evacuated, Nora McClarence's aunt, accompanied by her children, came to visit Nora and the other aunt she had been sent away with:

She talked to the lady of the house and also the aunt I was with. Lo and behold, before I knew it, I was knocking on my own front door. My mum and dad nearly collapsed when they saw me. They'd only just waved me off goodbye 24 hours earlier.

I did not know until I was in my teens the reason why we came back so quickly and spent the remaining war years at home. The widower my aunt had been sent to went to her room during the night and made nasty advances to her, so she refused to stay. My other aunt came and collected my aunt and me and home we came.

Some children decided that whether their parents made a visit or not, they were not going to hang around – they were going to escape back to their city homes. Alice Henning (now Richardson) was billeted with two elderly spinsters, and found it 'disastrous':

We were three boisterous children, especially my brother. I had just reached the age of puberty and I wasn't allowed to wash my hair when I had a period so I became quite lousy. We were very unhappy and decided to leave and go back to London. My youngest brother was plump and quite short and only six years old, and my other brother and I wanted to leave him as we thought he would slow us down, but he persuaded us to take him. I don't know how far we got but we decided to call in at a pub. We had nothing to eat and there were no road signs and we had become so thirsty. The lady in the pub saw that there was something wrong, but she gave us some water and something to eat and we left. As we trudged on, a police car stopped and took us back. They wanted to send us to the elderly ladies but I lost my temper and tipped up a desk so they sent us to another house.

James Forbes spent eight unhappy months in one home before eventually running away:

I used two pennies given to me by a school pal. I travelled approximately 12 miles by bus, then walked 27 miles to my home where my mother, who had been informed of my flight, was expecting me.

David Owen was eight and his two sisters five and three when they were evacuated. After various unhappy experiences he decided to make his way back to London:

In desperation I started out with them to walk to London. We got as far as Stony Stratford (John Wesley had said of it, 'Stony by name, but not by nature') before being discovered and returned on a bus to Ashton. I still recall how kind and concerned the police were.

After being told that he could not have sugar, Chris Portinari was caught helping himself from the bowl that had been left on the table. He was moved to another home, where two boys tortured him:

They would tie me to a chair when their parents had gone out, and went to fetch red-hot pokers that they held in front of my eyes. I had terrible nightmares and was always walking around in my sleep. I was sent away from there when three of us took down the knickers of the girl next door. I finally ended up in a spick and span place. Every day I would come home from school and it would say, 'Clean this, shine that, polish something else.' So I started to save up my milk money, a halfpenny a day, and I came home one day and wrote across the list of things to do, 'GONE BACK TO LONDON!'

My mother hid me for two days in the attic before telling my father. I think she wanted to break it to him gently and was in fear of authority. I wasn't sent back and stayed in London during the raids.

Pauline Silver, who was evacuated from Croydon to Newcastle, remembers that she left home with her little sister, but they were soon separated from each other:

I hated the whole experience and the family I was sent to seemed to live on nothing else but bread and I was permanently hungry. The family had one son aged about 18 and a daughter about my age, 12. At one meal the son suddenly coughed up a lot of blood; he was taken to hospital and diagnosed as having TB. Nobody seemed to be bothered that he could have infected us all.

However, after a while I decided that I was going back home, but not having a penny in my pocket it was a difficult problem. I picked up my miserable belongings, walked to Newcastle station and hovered around until I found out which trains were going to London. Waiting around till the last minute, I then dived between all the legs and jumped on the end of the train. I hid in the lavatory until the train had been going for about 15 minutes, then emerged and to my horror was confronted by a soldier with a red cap. I had got on a train full of Canadian soldiers going to London. I must have looked a poor little waif, as they took me to a carriage and sat me between eight husky young soldiers who all produced food. I shall never forget eating a delicious chocolate bar and cheese sandwich. One soldier gave me a rosary and said a little prayer that we both survived the war. I wonder who he was and if he is still alive.

Having got to London I then had to get to Croydon, and I found an 18 bus which went to London Bridge Station. I got on the bus and told the conductor that I was trying to get home, so he let me ride free.

At London Bridge Station I found a train going to Croydon, and as I had been travelling for about 12 hours by now, I just told the guard at the gate that I had no money and he held on to me until just before the train started, then handed me over to the guard with instructions to put me off at Croydon station.

Having got off I had about a two-mile walk to my house in the dark. When I got home my mother came to the door and to my amazement said, 'What are you doing here?' and slapped me!

The house in which one young girl found herself was in Salisbury, Wiltshire. Her eldest sister was an extremely determined girl who, after a short stay, decided that she was going to do all she could to get home:

The first time she ran away she took me with her. I can vaguely remember hiding with her under a train seat for quite a long time. Apparently her planning wasn't the best, and we got stuck in a siding.

For some evacuees, escape was never a real possibility. Either too far from home, or too nervous about being punished if they were caught and returned to their billets, they opted to suffer in silence in the hope that the war would soon end and they could go home.

Teachers were no substitute for parents, though many tried their best to fulfil the role. The procedure for assessing homes to ensure that they were suitable appears to have been almost non-existent.

Of the thousands of letters we received, understandably, those that told of cruel treatment were the hardest to read. It's true that hundreds of thousands of ex-evacuees did not answer our call. The majority of these would, like most evacuated children, have been treated with kindness and affection.

They probably felt that their 'ordinary' stories would be of little interest to anyone outside their immediate family, and so did not contact us. But evacuees who were treated badly have lived with their experiences for almost 50 years. The majority of phone calls and letters from such people have stressed the point that they have never told their story before. In deference to their wishes we have omitted or altered many of their names, and hope that by giving them the opportunity to speak we have lightened their burden.

An eye injury at birth had left Patsy with a bad squint. She was very tall for her age and had always been 'paralysingly shy'. Her mother had charged her with the care of her two younger sisters, but she found it hard to stand up for herself, let alone for anyone else. After one unsatisfactory evacuation she left home a second time, this time for Horsham:

The lady was a nurse. She did not want any evacuees, but had apparently been told that since she had four bedrooms she must take the three of us. She was constantly telling us that she did not want us there.

She told me immediately that she expected me to wash my and my sisters' underwear, and every evening we had to place our underpants into a pail of cold water to soak.

244

She was obsessed with us having bowel move-
ments before we left for school in the morning
and to this end we were fed Ex-Lax every even-
ing. If we did not have a bowel movement we
had to sit on the toilet until we did. I being the
eldest was relegated to the outside toilet, where I
had to sit morning after morning and bring her
to see the bowel movement before I could flush it
away.

Her favourite punishment was to lock us in a
cupboard under the stairs (where there was no
light) without supper. It is hard to know whether
the hunger or the dark held more horrors for me.

Every Sunday morning, afternoon and
evening, Joyce Lawson remembers, she used
to go to chapel. During the week, however,
things were quite different:

In the evenings everyone used to go out and we
used to come home from playing and had to
stand out on the step till someone came home to
let us in.

I got so soaked with rain some evenings that I
ended up with pneumonia. I was ill in bed. They
finally said I could have milk and gave me a
medicine glass of it. One swallow and it was
gone.

After being allowed up again I sat down to
breakfast and there was the little glass of milk.
After one smell I said that it was sour. Mr Porter
[not his real name] grabbed my nose and said,

'You want milk, you'll drink it!' and I had to swallow it, but he just let go of my nose and I was sick all over the table.

At school in cooking class one day they were showing us how to cook sausages, and during break someone stole a sausage. All the evacuees in the school were made to stand in the playground until someone owned up. The Welsh kids made fun of us but I don't think they realized how hungry most of us were.

Ken, my brother, had been caught again running away, so they had to inform my mother. My dad was away in the Army from 1939, but he came home on leave and Mum and Dad came up for a visit, I think to tell Kenny to behave himself.

My dad sat down in the front room and asked what had been going on. He went out to where Mr and Mrs Porter were sitting and she denied it all, but my mum asked who the doctor was and my dad went to see him and he confirmed it all. Mrs Porter even told my dad I hadn't had boils or pneumonia.

Dad came back from the doctor's and my mum had to pack our clothes. She asked Mrs Porter where my new hat and coat were that she had sent three weeks before, and Mrs Porter said it never arrived. I asked my mum what it was like and she said, 'Green,' and I told her that Rachel, a Welsh girl across the road, had it. So my mum and dad went across the road and came back with it. I knew it because I envied

Rachel in her new coat and hat, and all the time it was mine.

For Barbara Birchall (née Hollis), looking back is very painful. Her foster parents were extremely cruel, she says, and Barbara and her sister were often hungry:

We used to go out and tip over the dustbins for food. In the Harvest Festival my sister took a bite out of a tomato because she was hungry.

We used to go to pig sties and get the food from the pigs. We would get the scraps that others didn't eat at the table. She wouldn't let us have any water, so at night-time we used to creep down the stairs, go into the kitchen, climb up on a chair and we would drink the water from the drip pan.

If we heard her coming down the stairs we used to crawl into the coal cupboard, block our-selves in and stay there until morning because we were too frightened to come out.

Barbara and her sister both suffer from agoraphobia today.

John Munt was born in London in 1935, the unwanted illegitimate child of a domestic servant. His birth certificate says, 'father unknown'. In 1937, suffering from malnutrition, he was taken in by the Church of England:

My legs were bent and required leg-irons to straighten them. I was considered a bright, intelligent child. It would appear the Church of England had difficulty, considering the times, in placing their intended evacuees. In my particular case the selection was appalling. This was due to the inept discretion of an ageing bachelor vicar, although well intended, who thought he had found a suitable home in his parish for an evacuee.

My new home could only be described as a rural slum in a semi-detached utility bungalow, severely subsiding into the wet fen soil on which it was situated a few feet from the railway line, [as a result of] the vibration from the passing trains. No running water, gas or electricity, one coal stove in the kitchen and an end-of-the-garden toilet. Most of the house was freezing in winter.

My new family consisted of a very domineering 37-year-old woman and an absolute wimp of a husband whom she continually abused. They had a mentally retarded seven-year-old son. I was the intended playmate and companion who would hopefully bring the other lad around.

For the first few days John cried and cried. Little wonder; he was being constantly slapped and beaten. He was never shown any affection, yet was liked by everyone. He was polite, bright and did well at school. Perhaps this was at the root of the problem: his foster mother, he suggests, may have been envious for her son, who appeared to be the complete opposite. John was not allowed to play with other children and on countless occasions was locked, for hours on end, in a cold bedroom:

When this took place I escaped into the fantasy world I had created in my mind, for I lived a double life. There was the cruel, unhappy, real world of fear and despair, and the sanity-saving world of my mind – of loving parents and brothers and sisters and friends all with names, birthdays etc.

I was soundly beaten at least once a week with sticks, poker, wooden spoon – whatever was at hand – mostly when the husband was at work.

It was hard to endure this physical and mental abuse, and I often thought of suicide by drowning myself in the fen drain a couple of hundred yards from the house.

School was my salvation; it was like a refuge for part of the day. The neighbour complained and talked about my beatings and screaming but nothing changed. I suffered from severe headaches and vomiting and trembled continuously from anxiety. I had outbreaks of sores on my scalp, face and body as well as hurting all over from the beatings. I was always hungry and had a bad case of intestinal worms of which only I was aware.

When the old vicar came to visit he would ask me how I was, and I would say all right, because she would be standing behind him, with a screwed-up face, shaking her fist at me.

Relief finally came when the woman suffered a stroke and I was placed in a foster home on a farm. I was shown kindness – the first I had ever known, and was never hit or struck. I felt like a tormented animal let out of a cage. My spirits and health soared and I became a happy person.

Maureen was evacuated to Blackpool at the age of 10. She was 'not a very pretty child', she says, and remembers being the last to be picked. Her first foster home was a happy one, but gradually all the other children there with her were sent back home, and she was lonely. When she was 12 she was transferred to the home of a schoolfriend:

It was there that I had my first experience with a man that was not quite nice. He would tuck me in of a night and fondle me. I was terrified. Mind you, he never forced me. He would just say that I was an evacuee and if I said anything he would send me·back to where I'd be bombed...

Then one day I got really frightened. I thought he was going to put his thing inside me and I got really scared. And the next thing I knew I woke up in hospital. I'd been poisoned. You see, when I was in bed he never really did, you know, he just said, 'Oh, you'll like this – I'm going to put this inside you and it will make you feel very, very good.' And he had four children of his own. So I told him I was going to tell my teacher – and this was when I woke up in hospital. I had to have my stomach pumped.

My mum came down to visit and took one look at me and said, 'I think it's time you came home.'

Margaret King was four or five years old when she was first evacuated from her home in Dagenham, Essex in 1939. After staying in a number of different homes, she went to Norwich, this time with three of her sisters. Having waited in a hall until after dark, they walked the streets with a billeting officer, but finding accommodation for all four children together was not easy. Finally a woman agreed to take two of them and persuaded her next-door neighbour to take the other two:

The minute we got in she said, 'I wanted someone old enough to wash up and do the cleaning.' Our life had begun...

The Dukes [not their real name] had one son, Simon [not his real name]. To get to our bedroom we had to pass through a middle bedroom occupied by a Mr Loveday [not his real name] who I believe was some form of artist.

My younger sister hadn't been well for a

while with a swollen knee. No one seemed to bother about it. I don't remember ever seeing a doctor or anyone to talk to. I told Mrs Duke that she had been crying all night and she ignored me.

The next day I borrowed (pinched) a push-chair and put my sister in it, meaning to find a doctor or someone. I remember being told about a hospital and got on a bus with her. I still remember the massive gates and drive which I had to push her through. The doctor was very kind and it turned out she had to have fluid drained from her knee and she was kept in. Of course I got into serious trouble from Mrs Duke because of this...

Then Simon Duke started coming into our bedroom. He was 16 to 17 years old and I don't remember him going to work. He seemed always to be there... One night as usual Simon came into our room. After a while he started to touch my private parts and I got really scared. I had no one to turn to and no money for stamps to write home.

After a week or so I told Mr Loveday not to let him come through his room to us. Most of the time it was better if he was at home. I believe now he mentioned something to Mr and Mrs Duke because not long after he left. He told us not to be scared as Mrs Duke was locking our bedroom door each night. This she did and started going out of a night after locking us in.

One night the air raids were bad and we were

very frightened. I opened my window to try to call my sister next door when Simon climbed over the toilet roof below into our room. He cuddled both of us and my sister fell asleep, and from then until we left he had sex with me.

Six-year-old June Yewen (now Perez) was evacuated with her sister to Devon. Their foster parents treated them shamefully:

They withheld parcels or presents sent us and even locked my sister in a freezing cold bedroom with just knickers and a vest on because she had 'stolen' a biscuit from the cupboard.

I remember writing a postcard to our parents asking if we could come home. My father was appalled when he saw how we lived.

June was eventually sent to stay with a friend of a friend in Ledbury, Hertfordshire. ' "Aunt Nell" was an absolute saint,' she writes, and they have remained friends ever since.

Samuel Fawcett was taken to a miner's house:

When he came in he said, 'Who is he?' The lady said, 'He is an evacuee.' He said, 'What do we need him for?' She said, 'He will be all right for helping around the house.'

The first night I was there I was hungry. I thought I would have supper then go to bed as I was tired, but the man said to his wife, 'He had better fill the six coal buckets with coal and find sticks from out the back.' I didn't know anything about finding sticks or filling coal, as I had never done it at home as I was too young.

I was given three candles and a box of matches. I was put in a spench [cupboard] under the stairs in the back kitchen. I was locked in and told I could not come out until I had filled them and would get no supper. It wouldn't have been too bad, but to find coal amongst the slack you had to dig it out with your hands and fingers. The nails broke and the fingers became sore. I was afraid in the coal-hole; it was dark and weird by the flickering candle-light.

I had been taught at home in Liverpool not to play with matches and here they were giving me matches and candles which was very confusing.

Monica Dray (now Buckley) was evacuated to Westbury, in Wiltshire, where she moved in with a woman and her daughter whose only apparent motive for taking her in was to get the allowance, and who treated her like a servant. Her letters home were censored and the daughter turned out to be 'some kind of sadist' who used to beat Monica constantly:

The daughter told me my parents would he killed in London and I would never be able to go home...

The following is a letter which I wrote to my

parents. I came across it recently when my mother died and I was cleaning out her apartment.

I can tell you I cried buckets to think that she had kept my letters all these years – I can't imagine what the hell she was going through, worrying about me. I think this letter is indicative of the way the children must have all thought:

Dear Mummy,
I want my money I have only got 8d in money. I finished the pixy bonet what I was makeing I am makeing a coat to match it. We get a lot of tomtits in the garden. I saw some bombs drop near the convelasent it keeps on raining down here does it up there. xxxxxxxxxxxxxxxxxxxxxxxx all I have to say now xxxxxxxxxxxxxx from your xxxxxxxxxxxxxx Loveing Monica xxxxxxxxxxxxxxxxxxxxxxxxxxxxx

Monica's mother finally received a postcard telling her that her daughter was unable to attend school. The reason? Monica was unable to walk. Her mother rushed down to Westbury and brought her back. Monica was treated at the Middlesex Hospital and was soon back 'in my beloved London and with my family and I didn't care that bombs were dropping and the windows kept getting blown out by blasts'.

One girl, together with her sister and two brothers, was taken into the home of a kindly vicar, until he received the dreadful news that his son had been killed in action. They were asked to leave, and she and her sister were taken to a cottage owned by a Mr and Mrs Dent (not their real name), while her two brothers went to stay down the road, where two daughters of the Dents lived. The two boys had a grand time, but the girls were not so lucky.

They were sent to bed every night at five o'clock after a meal of bread and water. Every evening after school they faced a mountain of dishes as the wife and husband sat down to a hearty dinner. One day the husband caught a rabbit, skinned it and slapped the entrails in their faces, with strict orders that they were not to wash off the blood until the next morning.

The two sisters tried to run away but were caught and given a sound beating:

My dad used to send us parcels of sweets but we never saw them. We never knew we could complain, and any letters we wrote she tore up pretending that she had posted them.

One day my mum managed to get down to see us. She was on crutches after a fall. Mrs Dent wouldn't let her in, so we went down a lane and sat on a bench with her. Then my mum noticed my knees, which were in a bad way by then, and when she questioned us, it all came out – how Mrs Dent beat us and how hungry we were.

My mum was very angry but being on crutches was no match for our tormentors. She told us not to say anything but wait and she would see to it.

About two weeks later there was a loud knock on the door and there stood my mum and a big fellow called Danny who had come with my mum on the coach. They walked straight in and told me and my sister to pack our things. We couldn't get upstairs quick enough. Mrs Dent was screaming about money and my sister asked her where our parcels were, and Danny told her to fetch them so she ran upstairs and threw down the parcels – sweets scattered all over the place.

We got out of there and caught a coach home.

Margaret Jane Cox (not her real name) was instructed to call her foster mother 'Auntie'. She never knew whether there was a husband, but they shared the house with a son of 12, a young woman and two other evacuees.

Margaret became a punch-bag for the son, who would beat her mercilessly. His mother warned her against telling anyone, and she became very frightened. She would walk along the sands alone, glad to be away from the house. Her mother would visit when she could:

My mother asked about some bruises that I had. 'Auntie' passed the enquiry off with the excuse that I had been larking about with her son...

On the last Sunday that my mother visited me, I managed to slip a note into her bag which was at the side of her as she was sitting at the tea table, for it was always a good Sunday tea if she was coming. I did not have much hope of her noticing it amongst her things, but I prayed and prayed that she would find it and read it...

Normally I did not see any letters arrive. On this day there was a small envelope and it was addressed to me, with a note inside telling me that I was to return home with the one-way ticket enclosed...

All I remember after that was that it was me seated on the back seat of an almost empty Ribble bus, clutching the small cardboard ticket, and I was going home.

Twelve-year-old Helen and her three sisters were evacuated to the Isle of Skye. Their new home was a large house run by a woman who had two sons and three daughters, the eldest of whom used to beat Helen continually. Before she left her home in Glasgow, her mother had devised a wonderful escape code:

'If these people are bad to you, write at the bottom of your letter, "God save the King!"' I thought this was brilliant as anyone reading that would naturally think that we were being

very patriotic.

Our parents managed to get rail tickets to us. On the day we were supposed to travel, no one would help us, therefore we missed the one and only train. We couldn't use the original train tickets as they were stamped for that day. Mum then went to the police in Glasgow, who contacted the Skye police, and we got an escort away from that horrible woman.

Some children found themselves in the homes of people with strange occupations. Veronica, for example, ended up sharing the home of a prostitute:

I loved her. I really thought she was lovely. I was eight years of age and she used to give me money at night to go to the local cinema. I sat there night after night and, being wartime, the films didn't change as they do now. They changed once a fortnight. I remember sitting through 12 performances of Jeanette MacDonald and Nelson Eddy in Bitter Sweet, *and I used to come home in the dark and go around by the old churchyard where this old tramp was sleeping out. I used to taunt this old tramp and he used to chase me away. I made his life absolutely miserable (I was the only child wandering about this village) and then I'd go and get a bag of chips and I'd go back home to this lady.*

I stayed with her a long time and no one quite realized what was going on. I was always

259

scruffy and dirty at school but when you are at school you don't think of those things. When all your friends are in bed, you are going to the pictures, all the things they can't do, but it was fantastic.

She had all these men coming to the house. I can honestly say I never saw anything. These men were in bed with her, but I was in a little camp-cot and this sheep-dog used to sleep on my bed with me. But I thought she was wonderful, this lady.

Eventually the police got in touch with Veronica's mother and her movie-going days were soon over.

The most painful letters for ex-evacuees to write have been those concerning sexual abuse. Many, like Leah Mowcroft (not her real name), have never before told their story to anyone.

At the age of five, Leah was evacuated to Burnham-on-Sea, just half an hour's ride from where she lived. She had never been away from her family before.

It was at her second billet that the nightmare began. After staying in one foster home where they had been very happy, she and her eight-year-old brother, Paddy, were moved to live with a family of three boys and a girl. The house had four bedrooms – two doubles and two singles. Leah never saw her foster father and presumed he had

260

gone into the Army:

At first everything was fine, but I had to sleep with the three sons. Looking back I can only guess that they were about 14 to 16 years old. I was made to sleep between two of them.

Every night when they got into bed I would wake up and feel their hands going over my body and they would probe me with their fingers. I used to cry, but they would threaten me.

One time the 16-year-old took me into the other single room, took off my dress and pants, took his trousers down and made me hold his penis. I was very scared and frightened but did what I was told. I had never seen a naked man before.

One day his mother went shopping and again he made me go upstairs. This time he stripped me and his hands and fingers went everywhere.

I was always very sore and started to look ill. I was always sick and began to lose weight. Sores were beginning to come up on the back of my neck. I had beautiful long red hair and because of the sores I had to have my hair cut. The daughter laughed at me.

None of this was known at school until my hair was cut off. The head teacher knew something was wrong. She was very kind and tried to get me to talk about it but I was too frightened.

Then she had an idea. She asked me if I would like to write to my mother to tell her how I was

261

getting along. I cannot remember what I wrote, but the next thing I knew was that Paddy, me and the other evacuee were taken away from that home.

I can never forgive what they did to me, and it has affected me all my life.

Many evacuees had experiences that required the understanding of a loving parent. Janet James (not her real name) remembers a day spent at the beach:

We came out of the sea and dressed, still wet. Don't forget, we had no parents to see that we were dry. Later in the day four of us were sitting on the grass talking to the father of one of the evacuees and he suggested hide-and-seek. He showed me the best place to hide and that was where I lost my virginity. I didn't even know it was called rape or what actually happened.

I must have been in shock for some days, too ashamed and too frightened to say what had happened. I remember cleaning myself in the sea and washing the blood away and not even knowing what it all meant. Please remember that an 11-year-old then was a seven-year-old now. We had no sex lessons.

I sometimes wonder if this is why I'm in my third marriage now, always looking for the security that you need and want yet never knowing if it will ever be found.

Margaret Jane Cox (not her real name) was among a large group of children who were evacuated to Blackpool, where they were led to a group of holiday houses. When they stopped at one house, a woman looked her over and decided, 'I'll have her, she'll come in handy.' Margaret remembers:

That was me and without hesitation I was taken to where she lived and then the horror started.

My mother was a widow and had to work, so it was difficult for her to visit. This woman was accusing me of sending letters to my mother. Letters she never got.

I was beaten up pretty badly by her and her son. She entertained men and these men we had to call 'Uncle'. There was one in particular whom we had to call 'Uncle Grimble Destin'. I didn't know him but I had to call him that anyway.

I was Church of England but was sent to a Catholic school, which didn't matter to me. On occasion one of the nuns used to say to me, 'Why is your face black? Why do you have so many bruises?' and I couldn't say why because I was afraid.

In his initial letter in response to our request for information, David Nelson (not his real name) merely mentioned that he had been an evacuee, but gave no details of his experi-

263

ences. After thanking him for his reply we received a second letter, in which he said that if he were to tell his story he doubted that he would be believed. We wrote back expressing our interest and in return received his story, along with a covering letter:

First of all it's so important to me that you take my word for what I have to say. I have spent a lifetime with most of this bottled up inside of me. I am aware that none of this is what you want but you have finally released the 'floodgates' and for the first time since I came home on September 2nd, 1944, I am able to get it off my mind and in so doing will perhaps be able to relax like ordinary people. Even if you cannot use anything I have to say, I have the satisfaction of knowing that someone knows, for the first time since it happened.

In the pages enclosed with this letter, David describes how, when he was eight years old, after a very happy time in their first foster home, he and his sister were transferred to the care of a Mrs Storm (not her real name), who lived with her daughter, Sarah (not her real name), two years older than David. As his sister went upstairs to view their new home, Mrs Storm walked around him, slowly eyeing him up and down. He started to turn to face her and was shocked to hear her scream, 'Keep still you damned young shit!' She then cracked him across the ear so hard that his left shoulder hit the floor.

Dinner-time came. His sister, Mrs Storm and her daughter tucked into a hearty meal while he faced scraps:

Once I saw this, the only explanation I could think of was that Mrs Storm had heard of my bed-wetting and that this was some form of punishment, or that she really hated males. The job I had was to carry water to two large buckets which were kept on a shelf in the kitchen. It took four trips to fill each bucket. That evening I had a slice of bread and butter for tea. The others had cheese, pickles, chutney and homemade bread. For the first time in my life I became crafty and underhand because although only eight and a half years old I realized I was in danger from this woman and did not know why.

I was shown up to my bedroom, which was spotless. The usual double bed, with a chamber pot under it. She pointed to the chamber-pot and said I must keep it spotless. She went out of the room. I got undressed, put on my night-shirt and had a look around.

I found a boys' book called Up River *about a group of schoolboys who went on a camping/ boating trip, which I read in a few days. (I was and am an avid reader.) There was a clock on the mantelpiece that played a tune. It had no 'legs' on the corners, so the spiked drum that gave the tune touched the surface of the mantel-*

piece. The clock had stopped so I wound it up. It immediately started playing 'Soldiers of the Queen', but as the drum turned it transported the clock along the mantelpiece. I was delighted. To me it was a form of toy car. It ran down so I placed it back in the centre of the shelf.

Next minute Mrs Storm charged into the room and began ranting and raving at me so incoherently I could not understand one word she said. She must have punched me from head to foot until I was dizzy.

Next morning she called me down at 4 a.m. I dressed, went down to the living-room and stood around while she showed me how to lay the table and make Oxo broth. Her daughter's and my sister's broth remained unmade since they did not have to get up until 7 a.m. As soon as Oxo was made for the three of us she called her husband. He came down, drank his Oxo and at 5 a.m. left for work on a farm.

I washed up under her supervision. Every time I did something that was not to her liking I was punched – always in the same ear. (Today it is thicker round the sides and aches more often than my right ear.)

I quickly picked up this washing-up business – say over three or four days – followed by floor-polishing, window-cleaning, kitchen-floor scrubbing, lighting fires, polishing shoes, darning my socks, weeding the garden and fetching water. These jobs I had along with gathering dead sticks and taking them to the woodshed. There

266

was an alcove in there that had to be kept full. I was sometimes kept home from school to collect wood.

I began to realize that I may be in some form of danger from this woman. Much more likely to starve, so I began stealing. I would sneak out of bed at 2 a.m. and look for the cheese dish. I then carefully sliced off one end so that the cheese remained the same shape. When I got up that morning I actually went to school feeling full.

I learned what she meant by keeping the chamber-pot clean. I was not allowed to use it! So I used to pee out of the window, always afraid it would stain the outside wall. Dress, go downstairs, light the two fires, dump the old ashes outside, lay the table, prepare the Oxo, check both fires, take a sack and the water pail and go to the water pipe. I'd park the pail in the bushes, then go over a gate into a field that climbed very steeply, to a hollow tree where I kept a store of wood, fill the sack and go back to the water pipe where I filled the bucket, and then I'd go back to the house. This was my routine for seven days a week. I got to eat breakfast two mornings a week.

What happened was that I was told to sit down at the table with my hands in my lap while she stood behind me. Then, after a nerve-racking wait, she would tell me to eat. I'd pick up a spoon and after a moment of disorientation, find myself on the floor with the right ear and right side of my face ringing like a bell. On these mornings I was not allowed to take sandwiches to school so went without food all day.

On Christmas Day I had a clockwork tanker truck given to me. She let me wind up the lorry and as I removed the key she took the key and allowed the toy to run down. She refused to give me back the key. Remembering that I had lost keys to toys before and pushed cars backwards and released them, I did the same with the toy truck. It worked perfectly. At this she called me a 'Damn young shit!' and hit me over the head with a chair. (I have the scar today.) By now it was 11 a.m. so she told me to fetch wood and stay out.

It was after dark when I was allowed back in the house. I was hurting with a large bump on my head and freezing with the cold. She then made me wash in cold water. Her daughter was given the lorry.

One morning, when coming back from getting the milk, I tripped over the cat and shattered the jug. Mrs Storm hit me with the empty bucket. I ended up with lumps and bruises all over my head and a black eye. She kept me home from school and sent a note. When I went back, Mrs Kirby [not her real name], the schoolteacher, made me stand in front of the class while she read what it said. It explained that despite repeated warnings I had continued to climb trees and had fallen from one. I then got a lecture along the lines of how ungrateful I was worrying poor Mrs Storm.

We went to church each Sunday. One Sunday I listened to the preacher going on about 'suffer little children to come unto me' and making a big thing of this. At the end of the service I hung around till everyone had gone and asked the parson about this and explained how I was getting beaten every day for nothing. He was outraged and really shouted and raged at me. I went home and the parson showed up. I knew I was in for it. He spoke to Mrs Storm and when he left she really went berserk and bashed me with the kettle, a jar of jam and then the poker. My arm was broken between the elbow and wrist.

My mother came to visit and took my sister and me back home for a holiday. I told her bit by bit what was happening. She did not take much notice. But when I went back to Mrs Storm's house, my mother told her that she found it strange that I needed so many hidings as I had always been so honest and cheerful, but if Mrs Storm felt she had to chastise me then it was OK. My father came. He turned on Mrs Storm and said, 'I have to go back to the Army tomorrow, but I will be back in September or October and I don't want to hear that you have laid one finger on them.'

My father left the next day and how things changed. I had the same food as the others, I did not have to wash up, although sometimes joined in with the wiping up. I could use the chamberpot. Fantastic!

On 2 September 1944 David's father came back, with David's grandfather. They walked to Nettlecombe and caught a train back home to Southampton.

Many years later, David returned to face the woman who had caused him so much pain. The story of that return is in the last chapter of this book.

Freda Miller (now Tilley) was seven when she was evacuated to Shoreham from Peckham, in South-east London. Her brother, Bill, was thought to have mumps, so he was left behind:

When we arrived at Shoreham I was taken to the hospital to be looked at in case I had mumps. It seems nobody wanted me because of this, so in the end the doctor at the hospital took me home with him. Home was a very 'posh' house where he lived with his sister. They had a maid and in each room was a bell-push which you pressed to summon her. They also had an inside toilet and bathroom, which I had never seen before let alone used. I was given a large double bedroom to sleep in which contained twin beds and a wash basin. Very different from home where I shared a bedroom with Mum, Dad and Bill.

I was told to write home and let them know I had arrived safely. I wrote, 'Dear Mrs Miller ...', thinking that because I didn't live with her, she wasn't my mum any more. You can imagine how upset she was when she read that.

As he watched the bedbugs crawling up a wall stained with the blood of the insects he had squashed, Kenneth Barber trembled at the thought of the treatment he was going to receive from his foster mother in the morning. He had been living with her for six months and had received regular beatings. Now he was ready to do something about it:

I remember climbing out of the window about one o'clock in the morning to post a letter to my dad. He was in the fire service in London. About two days later at about the same time in the morning I heard a banging at the front door and a lot of shouting going on, so I went downstairs in my nightshirt and it was my dad.

He'd been at a fire, he still had his uniform on, all covered in black soot and his uniform was all burned and I heard him shouting, 'Where's my b..... son? Where's my b..... son?' He saw me coming down the stairs and grabbed me and I remember her saying even to this day, 'Let me kiss him goodbye.' And my father who had thrown a blanket around me and grabbed me said, 'Fuck off!'

It must have been particularly difficult for Ken's parents when he was evacuated. They were deaf and dumb and Ken was a right arm to them. He was 10 years old and had

271

no brothers or sisters. His father was a shoe-repairer. Ken wanted to go, but when he got to Cumberland he found the local children rather frightening, and the way they seemed to pick on the evacuees made him terribly homesick:

You know, when you are a child, you have your own personal secrets. Near to the house that I was billeted in there was a pit. It was an old ruin of a pit. We used to play cowboys and Indians around there.

I tended to isolate myself from the other kids and I used to write notes and leave them under a stone, pleading that I wanted to go home. You've got to remember, I was only about 10 years old. It all seems so silly now, I've never ever told anyone about this.

Some evacuees who were unhappy in their new environments were 'rescued' by worried relatives and taken home. Leille Hobbs (now Brandt) was miserable:

I threatened suicide so many times that finally my grandmother came and took me home. I was at the Hydra Hotel in Dunblane, Scotland. It had been occupied by troops before the school took it over. It was a massive building, cold and bleak.

There was an escaped convict hiding out some-where in the building. It was such a huge place and it was so easy with all the children in the building to avoid being caught. I remember the police coming several times because he frightened several of the children by turning up all of a sudden unexpectedly.

Pauline Castles (now Vickers) was one of 10 children. When they were evacuated, they were split up, and she, at the age of six, found herself in Brighton with three of her sisters:

I think we spent most of our time wandering the streets. When our father came to visit us he found us in the park in tears, so that was the end of that, straight back to London.

The woman who took Freda Risley (now Costa) in had not wanted an evacuee, but had been told that if she refused she would be forced to take a soldier instead:

There had been no attempts to find us homes before we arrived. It was all done on the spur of the moment, at least that's how it seemed.

I was actually a very quiet child – I had learned to read very early and could occupy myself without any bother. I was an only child and was used to playing alone, and I was terrified of being a nuisance.

I honestly think that, apart from the bother of looking after me and feeding me, I wasn't much trouble. But my hostess picked on everything she possibly could and I was regularly battered – I had lumps on my head, split lips, black eyes, but I was never kept away from school. As a teacher myself, I can't understand why my teachers never noticed or, if they did, took no action.

Possibly the worst thing, though, was that I understood what was going on – I knew there was a war on and that London was a dangerous place. I used to lie in bed at night worrying that my mother and father would be killed and I would not be able to go home. I supposed I'd have to stay where I was. Can you imagine the mental agony?

What brought it to an end was the German invasion of France. My mother realized that Essex was nearer to the coast than London was, swooped down and took me back home – to my enormous relief.

Leading an incredibly hard-working existence in her billet, eight-year-old Kathleen Kelvey (now Parsons) could hardly wait for her father to rescue her:

He came and took us back to London. I was so dirty and flea-bitten in my new mustard coat that I'd had new to go away in that my father made me walk behind him over London Bridge.

Some parents took their children back home for other reasons – because they seemed to be getting too attached to their foster parents. When one would-be foster mother first saw Kathleen Strange (now Mossman) and her sister, she was ecstatic:

She just shouted, 'Oh Bird,' – his name was Mr Bird but she always called him Bird – 'Bird, there are two little girls, isn't that wonderful,' and from then on we were treated just like her own children.

She used to play the piano and as we were Londoners she thought we were bubbling over with talent so she used to make us sing, and we loved it, even my shy sister.

One time, when we had been back to see my mother in London, she brought us back and as we got off the coach we just ran to Mrs Bird. Mrs Bird said that when she saw my mother's expression she knew. The next thing, my mother brought me back to London.

Mrs Bird had a breakdown over it.

Michael Caine was six and his brother three when they left home with their mother, stopping on the way to the station to buy a tin of corned beef for the sandwiches they were to take with them on their trip:

I remember having tremendous difficulty with my Mickey Mouse gas-mask, 'cause we all had to take a gas-mask with us. The evacuation from the school followed a standard procedure for that time. All children going away were medically examined to weed out those kids with colds or whatever. I remember that in that era there was a thing called impetigo ... you kept catching it off the dirty kids at school.

There were no buses to take us to the station and I remember holding my brother's hand and taking this tremendous long walk, but they did take our little cases to save us carrying them. Cardboard cases they were. No sooner had we set off than the first step I took, I stepped in some dog shit. Everyone was trying to figure out where the smell was coming from. So I'm going along and in those days there was a sort of very itchy kind of pullover that you wore next to your skin and to this day I would never wear anything like that.

Anyway, we marched off and were met by a group of great big WVS women in green uniforms. Everyone was very kind and very nice. I don't remember the train ride but I do remember being led into a great big village hall and my brother and I being picked out by this wonderful woman who whisked us away in this big car, probably a Rolls, to this great mansion with dogs and cats and it was lovely ... Mrs Warner was her name ... and we were there for two weeks, my brother and I.

Unfortunately it turned out we were too far from the school so we had to leave the house. I mean, I thought, boy, am I in for a great time here, and they took us away and they took us to another part of the same village. That was War-grave in Berkshire. They were semi-detached houses on the edge of the park. They didn't look too bad, but they split my brother and me up because of our age difference and put me with another boy who was six called Clarence. And we were put into this house and I was immediately aware that everything had gone wrong. I mean it was dreadful. The woman was asthmatic and the husband was a policeman and the whole atmosphere was obviously very, very different to what we'd left.

At first everyone was very nice and then the woman that had taken us there left and we sat down to eat. The woman said, 'Here's your meal,' and she gave us a tin of pilchards between the two of us, and some bread and water. Now we'd been in this rich woman's house so we said, 'Where's the butter?' And we suddenly got a wallop round the head. From then on it started ... not the husband, he was never there ... just her. What we later found out was that the woman hated kids and was doing it for the extra money. So that food was the cheapest meal you could dish up ... a tin of pilchards and dry bread.

Clarence and I used to sleep together and poor Clarence used to wet the bed, 'cause he was a very nervous kid. She could never tell who'd done it so she used to bash the daylights out of the both of us. So, of course, the more Clarence got hit the more he wet the bed. It was then we

277

started to get locked in the cupboard.

We weren't locked in the cupboard all the time, just when she used to go out shopping. You see, when we came home from school we were a bloody nuisance, she being asthmatic and all, and she had a boy of her own, about the same age as us, who she treated with kid gloves. In fact I think we were there to supply the money to give him the best of all possible worlds. We had no relationship with him at all. The only thing I remember about him was that he had butter on his bread. It struck me much later that it was really that lower form of lower-class snobbery and unbeknownst to me I was experiencing the British class system. With the 'filthy kids' from London with the 'funny accents'.

Anyway, as Clarence wet the bed more and more we started to get locked in the cupboard more. Like even when she and the son went to the pictures, in the cupboard we'd go. Then we started getting locked in the cupboard as a punishment. At first when we got let out we'd be shouting and screaming, till we realized that all that did was get us locked back in the cupboard again.

Meanwhile, my mother, who knew none of this, could not get down to visit because of the travel restrictions. And being on her own – my father was in France in the Army – made it even more difficult. Eventually Clarence and I were covered in sores, but they were on our bodies. Obviously we were let out of the cupboard to go to school and of course we never said anything, but one of the teachers picked up on us and realized that there was something radically wrong and sent us to see the doctor. And of course the woman we were staying with had given us very long socks to hide the sores on our legs. I mean we were covered in them.

At the same time Clarence had a broken arm. This had happened when we were coming out of the cupboard and the woman had hit him with a tennis racket. She told the school that he'd fallen over. You see, you have to remember the confusion of that time. There were hundreds of thousands of evacuees and these children were extra to the system, and unwelcome and looked down on ... the nearest I can think of, it would be like trying to evacuate black kids into Alabama white families...

Anyway, they sent us to the doctor and the doctor examined us. The woman tried to answer by saying, 'Well you know doctor, these evacuees come with these sores and I've not been able to stop them.'

They got my mother by sending her a special pass to get her on the train, and the incredible thing was that my three-year-old brother was staying with the district nurse and when they found him he was in a cupboard! He'd been in there for two days. In the same village.

My mother arrived and my mother is tough. She nearly killed this woman before taking us back to London.

Michael Caine is now a noted actor and Academy Award winner.

After a few months in her foster home, Faith Ford (now Bunn) tried to write and tell her parents how unhappy she was but her letters were censored. After overseeing what she wrote, her foster mother would remove the stamped addressed envelopes and seal them immediately. She also kept the two shillings Faith's father sent each week:

Monday was the day I loved and hated most. It was the day the long, neatly typed letter from my dad arrived and it was also washday. The outhouse at the back had the large copper built in the corner which had to be filled and the fire lit below. After many chores and after school, when all the washing was done, I would have to climb into the same water and wash myself and I would pray running home from school that he wouldn't be home early, that I could get in and out before I heard his boots coming through the stone passage.

Eighteen months later, after having smuggled a letter home through the mother of a friend who was also from London, my father came down on the night train on Friday. However, when I arrived home she had found out what was to happen and turned me out and told me to go to the hostel.

At the crack of dawn next morning, I crept out

to the railway station to await the London train and sat there until nearly noon, when the kindly station-master came and told me the London train had been in early.

I walked back to the hostel feeling very sad, but the matron told me my father had been there and would be back. I remember sitting there in the big hall where they were serving lunch, unable to eat anything, when I saw my father standing in the doorway with his bowler hat in his hand.

It was the most wonderful day of my life.

Betty MacMillan (now Pearson)'s foster parents had been on the stage and, along with their four daughters, Betty had a great time singing and dancing:

It was short-lived, however, because our mothers and headmaster took us away: it seemed these people were planning to take us on the road in a show.

One day, as Doris Thompson (now Pritchard) sat in her classroom, her foster mother came in and spoke to the teacher:

She told the teacher that I wet the bed and wouldn't do anything around the house, that I was very ungrateful and very cheeky. The teacher told the class and I insisted on going home that night. The foster parent took me back.

She told my parents that I had done all these terrible things and I ought to be whipped, and my father said, 'I'll deal with her after you've gone.'

I was absolutely petrified and after she'd gone he called me over. I went to him and he said, 'Forget about it. Put it out of your mind. You're home now.'

The house that Mary was sent to was dark and gloomy and, to make matters worse, the woman who owned it obviously did not like the tiny seven-year-old she had taken in. Mary remembers that another girl, Margaret Rose, was with her. The woman had 'this stupid son' who used to frighten Mary by jumping out at her in the dark:

I was terribly unhappy there and I remember a day when it was raining hard and she sent me outside. She bolted the door and I crawled into the chicken-house full of straw, and I stayed there until she came out and brought me in. She didn't want me in the place, you see.

The other little girl's daddy was a soldier and one day the lady said to me, 'You're to go upstairs and stay in the room and don't come down.' And she got Margaret Rose ready and made her pretty and she locked my door.

I could hear them talking in the kitchen below and I got a pencil and a piece of paper and I wrote a little note: 'Please tell my mummy to come and get me.' I waited until I heard the back door open and as soon as I heard

Margaret Rose's father's footsteps, which were heavy with his Army boots, I dropped my little piece of paper out of the window and dodged back quick. I was terrified he wouldn't see it and that the lady would find it and I would be in big trouble.

About a week after that I was on my way to school. There was a thick fog and I could hear footsteps coming towards me on the other side of the road. And I suddenly heard my mum saying, 'Is that you Mary?' and I said, 'Oh Mum,' and I went dashing across the road and she was quite horrified when she saw me. She took me back to the house and told the woman exactly what she thought of her and she said, 'How dare you send my daughter out on a morning like this. She's got holes in her shoes and no coat on,' and she said, 'What do you keep scratching your head for?' and she grabbed hold of me and I was absolutely full of lice, and with that my mum told the woman, 'I'll make sure you never get any more little kids to look after, after the way you treated her.'

Along with another lad, Vic Atkinson was billeted in a house in north Devon, where he had to work from dawn to dusk. Compared with him, he says, 'Oliver Twist had it good.' He never received anything his parents sent him from his home in Peckham. He and his companion planned to run away many times, but their plans were always thwarted.

His parents finally visited them and found, to their horror, two children as 'thin as rakes':

My dear old mum had to be physically restrained from decking the daughter (who had been particularly cruel). When she found out about the misappropriation of the money, which apparently she had earned by taking in washing, my mum behaved as I had never seen her ... it was quite embarrassing – but fun to learn all those swearwords.

The Government's re-evacuation programme, undertaken during the summer of 1940, had originally been intended to be implemented during air raids, but as the German armies advanced into France, it was quickly bought forward. The threat of an invasion overcame many people's earlier resistance to the scheme, and almost 60 per cent of those in the coastal areas to which it applied moved to the interior.

In early June, the Government put into operation a plan that sent a further 103,000 children out of London. A tour of London's shelters by the London County Council Education Officer, E. G. Savage, convinced the Government that even more had to be done to persuade parents to send their children to the countryside. Appalled at the unhygienic conditions of the shelters and fearing the harm that could be done to the children's health, he devised a method of disseminating direct propaganda to promote evacuation.

School Enquiry Officers were dispersed to visit as many homes and shelters as they could, to speak to the parents face to face. The results were disappointing. More than 60,000 were not at home and, even more disheartening, more than 100,000 refused outright to register for evacuation. Only 64,000 people were evacuated, and by 1942 the plan was suspended.

However, the failure of this scheme was to some extent offset by an exciting new programme of evacuation overseas. Encouraged by offers of help from private citizens in the Dominions and the United States, the Government established the Children's Overseas Reception Board (CORB), which, under the direction of Geoffrey Shakespeare, the Under-Secretary of State for the Dominions, rapidly brought together those eligible – children between the ages of five and 16 attending grant-aided schools – who wished to go abroad for safety.

Children with defective teeth were instructed to have treatment before their applications could be forwarded, while those suffering from scabies, impetigo or lice had to be completely cured before applying.

Since there was to be no charge for the sea

voyage, the response was strong. Working day and night, Shakespeare and his staff sifted through 210,000 applications by 4 July. Shakespeare estimated that 94 per cent came from working-class families.

A major problem would lie in getting the evacuees to their destinations safely. This would not be easy since, with the fall of France, the French Fleet had joined the new Vichy Government, and posed an extra threat in addition to the existing danger in crossing the Atlantic.

Unfortunately for the scheme, rumours began to circulate that the rich were taking the shipboard places that should have been allocated to working-class children. It was true that many of those who could afford to escape to the safety of overseas homes were doing so, even at the risk of being sunk on the way. However, the rumours were never proved, and the Government was quick to remind everyone that the CORB had been devised to accommodate all classes.

Within two weeks everyone began to have second thoughts. The passenger liner *Arandora* was sunk off the west coast of Ireland with 1,500 Italian and German internees on board.

Meanwhile, the arguments continued in the House of Commons as MPs stood to denounce a programme that was thought by many to favour the rich. In order to placate its critics the Government decided to cancel the overseas programme. The announcement was followed by an uproar, leading Churchill to issue a statement that the programme had been postponed, not abandoned.

An investigation of the allegations suggested that the critics had been right. Passenger lists for July 1940, when Shakespeare reviewed them, showed that a large number of privileged children had indeed benefited from the scheme.

Nevertheless, many children of all classes did take part. Tim Willis spent his seventh birthday on board the *Duchess of Richmond*, which set out from Liverpool in September 1940. The trip to Canada took from 25 September to 6 October. There was good reason for its taking so long:

The ship had many evacuees but also many troops, so most of the time we followed a zigzag course. We were shadowed by a U-boat that was sunk in the night by a motor torpedo boat. We were not in convoy, but I remember two ships that also sailed with us, but after several days we were on our own.

We docked at Halifax and the troops disembarked and then we sailed up the St Lawrence to Montreal. The colours of the leaves on the north shore were unbelievable and unforgettable.

I heard that the ship that sailed before ours was sunk with the loss of many children, and that ours was the last ship to carry children to Canada.

Sheila Davis (now Vogel) was shipped to the Bahamas in August. She was 12 years old when, along with her mother and brother, she boarded the HMS *Orduna* for Nassau. The voyage was not without its exciting moments:

I was very seasick and I remember my mother rushing off to search for my brother when the alarm rang. We were almost ready to get into the lifeboats when the woman next to us began screaming her head off. My mother turned around and gave her one almighty crack across the face and said, 'For God's sake, stop screaming and look after my daughter,' which she did.

My brother looked across the ocean and said, 'Look Sheila, people are swimming.' And the ships were sinking all around us. Thank God we never got into those lifeboats or it would have been the end of us.

I woke up one morning to a great blast and, from lying down in bed, I was suddenly standing up, blasted out of my bed. A torpedo had hit the ship. After this the Captain decided to leave the convoy and we woke up to find ourselves alone at sea.

A journey that would normally have taken five to six days had lasted three weeks by the time the ship finally pulled into Nassau.

As the neighbours sang 'Goodbye Sally, I must leave you', Grace McInnes (now Forrest) left her street and climbed on to one of the many buses waiting to take her and her fellow passengers to the docks. There she was to board a ship bound for Canada:

As the bus pulled away I banged and banged on the window screaming my mother's name, so that she would see me and wave goodbye. The last glimpse I got as we turned the corner was of my little sister in her little crushed-strawberry coat and pantaloon set, and her little bonnet trimmed with velvet, but they did not see me.

Jean McVey (now Murphy)'s mother had an uncle living in Hamilton, Canada, so it seemed as though it would be a good idea to send Jean over there to live for the duration of the war. It was the middle of the night and in mid-Atlantic when the siren sounded to abandon ship:

We all got into the lifeboats. The frightening thing was the lifeboat dropping on to the sea and we were out on the sea for hours until morning. I was seven years old at the time.

It was a very dark night with guns firing all around us. We were surrounded by a huge convoy protecting us and we lost five of the convoy that night. They were all sunk. I was too young to turn around and look at the names of the ships.

I do remember a French Canadian gentleman in our boat and I always remember the song 'Alouette' because he taught it to us and we sang it over and over again as we were on the sea.

Jean finally got to Canada and stayed there throughout the rest of the war.

Richard Price was seven when he, his mother and his three-year-old sister set sail across the Atlantic:

My father took us to Liverpool from our home in Leeds the night before we were due to sail on the RMS Nova Scotia. *That night the Germans bombed Liverpool and we spent the whole night in the basement of the hotel...*

The following morning my father took us to the docks and we boarded the RMS Nova Scotia, *a 14,000-ton passenger ship which regularly sailed from Liverpool to Canada and New England. We had a three-berth cabin and I was tremendously pleased to have the top bunk. At night we left the dock and anchored in Liverpool bay to await the rest of the convoy – the* Nova Scotia *was to be the flagship – and again Liverpool was bombed.*

The following day, which I believe was September 20th 1940, we sailed north-east from Liverpool around the northern coast of Ireland in a convoy of some 30 ships. We had an escort of three frigates. In the first days we went through regular boat-drill, and on the third day out ran into a storm. It was then that I realized I had good sea-legs and was tremendously pleased to have five stewards waiting on me at breakfast – they had nobody else to talk to.

About the sixth day out we were summoned to action stations quite early in the morning because one of the ships had been torpedoed. The escort had left us the previous night because it had been thought that we were then outside the range of the German U-boats. How wrong they were. I can still remember seeing a second torpedo pass our stern and hit the next ship in line, and asking my mother why we were not stopping to pick up people who were sliding down the decks into the water, and her having to try to explain that if we stopped we would be a sitting duck and therefore could lose our lives.

I was later told that we were the last ship to be allowed to sail with children aboard, because a few days before we sailed another ship had been torpedoed, with the loss of a lot of children's lives.

On 13 September the *City of Benares* weighed anchor and slipped quietly out of Liverpool. On board were 400 crew and passengers, among them 90 children and nine escorts who looked over the rails of the ship and watched the rest of the convoy.

Within 20 minutes the *City of Benares* was

beneath the waves. There were just 100 survivors, including two escorts from the CORB programme and seven children.

In Glasgow, 600 children waiting to leave were recalled home immediately.

On 30 September the CORB programme was cancelled as 600 more children were about to board a ship.

It was sunk six hours later.

Colin Jones had a lucky escape. His passage had been booked on the *City of Benares,* but at the last minute there was a change of plan. Colin's son, Paul, writes:

It was noticed that his teeth were in bad condition, so the ship sailed without him. It could be said that my father's life was saved by his rotten teeth.

Lorraine Thornton (now Holmes) was 10 years old. She had relatives in Canada and her parents decided to send Lorraine and her brother there for safety. Dressed in their best clothes, they stood waiting at the station for the train to the docks:

When the time came to say goodbye, my mother just could not let us go. She said that she had a premonition that something dreadful would happen to us and she would never see us again. Whatever the reasons were, we were very fortunate. The ship we were to go on was sunk.

Another correspondent recalls:

At the beginning of the war all parents in our town were asked if they would like their children to be evacuated to Canada or the USA. Everyone in the neighbourhood decided against it except one couple who had two sons aged about 12 and they felt it would be safer for the boys to go. Not long after they had left, their mother woke one night having had a nightmare in which she could hear her sons calling her. They had sailed on the City of Benares *which was torpedoed...*

Both of the boys died, but for the next 40 years, on the anniversary of their death, I always used to see a memorial notice in our local newspaper and always felt so touched by it.

Betty was one of 13 children who left Surrey to link up with 100 more from various other parts of Britain who were to be evacuated to New Zealand. They assembled at a school in Liverpool and four days later boarded the SS *Rangitata:*

We were part of the convoy when the ship City of Benares *was torpedoed. I can still remember that night, being got from our cabins with just our coats and life-jackets over our nightclothes and taken to the first-class lounge where we were bedded on the floor.*

Our captain broke convoy and daylight found us alone and safe. It took seven weeks to reach Wellington.

With the sinking of the *City of Benares*, the overseas evacuation programme came to an abrupt end.

By the end of the summer the second wave of evacuation, involving those living in the coastal areas closest to France, was complete. Nearly half the urban coastal population of East Anglia and two-thirds of that of Kent had moved to safer locations, and almost 100,000 children had left London, many for the second time.

And what of those who were left in these areas?

'Stay put!' said the Government.

In the face of what was to come, this was not going to be easy. The number of German aircraft appearing over Britain was increasing as the Luftwaffe made use of their newly acquired bases in France and Belgium. Single planes or small formations regularly tested the air defences as they reconnoitred the ports and airfields. On 28 June the Germans had bombed the Channel Islands in broad daylight, killing 30 civilians and injuring 40 others.

Doris Amelia de Carteret was evacuated from Guernsey in 1940:

One day we had been on the beach and when we came home my mother said, 'Sit down and have your teas, Dad and I won't be long, we have to go and see your teacher at school.' When they came back my mother had been crying but all she said to us children – me and my sisters, Kath and Margaret – was that we had to go to bed now as it would be dark when she called us up and we were not to be scared as we were going to England. I wasn't worried; I was excited as I'd never been off the Island.

Anyway, about four o'clock in the morning we were dressed and ready to go up to school. We were only allowed a pillowcase each with clean underclothes. We were all down at the school and our names were taken and we were put on buses. My dear mum handed me my youngest sister and said, 'Doris, look after Margaret,' and I said all right. So she kissed us all and told us to behave, and the buses set off for the harbour.

We got out and had to stand in line – we stood from 7.30 till nine o'clock because they had to unload a cattle boat so we could use it. We were allowed on and I was very excited, but there were some poor children crying for their mums and when the boat sailed some were very sick, my sister Kath being one of them. By the time we arrived in Southampton the boat was a mess with sick everywhere.

Anyway we got off and I told my sisters to fol-

low me... We went into a big hall where we were given a meal and had a wash, then we all had a label tied on us with our names and which school we had come from. Then some lady said to us, 'Now, children, we are going to take you to the trains.' The lady in front had a torch and just said, 'Follow the light' – it was black-out time so there was no light at all – so off we went...

On the table in the train was a big bag of food for each of us and the teachers said it had to last for 24 hours so 'Don't eat it all at once.' We had to sleep where we were; we didn't mind as we were tired. When we woke up we could lift the black-out curtains and it was lovely – we saw all the green fields and our first black cows – it was great. We had never seen cows that colour before and we had a great time counting them.

Doris finally arrived in Scotland, and it was only then that she discovered that her youngest sister, Margaret, had been lost in Southampton. She was too scared to write and tell her mother, and it was not until some weeks later, when Doris and Kath were reunited with their parents and four brothers in Yorkshire, that the rest of the family learned of Margaret's disappearance:

The first thing my mum said was, 'Where is Margaret?' and I said we didn't know, she had never been with us in Scotland at all. Poor Mum, she did cry, and she said, 'Where in heaven's name is she, poor girl?' Being a child I thought, 'Why the fuss? She is bound to be with someone,' but little did we know it would be another year before we would find her. She was picked up in Southampton by French nuns with her mate and taken with them. They landed up in Stockport and she was billeted out with a farmer and his wife, who were very good to her.

This, at least, was one story with a happy ending.

8

The Terror Begins

As the summer months passed, enemy activity was stepped up. Although it was apparent that these summer raids were a form of practice for German pilots for heavier raids in the months to come, the number of civilian casualties was increasing.

In early August Field Marshal Goering decided that the time had come to finish with the rehearsals and begin the show. The number of daily flights made by enemy aircraft began to rise, until on 13 August nearly 2,000 German aircraft launched themselves against Britain. The Spitfires and Hurricanes took to the air and met the enemy head on. As the figures poured into Air Force Command it became clear that Britain had achieved a remarkable and desperately needed victory. The Prime Minister stood in the House and declared, 'Never in the field of human conflict was so much owed to so few.'

On 24 August the first daylight bombing of London took place. Bomber Command retaliated and on the nights of 25 and 26 August dropped bombs on Berlin. It was the beginning of all-out war on the capital cities of both countries.

The Battle of London began on 7 September. Most evacuees had left for safety just a year before; many had since returned and were now about to leave again. Maud Wheeler stood watching the flames as German bombers set the docks of London afire, and decided that it was no place for her husband, her son and herself:

We packed a few clothes and with our canary in a cage we arrived in Huntington, where we were met and taken to Trinity Church. I remember how we slept that night without the drone of enemy aircraft and the screech of bombs.

I looked for work and soon found a job in a café. I also noticed a sign on a board of the George Hotel saying that they were looking for a cook. I walked into the yard and said to the manager, who was sweeping the yard, 'Boy, can you please tell me where I can find the manager?' He looked me up and down and said, 'I'm the manager, our porter has joined the Armed Services.' 'Well let's start again,' says I. 'I know where there's a good chef going cheap.'

Well, he told me to present myself and my husband at his office after lunch, and my husband got the job of head chef and I got a part-time job as breakfast cook.

Those leaving the cities for the safety of the countryside now knew full well why they were going, and needed little persuasion. The peaceful period of the 'phoney' war was over, and now bombs were falling. Mildred Horne was married and living in London with her nine-month-old son. After countless sleepless nights, she packed and left. She soon regretted her decision:

The farmer's wife who took me inside her poor home showed me a bed with a mass of springs, a very dirty blanket, no pillows. I had nothing to eat; neither did my little boy.

I went to bed and cried, as I had left loving parents to avoid the bombs and I got an inhuman woman.

I walked a mile the next day to buy food and after eight weeks I could stand it no longer and returned home to face the bombs.

Nothing had seemed to be happening during the early part of the war, so Peggy Mamie Bottomley (now Stevens), like thousands of others, had returned to London. People were given fire-drill training, and made sure that a bucket of sand, a bucket of water and a stirrup-pump, in case of incendiary bombs, were ready on the front porch. Firemen seemed to have little to do and families carried on their lives in the same relaxed fashion as usual:

One Saturday afternoon my mother sent me to the corn-chandler's to get some chicken food, and while I was down there the siren went. I started running home and my mother was waiting at the gate for me and we all went down to the shelter at the bottom of the garden. Dad had put the shelter up and put boards down inside for us to put our mattresses down.

A lone German plane had dropped its bombs before going home. That night the sirens went again and we were really at war. We were bombed very badly that night, and when we came out of the shelter next morning, people were picking up pieces of china and sticking up windows. My sister and I went looking for shrapnel.

We were bombed night and day for weeks on end. Every night we went down to the shelter at about six o'clock. We took all the washing off the lines so that the Germans couldn't spot them. We never went anywhere as my mother didn't like us to be out of her sight.

One Wednesday, to take our minds off the war, Mum took us to a matinée at the pictures. We saw one picture, but just as the second started the siren went. Mum said that we should try and get home as it wasn't far, but as we got to the railway arches the bombs were falling and an air-raid warden told us to take cover. Just as we got to the paper shop we heard a bomb coming down. I went under a billboard and my sisters flung themselves into the garden. Mum and the baby and the air-raid warden flung themselves against a door. When we all turned round there was a big crater with the water mains and the gas mains burst. We were lucky to be alive.

It was a very unsettled life, and we never knew from one day to the next whether we would live to see another day.

Ronald Crane and his family were hop-picking in Kent. One day, when he and his brother returned from getting the milk, one of them remarked to their mother, 'The war's started.' He was rewarded with a 'customary belt around the ear'. As the months passed, the boys found that being in the fields of Kent gave them a front-row seat for the spectacle taking place above their heads:

One Saturday afternoon we were back at the huts and watched as hundreds of German planes flew overhead on their way to bomb London. This was the beginning of the blitz.

When we returned to London the raiders came over every night. There was a large anti-aircraft battery about 150 yards from our house, and though we went into the Anderson shelter, we couldn't sleep because the concussion from the gun would make the shelter jump.

My stepbrother turned up one night straight from being picked up from Dunkirk, still wet and filthy from the beaches. I answered the door. I didn't recognize him and called his mother and she told him to 'Piss off!' and slammed the door in his face.

When my old man joined the Army my brother and I gave three cheers, because although my mother was handy with her fists, we could keep out of her way. With him, he made us go to him, and the longer we took, the more we got.

When the time came, we were more than happy to be evacuated. It had to be an improvement on what we had.

Eileen Welby (now Hudson) often hid under the kitchen table as the bombs fell:

I had a son aged four and a new-born daughter of six weeks. One time I lay on top of my son in the gutter to protect him against machine-gunning. After that we were evacuated.

Philip Gain's father was in the Home Guard:

When the siren went he would march us down to the cellar.

D. I. Parkes remembers watching two children being delivered to school by their ambulance-driver father in his ARP uniform:

They were a boy and a girl about seven and eight. Their mother had died eight weeks before. Four months later the father was one of the few in Leeds to die in the air raids.

The evacuation of the cities once the raids had started was very different from the evacuation that had taken place before the war and during the lull, as Ivy Bland (née Hutchings) remembers. She was an elder daughter who stayed behind with her father and helped her mother and sister prepare to leave:

I stood at the side of my mum. We were all very apprehensive. An air-raid warden was shuffling mums and children into a straight line when suddenly planes flew overhead and the siren went. Everyone cried out in fear and ran for the shelters.

As we scattered this way and that the air-raid warden was blowing continuously on his whistle.

Dennis Cooper was 11 and lived in London. After a few nights of the blitz, a close call resulted in the windows being blown in, and his parents decided it was time to get him out of the city:

I was put on a train at Euston with a suitcase and told I would be met at the other end. The trip took six hours due to bombing in the Midlands. It gave me my first experience of being alone in the world and of having to stand on my own feet.

I was very much the grubby little evacuee in a surrounding where they dressed for dinner and little boys were to be seen and not heard.

Maureen Davis (now Mancha) and her family took their furniture and loaded it on to a lorry:

My grandma and my grandfather were there and we all sat in the back of the lorry in armchairs. Before we set off, Grandpa came out with a po and threw it on the back. 'Here, take this, you may need it!' he said.

When bombs began to fall on Hull, Jean Birch (now Carberry) sat in the air-raid shelter listening as buildings crashed to the ground. The shop next door had its front blown out, and the fumes from the burning wood made Jean cough and her eyes water:

That night there was a loud banging on our shelter door. We all screamed. We thought Hitler had come to get us. It was the air-raid warden come to tell us that an incendiary bomb had landed on our roof and hadn't exploded.

He had come to lead us to the safety of the church hall. As we rushed through the streets there was glass and shrapnel falling all around us. We could see the German planes above us. They seemed very low. Just as we reached the church hall a land-mine fell in our street and flattened it. Had it not been for the air-raid warden we all would surely have been killed.

The next day we learned that most of my school chums and their families had been killed. In all we moved into six different houses. They all got bombed.

By now my mum said, 'Well, enough is enough,' and had us all evacuated.

The air raids finally made B's mother decide to send her daughter to the safety of the country. Nevertheless it took time for the little girl to forget her 'city under siege' habits:

When I went to my first billet, whenever I heard a noise I used to sit under the table and sing 'Knees up Mother Brown', but after a while I was all right and the effects of the bombing didn't bother me any more.

D.I. Parkes was a reception officer in Leeds and remembers how careful she and her colleagues had to be with the mothers and infants when they arrived:

Life had been very hard for them for some months. The big difficulty we found was that at the sound of an aeroplane, without waiting for the siren, everyone silently vanished. No panic, no noise, they just disappeared under anything that would give them shelter.

Those living near Folkestone in Kent suffered so many raids that it got to the point where they never took their clothes off for weeks at a time, remembers George Tavener:

We could tell by the sound of the engine whether the plane was British or German. Bombers and fighters were shot down around us and our planes used to come back all shot up, engines smoking, fuselages full of holes, tails missing, skimming over our heads at roof height.

All the households were sent circulars advising us to evacuate, and we decided after much soul-searching to go.

It broke my heart to have my cat put down. I took my bike to pieces and buried it in the garden because we had been told to leave nothing behind the enemy could use.

306

It must have been particularly difficult for mothers who had husbands fighting overseas. Many felt that they needed their families to be close, but the thought that their sons and daughters might be in as much danger as their husbands prompted them to send their children to places where they would be safe. Shirley Izenman (now Robinson)'s father was in the forces overseas, and her mother had sent Shirley and her brother to Stockport. They were pushed 'from pillar to post', and Shirley begged her mother to bring them home, at least for the wedding of an aunt:

After the wedding we all went over to a friend's house because they wanted to see me. I remember hearing a crash and everybody said, 'It's OK, if you hear it it's all right.' And the next one we didn't hear. I was screaming; I had broken an artery and I was bleeding to death. They rushed me to hospital, where I was in intensive care for quite some time. I had one operation after another. I lost count after about 35.

The doctors and nurses were marvellous. They saved my arm, but I am scarred all over from head to foot. It was the second last raid of the year. I was having operations until I was about 20 years old and they are still digging glass out of me.

Finding oneself in an area that has recently

been hit by explosives can be a strange experience. The dreadful quiet that follows the noise can have an almost dreamlike feel. Jill Perry (now Cullimore) rushed to a friend's house immediately after a bombing attack and found that her friend had been killed:

The friend's house was completely sliced in half. One could see fireplaces and curtains waving about at the gaping holes where windows used to be. I imagined the body of my friend being still down in the crater.

I was home from evacuation for a two-week holiday and used to cross off the days in my diary until the fortnight in Woolwich was over and, yippee, I was delighted to catch the train from Waterloo to take me back to Ilfracombe again.

Once a child had found a home with a foster family in a safe area one might have assumed that the child was out of danger. Not in Stanley Wright's case. The family he was eventually billeted with decided to move to London. Stanley had been evacuated from London to Great Bookham in Surrey, where he lived for about three years before finding himself with Arthur Turner and his elderly mother:

Mr Turner was blind and since he had a house

in Clapham decided for certain reasons to go back there to live. Naturally he took his unpaid guide with him. In consequence I found myself evacuated but dodging bombs in Clapham.

Eventually the authorities caught up with Mr Turner and removed Stanley from his care.

One correspondent was a lorry-driver in London during the blitz. He worked in the docks, one of the first areas to be bombed:

As people were bombed out we used the council street-cleaning lorries... Bedridden people, mothers and children were all taken to safe areas. To see these people at night asleep on the floor of a church hall was very sad. Next day we were back in the Stepney area using the same trucks to pick up those killed overnight. Some were only parts of bodies. One night the mortuary was hit and sacks of bodies were strewn around. We picked them up and took them to a communal grave.

It was a flower-pot that finally prompted Joan Boulton (now Orger)'s guardian to grab Joan and move out:

One day a land-mine dropped on the local church, killing many of the people sheltering there. This same bomb blew in all the windows and caused the aspidistra to hit Mrs Philby, my guardian, as she was bending over seeing to the bedding for her husband and my dad who slept under the table.

This was the end of the tether for her, so she just packed up and left with me to go and stay with her daughter in a remote village.

When Joyce Stone (now Housden)'s father got called up, her mother decided to have her evacuated again:

A barrage balloon exploded on our house, so my dad took me on a bus. He hadn't a clue where he was taking me and he went to this pub and asked these people to take me. My dad didn't know them... When I left there, I was in a terrible state.

Reg Castle also ended up in a pub, along with a talented sister:

We went to the Fox and Hounds in Orsett. My sister served in the pub and also played the accordion.

Jean Chapman (now Wootton) was almost 12 when she left her home:

I crawled out from the air-raid shelter as the all-clear sounded. My grown-up sister, Gladys, her three-year-old son, Jimmy, and myself washed, dressed and were given a good breakfast before setting off on the journey. The family clustered around us making fond goodbyes, and when little Jimmy said to my mother, 'I've kissed your dog goodbye, Grandma,' she burst into tears.

As Geoffrey Brogan, a billeting officer, loaded a group of children into the car and took charge of a large envelope containing their ration books and identity cards, he could not help noticing that all the children had one thing in common:

They were all showing signs of nervous twitches as a result of the bombing. I used to try and chat up the kids and get them laughing to allay their fears.

One little cockney lad was sat rather grumpy in the back seat of the car and I said, 'Is your daddy a soldier?' and received a surly reply, 'No, 'e ain't a soldier.' I got the same reply to sailor and airman, so I tried, 'Does he go to work, then?' The reply was, 'No, 'e stops 'ome and minds the fire 'cause the police are after 'im.'

I was somewhat interested in the contents of my large envelope when I returned to the office. The young lad's mother was listed as a sales assistant at Woolworth's, with the 'whereabouts of father unknown'. I could have told 'em!!

While Betty Williams was in a grocery shop on an errand for her mother, she stopped to speak to one of the neighbours:

She was going to the country until the bombing was over. I went back and told my mother and she said, 'Would you go away like that and stay with some nice people until the bombing is over?' I said no, I wanted to stay with her.

A few days after, I came home from school and my mum told me to go and look under the stairs. There was a new satchel and inside were pyjamas, socks, hankies. I was overjoyed. One thing I really wanted was a new satchel. Then she broke the news that my two younger sisters and myself were to be evacuated.

One day, at the age of four and a half, Jenny Brooks (now Duckworth) was walking to school after a particularly noisy night of bombing. As she turned the corner a shock was waiting for her:

The whole road had disappeared into a crater and the adjacent houses were just shells.

A warden told me to go home and that the school had also been hit. We found out later that a direct hit had flattened the school the previous evening. As a result, what had been more or less a voluntary system of evacuation was now compulsory.

Soon after the blitz started, Joan Lynch (now Day)'s father tied five brown carrier-bags together, like a bolster, and threw the bundle into a first-class carriage of the train his wife and children were to travel on, whereupon it was promptly thrown out again by a porter:

You can imagine the salty altercation that followed.

My mother told us that one of the lady's spinster sisters would be meeting us in a very old car. We thought she said gold *car, and were patiently waiting at the station when this old car drew up with the lid down. It had an enormous old-fashioned klaxon horn, which we thought would make a great old-fashioned honking noise, but as it drove off there was a pathetic 'beep beep'. We were rolling on the floor in hysterics, all being kicked by our mum. Furthermore we were told that the other spinster sister had a glass eye and we mustn't stare. You couldn't have said a worse thing to us at this stage and we were mesmerized as we had never seen a glass eye.*

The lady took a great fancy to my little brother of two, whose language would have done credit to a docker. She used to say, 'Dear little chap, what's he saying?' and my mum, ready to sink through the floor, would say, 'Don't ask me, he's got a language all his own.'

Eileen Huddlestone (now Ashby)'s mother held on for as long as she could, but the raids became more and more frequent until they were just too much for her. At the beginning the family shared an Anderson

313

with Eileen's aunt and her family across the street, but they were finally driven out by Peggy, a large smelly spaniel who took the most comfortable spot in the shelter. Since there were nine humans sharing, it seemed hardly fair:

My dad called it the black hole of Calcutta. We had a choice of positions. On the floor amongst the feet with smelly Peggy or sitting upright on a small bench that ran the length of the shelter. Condensation and earwigs fell in equal number from the tin walls.

Somehow I managed to get to school and their shelter. Here we would be herded together to sing songs by an anxious teacher. I can still recall 'An Apple for the Teacher' being bawled at the top of our voices.

If it was my dad's half day he would come and get me from school. I would ride on the crossbars of his bike and we would make quite a game of dodging the shrapnel and bombs before rushing to the shelter the moment we got home.

Eventually we got an Anderson of our own. It was quite cosy, complete with a little pantry. We had a damp blanket across the door, in case of gas, Mum said. I never knew what she meant.

Later on, after some awful raids on London's East End, we left our shelter one morning to find, standing on the doorstep, dazed and in a sorry state, my elderly grandad and my mother's two spinster sisters, dressed only in their nightwear and overcoats. A bomb had scored a direct hit on their house in Bow, so now homeless they had come to us for shelter.

It seemed they brought the raids with them. Bombs fell on our district, each raid heavier than the last, so one day at the end of August we packed some clothes and walked to Chadwell Heath station. Mum said, 'Well kids, we are going to live in the country.' It didn't mean a thing to me.

Mum carried my sister Maureen – she was only three – and Dad carried the cases. Not his. He wasn't coming.

It was like a dream, wide open spaces, the rivers, the trees and most of all the rich ripe corn, swaying like a golden sea. Much of my younger life had been spent in Bow. I'd never imagined such wonder while playing swings on a lamppost or walking the crowded pavements of the East End.

Those who had turned down the offer of an Anderson shelter regretted their decision once the raids started. As early as the Munich crisis, Dorothy Ritchie remembers, Government representatives had gone round from door to door asking the occupants of each house whether they would like a shelter installed in their garden. It was free for those who earned less than five pounds a week. Although Dorothy's father qualified he had refused the offer. He was soon kicking himself when, in May 1941, German bombers turned their attention to Liverpool and the busy docks became a favourite target:

They had a clear run. No ack-ack guns were in place for the defence of the city. All residential areas suffered damage and loss of life.

It had been the practice for some time to disperse ammunition trains on to local sidings, and when one of these trains suffered a direct hit, the whole of the area for a wide radius was damaged, ammunition still flying through the air many hours after the bombers had left for home – none brought down of course.

Fortunately our family had been given places in a neighbour's Anderson shelter, but our home was wrecked. Hastily improved 'rest houses' were set up to house the homeless and those who preferred to remain with their home were given 'relief' in the form of a cash payment to cover essentials.

The cry went up, 'Evacuate the children!' London kids had long been evacuated but no large-scale evacuation had taken place up north. Now it came near to panic. People could be seen leaving the city in droves every evening to camp out in the surrounding countryside; all types of vehicles came to be used, from old prams to horse-drawn carts and everything in between.

My school, which was a girls' one, was split in two. My half were taken by coach to an unknown destination, mother giving me a stamped addressed postcard to post with the address as soon as I knew it. After delays of one kind and another, we set off, and duly arrived at a little tiny village in the Wirral peninsula, and took up residence at the local manor. This was very exciting. Elegant staircases, huge rooms, ballroom – all empty of furniture except for narrow iron truckle-beds with Army blankets on them. Much to our delight we found we now had our own private swimming-pool – the very first private swimming-pool any of us had seen other than in the movies...

Within hours someone discovered that the local village shop still had goodies on its shelves, and we descended upon it like vultures, oohing and aahing over lollies, bubblegum, chocolate bars – which had long disappeared from city shops (not yet on ration but under the counter only for favoured customers) – and, the treasure above all others, pipe-cleaners, which we girls bought in quantity (eventually the shopkeeper limited purchases to two packets each). We used these, as was the fashion, to curl our hair in tight little curls. Next day the shop presented a very different picture. The little window was bereft of a single item; its shelves were stripped bare.

Dorothy was subsequently evacuated again, this time to a farm in Shropshire:

It was here that I had my first experience of country life. How I cried when calves were

317

separated from their mothers. I knew the feeling. But consolations were many: that first Christmas I proudly struggled home after a tedious five-hour train journey which normally took an hour and a half – all trains ran late and standing room only was the norm – carrying the Christmas turkey in my bag.

I was certainly better fed in Shropshire. The farm produced fresh eggs for which one searched around the farmyard to find where the capricious hens had hidden them... Going home was the event we planned for many weeks, and usually we were able to take with us a few fresh eggs. By this time one per month was the ration, and all city people had was the dried variety out of a tin from the USA. Occasionally I would take home a piece of fresh pork or a little home-cooked bacon, which was accepted with much appreciation.

On one of my weekend trips home I was surprised to find 'my' bedroom was no longer available for me. My mother explained that the registration officer for the area had called at all the homes in district, and any that had vacant bedrooms were allocated building workers who were being rushed in to build an ROF factory.

Eventually it was decided I could come home, join the work-force and 'do my bit'. However, I kept in touch with my second family, never forgetting their many kindnesses and loving care given to homesick city kids.

One morning Maureen Ford (now Agassiz)'s dad came home from his air-raid warden patrol and told the family to look out of the window:

It was hideous! The road was like a switchback, the garden torn up and our lovely rose-bush was sitting on the porch over the front door. We were also told our friend two doors away (a little boy with a crippled leg) had been killed. After that we moved to West Molesey and got a Morrison shelter. This was like a big iron table. We had it in our kitchen – the top and legs were iron and there was like a wire mesh around the sides.

We all slept in there every night. By the time we got us four girls in there it was a bit squashed. Later we found it wasn't safe enough, finding large chunks of ceiling on top of it. We were worried more about incendiary bombs being used. So we moved shelters, this time to a big dug-out down the road. It took about 50 people and had bunks down the sides. We spent most of the daylight hours playing on top of it and when the siren went, instead of running inside it for shelter we used it to get a good view of the dogfights.

As the year neared its end, other cities became German targets. Bombs fell on Birmingham, Southampton, Manchester, Sheffield, Portsmouth and Leicester. Many of the parents whose children were safe in the countryside breathed a sigh of relief. At least now they could feel they had done the right thing.

On 29 December, as the pasted pieces of paper that decorated many homes were beginning to sag, London was once again subjected to a massive bombing attack. The 'second fire of London', as it became known – coming more than 250 years after the first – was seen by the eyes of the world via photographs of a resilient St Paul's, against a backdrop of flames, refusing to say die and telling the world that for Britain there was no surrender … ever.

Despite the newsreels and radio reports about how thousands were suffering increased raids, evacuees continued to return home. In many ways this was the most defiant of all the acts of courage being played out in Britain. Women and children, the so-called weakest members of society, were saying, 'I don't care what the hell it's like, I'm going back.'

John Pierce went back to London and stepped straight into the front line:

I became a telegraph boy. I came up each day to London from Croydon, and some days I didn't finish until eight o'clock so I was walking through most of the bombing before I even started for home. I worked out of Church Place, Piccadilly until I arrived one morning and it had been bombed.

One night I was going up Sackville Street to a bookmaker's and by the time I got there the office had been bombed. I met a policeman at the top of Savile Row and he said, 'Where are you going, son?' and I said, 'Well I've got a telegram for Joe Lee,' and the bobby said, 'I don't think he'll be interested, he just had a direct hit.'

May Tranter (now Cashmore) made her way back to Coventry with her mother, who was sick with TB:

She was admitted to hospital, where she died. We were very lonely and used to go back to Coventry to see my father on every occasion that we could.

My brothers were in Coventry on the night of the blitz and they spent the night under the stars which were shining as the bombs fell around them. It was the most terrifying time of their lives.

As Dennis Galvin's train pulled into Paddington Station, the first thing he noticed was how black London was compared with the area in Wales where he had been evacuated:

It seemed strange going all across London not being able to see anything.

There was a little family gathering that night

321

to welcome me back. I had acquired a Welsh accent and of course that was the fun of the evening. I had changed from an East End cockney Londoner to a Welsh one.

Living as we did you'd be sitting playing a game of snakes and ladders and the next minute there would be an explosion and you couldn't see your finger in front of you. It was all the soot and the plaster. You couldn't even get out of the front door. That's what it was like for us all the time.

Stephen Hardy remembers the night his house was hit:

The Germans and Italians were giving us hell that night, the night we received the direct hit. I remember saying to my parents, 'If a bomb hit this shelter it would bounce off, wouldn't it?'

Jim Unger, the creator of the newspaper cartoon 'Herman', recalls:

I think I was three. I do remember that on the train I evacuated my pants so I know I was only three and not 27. I left with my aunt Vi who was my mum's youngest sister. There was Mum, Vi and four kids, so there was quite a crowd. Well, more than a crowd. I mean, I remember vividly being at the railway station with a vast array of strange people and I remember that we all had big labels on us. Like we were something out of a department store. Someone gave us huge mugs

322

of cocoa out of large enamel pouring jugs. The cups probably held a pint but to a three-year-old it was like a gallon.

Anyway, we headed for a place called Merthyr Tydfil in Wales. There was nothing there. I don't remember getting off the train but I do remember ending up over a pub. My mum and her sister slept in a double bed and we were scattered around the room with the littlest in a drawer. Every night we'd have the coal miners come to the pub and loosen up a bit. Being Welsh they'd start singing. Nobody got any sleep. Within weeks my mum had had enough and brought us all back to London, in time for the blitz. They never started bombing until we got back.

Carole Foster, who was a teacher, also returned to London:

At one time, hearing bombing in the distance I told my class to get under the desks. I myself saw the pilot of one machine as he passed by the window. It was 12 o'clock and the mothers were in the playground waiting to collect the infants. The bombers machine-gunned the mothers.

Another day a colleague said, 'I heard you had been killed. I will take your photograph as you may not be here tomorrow.' I still have the photograph.

John McLaughlan used to sleep in the same room as three of his sisters. When the siren sounded in the distance he was always the first to hear it:

I would wake my sisters and say, 'Air raid coming,' and they would tell me to shut up and go back to sleep, but after a few minutes our local siren would sound and I would tell them, 'I told you so,' and we would all get up and go to the Anderson shelter in the garden...

My other sister and brother would sleep in the back room, and one night there was this terrible raid. My eldest sister shouted at my dad, 'We've been hit! Hughie and Helen are in the house.' I peeped out of the shelter and looked up at our house. There were no windows left. They had all been blown out. It turned out that when my dad and sister got to Hughie and Helen's room they were still asleep under the blankets which were covered in glass. My dad blew his top and from then on they had to sleep in the shelter with us every night.

Jim McGinlay remembers the air raids very clearly:

...the bomb had fallen on the road between St Luke's Church and the small swing-park close to our flats. It left a big crater in the road and shrapnel had chipped all the front off the church. My mother was convinced that they had bombed the swings because they looked like a military exercise yard.

There was an air-raid warning one evening and we couldn't find my sister. She had a new pair of gold tap-dancing shoes and was tap-dancing on one of the stairways after everybody else had left for the shelters. I remember my mother running towards the green carrying me and dragging Kathleen still wearing her shoes. The racket these made in the deserted streets was quite incredible. My mother was panicking, convinced that the German pilots could not fail to be drawn towards the noise.

When Mark Donald Woodman arrived back in London, he and his classmates were told that after school each day they must go to the air-raid shelters across the common and wait there until six o'clock, at which time they would go into the shelter and take their allotted places:

Well, with all the ack-ack gun emplacements that they had around the common we were more interested in that. I went home and my sister Eileen said, 'You'd better get back to your allotted place.' Anyway, we didn't go and we went into the shelter in the garden which was our hide-away. A bomb took away the corner of our house which buried the shelter.

My mother was down in the pub thinking we'd gone to the Clapham Common shelter. She went down to the shelter after she'd been to the pub and caused a bit of a fracas because we weren't there. She got arrested and spent the night in the police station.

When she was let out in the morning she was faced with this devastation. Where we were buried in the shelter we could hear activity outside but they couldn't hear us. We heard this voice, 'Where is me boys, where is me lovely boys?' They finally got us out the next afternoon and my mother grabbed me by the collar and started beating me, saying, 'Why don't you do as you're told?'

The policeman put his hand on her and said, 'Aren't you glad to see your son alive?' and she began to tongue-lash him.

Sylvia Smith (now Shaylor) was brought back to the city by her mother:

I found it absolutely terrifying. In our block of flats we had a shelter in the garden. We used to all run down from the tenement house when the sirens went, and one time I got left behind and I had to crouch in a corner. When my mother got into the shelter she found I was missing, but they wouldn't let her out until the raid was over. I sat in the corner with my arms over my head just waiting and terrified.

Many German planes were shot down during the raids. One came down close to where William Smith and his friends were:

Naturally we all ran over and the kids got there before the authorities did. They were more concerned about getting kids away from exploding bullets, and all we cared about was getting what we could as a memento.

Anyone who has been on the receiving end of virtually any object falling from the sky is not likely to forget it in a hurry. Charles Foster remembers listening to the sound of the bombs when he got back to London:

The air raids were getting worse because every night we used to sit in the air-raid shelter. Those whistling bombs were terrifying, and as soon as we heard the whistle someone would say, 'Oh, this is our one.' My father said, 'I think you have to go away again,' and this time my mother came with us.

Meanwhile my uncle was having a farewell party at my house in London. There were two aunts, two uncles and three cousins as well as my father, 13 altogether of my family, and the house received a direct hit and they were all killed. Someone came down and told my mother. She took us on her lap one at a time and told us what had happened.

We never got any compensation for the house that was bombed or a pension for my mother until after the war, so throughout the war we received nothing. My mother had to go out to do scrubbing for other people. She had five young children. She did three jobs to keep us together. I worked during the day and did a gardening job in the evening. I was 13.

Incredible as it may seem now, many theatres in London and other major cities began to reopen. A notice commonly seen on plated shop-fronts was 'Open for business', and theatres decided to do likewise. It is to their great credit that so many actors continued to perform at that time. Certainly there were few enough treats around, and a trip to the theatre was an ideal way of taking one's mind off the war, if just for a short period. Margaret Munro (now MacCormick)'s father decided it was just the thing:

One Friday evening when I arrived home my father informed me that he had been given tickets for the theatre, The White Horse Inn. *During the show an air raid was announced and we were told that if we wished to go to the shelters we should leave now. My trust in my father was so great that I stayed by him and watched the show to the end.*

Only on leaving the theatre did we realize Clydebank had been badly bombed, with over 1,100 people dead. This, then, was the Clydebank blitz. In one house alone the 11 members of the MacDonald family died.

When the bombing eased up a bit, Jean

Birch (now Carberry) and her little sister thought the war must be over:

So instead of just playing in our garden we decided to go to the park, where we were playing when the air-raid siren went. German planes seemed to fill the sky in minutes. We two thought we must be the only two people in the world. There wasn't a soul about. We ran like the wind to get home to our shelter, trying to avoid all the shrapnel.

As we ran across the road an American jeep came from nowhere and I was knocked down. I lay in the road screaming in pain. My knee had been shattered. A policeman saw me and picked me up in his arms and ran through the streets to my home. After the raid I was taken to the children's hospital and was there for six months. I must tell you that the jeep didn't stop after it knocked me down.

While I was in the hospital the raids seemed to be getting heavy again, but we were not taken to any shelters. We had to lie on the floor under the bed and a nurse would lie on top of me to protect me.

Whoever the man was who knocked me down, he must have had a guilty conscience, for I received chocolates and flowers all the six months I was in hospital.

Joan Mary Hay (now Barrett)'s mother collected her and took her back to London where, from a child's point of view, she had a 'smashing time':

For one thing there was no school. One had to go and collect homework – for a year, I think. We watched plane-fights in the skies and after air raids were out as soon as possible to collect shrapnel. It was still hot, sometimes, and the most desirable bits were very jagged and discoloured by what we considered was blood. We used to swap it and it was considered a very good currency! War in fact never touched me emotionally. I do not recollect ever being frightened, just fed up that my sleep was interrupted by having to go to the air-raid shelter.

Betty Hill (now Sheahan) went back to Kent during the Battle of Britain after she had taken her final exams:

It was a nightmare journey that took hours to complete. At times we had to go back towards London by bus, as the railway lines that led to Folkestone had been bombed. It was the day that Buckingham Palace had been bombed, so we went from station to station in our quest to find a train going to Folkestone. I was shocked to see street after street of houses so badly damaged that they looked as though they had been pushed over like packs of cards.

Tony Brown remembers a bomb that fell on

the corner of his street, killing about 30 people and destroying his father's fish-and-chip shop:

The ironic thing about this was that the corner was occupied by the headquarters of the British Fascist Party (Oswald Mosley's lot), who used to come into the shop during the late thirties for 'two twos and a penn'orth' after a strenuous night demonstrating and beating up people 'up west'. Their building was completely destroyed.

Ellen Campbell, who used to take in evacuees, was living near Coventry:

My husband dug a hole in the ground with boards across for me to shelter in. It was very damp and I hated it. He would go off on Home Guard duty and tell me to get down there quickly as the Jerries were coming over again. I think it was the night they bombed Coventry and I said, 'I can't, I can't find my knitting needle.' I won't tell you what he said.

Some evacuees were forced to return by bad news from home. Violet Sutton (now Goode) went back for the saddest reason of all, and one that was common to the experience of many evacuees – for the funeral of her parents. It was, as she recalls, 'the most traumatic event' of her life:

The air raids on London started early ... first the oil bombs, then the incendiaries to set them on fire, then the waves of bombers dropping high explosives. My father had gone to the skin market to help them extinguish fires. At about 9.30 p.m. my mother decided to take some supper to him. My mother stayed there because the raid by now was very heavy, with bombs falling all around. Just after midnight a stick of bombs fell, hitting Guy's Hospital and the skin market. My father was killed outright. My mother was badly hurt by flying glass. It was difficult to get her out owing to the fires and Mum was dead before they could get to her. My eldest brother on his way to the market was knocked unconscious.

My brother advised me by telegram, and I was to go up to London for the funeral. I was now 15 years old and my world had come to an end. I remember the train journey, being so numb ... I couldn't even shed tears ... to me it just wasn't true – but that soon changed on seeing my brother. Many of his schoolfriends had been killed that night. It took many hours to bury them all at Nunhead Cemetery.

I recall the funeral procession ... just my brother and I in the first car, relations following. On each side of the road large numbers of people stood. I thought when I saw all the people that my parents must have been well liked. It was 40 years later, when I read the book Bermondsey at War, that I found out that the Mayor had been killed in the same raid and his funeral was *behind ours.*

With the German occupation of France, the enemy were so close as to be in a position to hit just about anywhere in Britain they chose. Nowhere, in fact, could be guaranteed to be a 'safe area'.

The cities were clearly the most attractive targets, since they not only had the most worthwhile bull's-eyes but could be counted upon to contain the greatest number of people at any given time. However, this did not mean that evacuees in the countryside could be sure that they would never hear the sound of enemy aircraft. Like all pilots, the Germans frequently lost their way and were forced to drop their bombs on areas other than those marked on their maps. Freda Berry, who had originally been sent to the Isle of Wight, where she stayed in a home with 16 other children, was eventually moved because the area was so prone to enemy attack. Her next billet was in an incredibly beautiful and peaceful village in Sussex:

It was ironic to say the least, us being evacuated to such a beautiful and peaceful place, as the local school received a direct hit from a stray German plane. All 48 children and teachers lost their lives, but no evacuees perished as we had our schooling separately in the 'Iron Room' in nearby Petworth.

J. Wilson remembers the raids on the town of Stonehouse in Scotland, where she had been taken into the home of an old lady:

We were only five miles from Clydebank. The raids were aiming for the shipyards, in fact Clydebank was nearly destroyed. Our house was on Main Street and the front door opened on to a footpath. I only remember that I wouldn't let my dolly out of my sight. I can still see the house, the old lady with white hair and me standing with this doll.

I remember seeing the building we lived in on fire after a raid. We stayed in a tenement square. The hills around us were full of bomb craters, with some unexploded.

George Russell was probably reliving every child's dream as he looked up at the sky and watched the action overhead:

I remember a Heinkel III that was shot down over our heads by three Spitfires from the Edinburgh squadron. It came down in a shallow dive, but disintegrated in hitting a series of stone dikes and scattered itself across three fields. By the time we got there, some farmers had the bodies covered and were keeping the kids away.

Life was full of excitement for Jean Kidds (now Joy). Every morning she would go with 'Uncle Dally', her foster father, to help him collect the crab-pots and fishing-nets off the Cornish coast. At five o'clock in the morning they would be out, and on their return Jean would make her way to school – until one morning:

We went out as usual and I heard this cry in the sea. We picked up this German pilot who was floating in the sea. He'd come down after bombing Plymouth and we took him back to the fishing village and all the villagers wanted to put him on the point and shoot him. (They didn't.)

Then another day we saw this Polish ship. There were two planes above it and it was fascinating watching the tracer bullets going up and trying to get this plane down. Eventually they hit the boat and it went down. When it went down it shook the earth. I was nine. The one I was evacuated to, he was the coxswain of the lifeboat and because he was, I was allowed to go in and clean all the brass. And this was the boat that was used to go out and get some of the survivors from the Polish ship and they came back pretty badly wounded.

Seven-year-old Donald Baker, who had been evacuated from wartorn Birmingham to Alfreton in Derbyshire, must have wondered why he had bothered to leave home at all:

We were sent there for safety, and on the second night an incendiary bomb dropped on the house next door.

Ethel Hartley, who was the headmistress of an infants' school in Clacton-on-Sea, remembers that soon after one group of evacuees had arrived, they were followed by another visitor:

We received a Heinkel with two magnetic bombs which gave us the unwelcome distinction of having the first civilian casualties, and we had to organize the immediate return of the children to London.

After waving to the two pilots of a plane overhead, Stanley William Shirley and his friends were suddenly horrified to see that the plane was in trouble:

The Fleet Air Arm Skua aeroplane crashed in a field. Both crew were killed. Waving to them one minute, dead the next. Looking back on it now you realize that the pilot was a hero when he was coming down because the engine was not working properly. He realized he was going to crash into houses grouped near the church. He banked the aircraft, a wing scraped the ground in a ploughed field and turned over and over. We collected lots of live bullets and a Very pistol. After a few days the police came to pick them up.

Sheila Mayne (now Fellows) was playing on the cliffs in Brixham, Devon, when suddenly she heard a 'terrible noise':

I was paralysed with fear. I couldn't look up and then all the bullets started whipping around us and the teachers ran around us bringing us down with rugby tackles. One got me down. Two of my friends got hit. This experience didn't leave me till well after I was married. Every time I heard a motor cycle go by it affected me...

Then my mother was evacuated with us to Nottingham and in my school there, whenever I'd hear a motor cycle I would dive under a desk. Of course, they hadn't had any war in Nottingham, but the headmistress explained to all the school what had happened to me.

Harold Silver's first destination was Peterborough, where he stayed with a foster mother who was 'kind but domineering'. The foster family had two holiday homes in villages on the east coast, and Harold was taken along with them on vacations. Life in the flat fen country was never dull. Several planes crashed in the fens and it was not unusual to see their tail-fins sticking up out

337

of the mud:

We used to have fun if we could get into the cockpit and fire the remaining bullets into the ground. We helped a pilot to safety on one occasion (well, we walked with him and carried his parachute and other gear back to the village).

Our house had a westerly aspect and my bedroom at the back overlooked the dairy farm, and one morning about 7 a.m. I heard the distinctive drone of a German plane. I looked from my window and there it was, heading straight for our house. It was about 500 feet up and I raced to the master bedroom at the front and we witnessed the sight of the plane, only 200 feet up or less, with guns blazing, demolishing a Lewis gun (the only one) in the Army camp on the other side of the road where we lived. The plane was shot down, we learned later in the day, but no sign of the pilot.

This incident occurred about two or three weeks before the horrific bombing of Coventry, and there were plenty of rumours around as to that pilot's possible involvement in locating targets in the Coventry area.

Freda Hallett (now Strain) and another evacuee named Norah used to sleep in an upstairs bed together. The house was near the aerodrome at Weybridge, so at times the bombing was intensive:

A bomb dropped in an adjacent field one night and from then on Norah and I slept under the grand piano in the living-room.

As I was returning from lunch one day, the siren went, and I began running to school for shelter. The Germans decided to machine-gun the area and as I ran across the street a cyclist knocked me over and down. I arrived at the school with scraped knees and elbows. I said nothing to my foster parents about my scare. But they found out. I got a good telling-off and was sent to my room.

Patricia Perriman (now Taylor) had a dreadful experience:

My friend Edith was killed when a plane jettisoned its bombs. The old lady she lived with had tried to shelter her by lying on top of her. By 1942 there had been an invasion of another kind. American, Polish and Commonwealth servicemen could be seen everywhere. Kind and generous to a fault, they were quick to show how much they loved children. Maybe it was because both groups were apart from their families that they felt a kinship. Many of the servicemen from overseas must have been sorely missing their own children or younger brothers and sisters.

Shirley Rogerson (now Evans) and her sister were evacuated to Fleetwood in Lancashire, where they were taken in by a vicar and his sister. Shirley remembers American soldiers being invited to the vicarage for afternoon tea. She has many other memories too, some jogged by her sister:

I can also remember going up the street swinging on the hands of two soldiers. A very vivid memory is of seeing an RAF plane down on the beach with dead airmen in it, and I have for years wondered how I happened to be down there, as we were very strictly looked after, but ... last year my sister and I were talking about it, and she said, didn't I remember that each day we were allowed to go down and see the marionettes. It used to cost a penny, and whilst there we heard about the plane and took off down to the beach. She also reminded me that a lot of people were stealing pieces of the 'new glass'. Looking back I feel sure that it was Perspex.

Another very vivid memory is of seeing lots of little boats come into Fleetwood with wounded soldiers in them. Everyone I've told says they couldn't have come from Dunkirk, but I can't think where else they would be from...

Later on we were evacuated to North Wales... My sister and I were the only children in the school who didn't speak Welsh and we felt very out of it.

Whilst living at the vicarage, we were taught that if you wanted anything badly enough and prayed hard enough you would always get it.

Well at the school in Wales they had a raffle for a rabbit, I can still see it, holding a carrot and dressed in blue gingham. I prayed my heart out for that rabbit and was quite sure I would win it, and even to this day I can remember that I couldn't believe it when someone else won it.

'Got any gum, chum?' It is a cry that many ex-evacuees will remember as if it were yesterday. The moment an American uniform appeared, the children would start the chorus, laughing and giggling, tugging at the wearer's sleeve. Invariably the tug would be met by a huge grin, and small packets of gum would be distributed.

Dorothy Bruce (now McLellan) did her sleeve-tugging in Great Torrington, in Devon. The Americans there adopted a London evacuee each:

The one who adopted me was named Dersey Polski, it sounded like to me, but he always laughed when I called him Dersey, so I'm sure I pronounced it wrong.

Anyway, the soldiers were very good to us. On Saturdays they took us to the matinée and on Tuesday it was sweet-ration day. When the circus came to town they gave us a great time.

Then, as always happens, all good things come to an end. For me it was a night I still remember. We were woken at midnight. I was taken from my bed, the streets were full of Army lorries.

341

They had stopped so I could say goodbye to Dersey.

When Eunice Mackenzie (now Lawrence) and her sister stopped in the centre of London to ask directions, it was an American soldier who came to their help. They had been evacuated and had run away, and were now looking for a number 46 bus to take them home:

He stopped and asked a passer-by, and once he found out where to catch the bus he gave us the money for the fare.

When Eunice and her sister arrived back home, their mother shipped them straight back to where they had come from.

John Ancliff was an engine driver and can remember the lucky evacuees who were billeted in Tollerton, Nottinghamshire, where an American Air Force squadron was stationed:

They gave the kids a swell party every so often and things they had never seen. The kids used to go to the air-base with their cycles, letting the Yanks put them on the crossbars of their bikes, and ride down to the bus stop about one and a half miles away so that they, the Yanks, could get a night out in Nottingham ... then the kids would be off again for another customer for two-

and-six a time.

In a small cottage in Blandford, in Dorset, Jill Fisher (now West) and her mother attempted to survive the millions of fleas. Their home was 'alive with them'. When her mother complained, she was told, 'We didn't expect posh people':

She obviously hated having us and we certainly didn't like her! But it was better than being bombed I suppose! I loved it. The American Army was based there. We kids bummed gum and 'life-buoys' from passing convoys, yelling, 'Got any gum, chum?' and we were always showered with goodies from men missing their own kids, I daresay.

My poor mother dealt with an MP at the door who was complaining I had climbed a lamppost (in shorts) with all the boys and had had an audience of soldiers watching my legs. I was 11 years old and an innocent tomboy, and I just couldn't understand why I was read the Riot Act and couldn't wear shorts again. I was one of the boys.

If I can give you a picture of a small Dorset town, then: Americans, evacuees, locals, I think 24 public houses – I'm not quite sure of the number – and all us kids standing around the doors, asking for 'Gum, chum' and receiving money, sweets, gum and lots of affection from men who had imbibed!

Prisoners of war were another group of people who sometimes ended up living close to evacuees' new homes, since their camps were deliberately sited away from the cities, often deep in the countryside. One day some German POWs were brought to the area where Raymond Carabine was billeted. They were marched from the railway station through the town:

We were disappointed because none of them wore their steel helmets or looked nearly as horrible as we expected.

Italian POWs were working in the fields near the village where Kathleen Strange (now Mossman) had been taken in:

They used to sing 'Rose Marie' and it sounded lovely. They were happy and smiling, and one Christmas they gave us oranges they must have got from their Red Cross parcels because we certainly didn't have any. Some of them were allowed to walk around the village; some of them worked on the farms.

They brought some German POWs down and that was a totally different thing. They didn't bother looking at the children at all. They were not happy and the first thing they were going to do was try and escape. There was a lot of trouble between them and the Italians.

344

For 18 months the village smithy and his family shared their home with me and although, looking back, I can see that like many evacuees I was useful cheap labour, this did not mean that I was not cared for in a loving way. From a tiny room upstairs I listened nightly to Mr Roberts emptying the day's takings from the smithy on to the kitchen table. In shirt-sleeves and cloth cap (I never knew him to take it off), he would set the coins in neat little piles like an army of toy soldiers preparing for war. Years later I would miss the sounds of the family's lilting Welsh accent, and shall for ever think of Wales as a second home. The little Welsh I was forced to learn was not needed. I knew they cared.

They gave me the opportunity to be a part of the country way of life. I would be up each morning at six o'clock to feed the pigs and chickens before school, a routine that awakened in me a love of animals that I have to this day, and after school would go to the forge to pump the bellows.

I was almost 15 when it was time for me to leave school and make my way back to London. I had been away from home for more than two years, years that I would look back on with fondness because strangers had taken me into their home and shown me love.

South London was an even less inviting place than it had been when I left. Although it was wonderful to be back home with my family, the area had suffered heavy bombing. Few structures had escaped damage, and crippled buildings everywhere struggled to stand erect as they awaited the next attempt to push them down.

My first job was in the East Street Market. A friend's father was kind enough to let me help sell fruit from his cart. Unfortunately the money was not good and I moved on through a series of jobs until I finally found myself working for a kind man called Mr Francis, who made handbags.

He followed the law and allowed us to stop work at the first sound of an air-raid warning and make our way to the shelter below the building to wait for the all-clear. Unfortunately my friend and I were much more interested in the aerial fights going on overhead, and as the rest of the workers in the building made their way to the basement, we headed for the roof. It was not long before Mr Francis noticed our absence and decided that instead of his paying good wages for us to stand around on the roof, we might just as well stick around beside our work-bench.

The weeks passed and the daily routine continued – work during the day, shelter during the night. Every evening, hundreds of families shuffled down to shelters, carrying their bedding with them. The shelter my family used was Borough underground station, one stop from London Bridge and in the heart of cockney land. I had tried to sleep there with my mother, my sisters and the baby, but had found it impossible. The last train to leave the platform dragged with it the only vestige of fresh air left in the tunnels, leaving the stench of stagnant waste in the toilet buckets to glide along among the bodies of those who lay there, coughing, attempting to sleep. On each of the three nights I spent down there I attempted to overcome the need to vomit, but by the fourth night I was forced to give up and take my chances with my father, the shy First World War veteran who would rather risk the danger of a thousand bombs than be forced to sleep alongside strangers.

He was the worst of companions with whom to share danger. Within minutes of his head's hitting the pillow he would be asleep, and nothing on earth would wake him. With the covers pulled up to my neck I would lie awake for hours, repeating over and over the Lord's Prayer as bomb after bomb fell. The ack-ack gun on a train that moved back and forth through the area was little comfort; each firing made the building shake and the windows rattle far more than the bombs did.

My arrival home coincided with a change of fortune for the Allies. There was good news from the Mediterranean. An attempt by the Italians to force their way into Greece was crushed. More good news followed, as half the Italian Navy was put out of action by a daring Fleet Air Arm attack on the port of Taranto. For the Italians, bad news came in threes. Headed by General Graziani, a large army set off through North Africa and headed for Egypt. In December they found themselves facing General Wavell who, at the head of a British force, mounted an assault. In two months the British troops advanced 500 miles and destroyed an army that outnumbered them by five to one.

However, help was on the way for the routed Italian army. A German lieutenant-general was about to become a household name in Britain. Rommel landed on the shore of North Africa and, at the head of a combined German and Italian army, this brilliant tactician began to force the British troops back to the Egyptian border. On the way he deliberately bypassed the coastal town of Tobruk, and on 21 June 1942, with no means of escape, the garrison was forced to surrender.

It was an area of the world that we as a family were deeply concerned about, since the last news we had received from my elder sister's husband was that he had arrived in

North Africa.

By this time I had left Mr Francis and his handbags for a job beside my sister, making diaries for a large company called Letts. Every day, during the half-hour for lunch, we would hurry home to see her young baby, who was being looked after by my mother, and to listen to the latest news reports. Within weeks of the fall of Tobruk, the telegrams for the next of kin began to arrive. My sister received one. 'We regret to inform you that your husband has been reported missing in action and must be presumed dead.' The months that followed were hideous as the family tried to help Doll overcome her grief.

Three months after this disastrous news came word from the Red Cross that Doll's husband was safe. He had been seen in an Italian prisoner-of-war camp. It was a wonderful day for all of us, especially for my sister who, with a young baby to care for, could once again look forward to the day her family would be reunited.

In August Churchill flew to Alexandria to make a change in the leadership of the Eighth Army, which had now been pushed back to the Egyptian border. Field Marshal Alexander was placed in overall command. He appointed a man who, like Rommel, was to become a legendary figure – General Bernard Montgomery. Churchill had just one order to give before he flew on to Moscow: win a major battle. By October, Alexander and his new appointee were ready. With 250,000 men now ready for action, they began with one of the biggest barrages of the war and on 23 October, with a Scottish Piper leading the way, they set out from El Alamein and began to repulse the German Army.

By November General Montgomery had given the British public something they desperately needed. A victory. Church bells rang throughout the country and evacuees everywhere began to believe that maybe, after all, they would see their homes again.

At 11 o'clock on the night of 15 September 1944, a new flying weapon appeared on the scene. The V1, or 'doodlebug' as it was nicknamed, was a small plane without a pilot. It carried a high charge of explosive and was catapulted from the Continent in the direction of London. The principle was incredibly simple. With just enough fuel to make the trip, when this ran out, the plane would drop.

The first time I saw a V1 was from the balcony. It was late at night and, my mother and sisters safe in the underground shelter, I had left my father asleep and wandered out into the clear night air to watch any action. It was not long in coming. A small plane was making its way up the Thames and was

caught in the searchlights. I watched with excitement as bursting shells puffed and
exploded around the aircraft. As it got closer,
I became aware that a flame was coming
from its tail. I rushed inside to tell Dad, who
quickly turned over and mumbled something
that sounded like 'That's nice!' I ran back
outside and was in time to see the flame go
out and the plane disappear in the night sky.
Suddenly there was a familiar swishing noise
and, as I dashed for the stairs, an explosion
and a fierce gust of wind that blew me right
down them.

The next morning we discovered that our
local post office had received a direct hit.

Within days the Government issued a
statement to the effect that Hitler had
begun a new form of warfare.

Two weeks later I had another opportunity
to witness the doodlebug in action.

I was a member of a cricket team, which
met on Sundays and enjoyed the distinct
honour of never winning a game, and which
the captain claimed was the strongest team
since it constantly held up the rest of the
league.

On a typical Sunday morning, as we pro-
gressed towards the inevitable result, the air-
raid warning sounded. All the players looked
anxiously up at the sky, as we awaited the
arrival of the now familiar doodlebug.
Ginger Baily was the first to hear the sound

of the 'motor-bike engine'. We all held our breath as we watched the small rocket plane approaching. We all stood with our hands together, asking God please to give the plane enough fuel to pass over us and head for somewhere else.

Suddenly it happened. The engine stopped and the plane began to glide. It was like a re-enactment of a Charlie Chaplin movie as all 22 players ran for cover, banging into one another as they ran.

The plane landed in the corner of the field and exploded.

That afternoon, during a friendly card-game with Sammy Verigo, Arthur Biggs and me, the same Ginger Baily, with ears as sharp as a deer's, held up a hand for quiet.

Once again, Ginger could hear a V1 approaching. We dived under the table as the engine cut out and a loud swishing noise overhead told us that it was going to be close.

We ran through the streets towards the pillar of smoke that was rising from Arthur's street. I can still remember Arthur's face as we turned the corner and saw that his house had been hit. We scrambled over the bricks and into the ruins in time to see his mother and father staggering out of what had once been their home.

'Where's Gran?' shouted Arthur.

His dad turned, ready to follow Arthur,

who was already at the foot of a sloping staircase. Suddenly an old lady appeared at the top, covered in soot and dirt.

'Wot the bloody 'ell was that?' she shouted, and was greeted by roars of laughter.

Like all children who witnessed the air attacks on Britain during the war, I had become a fanatic about aeroplanes, whichever side they were on. The sound of an engine or the fleeting glimpse of an airborne intruder was enough for us to know its name and certainly which side it was on.

Within weeks of arriving back in London I had joined the Air Cadets. At just over 17 I had volunteered for the Air Force, hoping that one day I would be zooming amongst the clouds, hot on the tail of a weaving Messerschmitt fighter.

Two weeks after passing the initial test, I received a letter from the Air Ministry informing me that they no longer needed pilots, but since I had volunteered for the Armed Services I would soon receive my call-up papers from the Army. After three and a half years of regular evening study, my dreams of becoming a flyer had been crushed. I have never trusted any Government official since.

Once again I left London, now a young man determined to make good despite the turn of events. The year was 1944, and I was about to escape a weapon that was to prove to be the forerunner of the rocket that would take man to the moon – the V2.

The first V2 landed with a shattering explosion in London on 8 September. So shaken was the British Government that it was not until November that the nation finally heard the terrifying news that London was now under attack by a weapon that gave no warning of its approach. By the end of the month, the factory beside our house had received a direct hit. It came at five o'clock one evening, as workers waited for buses to take them home. Many of them were killed.

Just seconds before the explosion, astonishingly, my father had shoved my mother under the table. Years later he would claim that four years in the trenches in France in the First World War had developed a built-in alarm system that warned him when anything with an explosive head might be coming his way.

The V2 rocket blew in the windows and the door, and although Mum was cut about the head they had both escaped more serious injury thanks to Dad's quick action.

Other Londoners were not so lucky. Shirley Izenman (now Robinson) was in her house:

When we received the hit by the V2 the little baby next door was killed. The mother was in with us showing us his new Easter outfit.

Jean lived in the East End of London where, after V1 and V2 attacks, she returned to school to face the shock of seeing the chairs of classmates standing empty. The underground that had previously been such a safe haven had suddenly become a prison after one particular disaster that stands out in Jean's mind:

...176 people were killed through one person tripping down the stairs and others falling on top of each other.

As the Allies advanced through France, they raced to get to the launching pads of the rockets and stop the hideous weapons at their starting-point. Slowly they succeeded, as one after another of these targets was overrun. But not before people like Ted Riley and his family had suffered the effects of the last of the V1s:

We were bombed out at Brixton and moved to Sutton, Surrey to a so-called safe area, where we got a direct hit from a V1 which killed my younger brother and injured my sister.

Happily, the danger from the air began to subside. The years of horror that had brought so much pain were almost at an end.

What might have been the fate of many

evacuees, had they stayed in the cities, could now be seen in the safety of newsreel cinemas, as British Bomber Command selected the German city of Dresden, a non-military target, to show the might of Britain's air arm. This city was later to find itself with the dubious honour of holding the record for the highest number of people killed in any single air raid, higher even than in the atomic attacks on Hiroshima and Nagasaki in Japan.

The bombing of Dresden may have served to reinforce the British Government's conviction that their decision to evacuate the children from their own cities had been a right one.

Most of the evacuees would not agree. They would never be the same again. Fifty years would pass and they would still remember the brown luggage-labels tied to their coats and the cardboard boxes containing gas-masks strung around their necks. Some would look back fondly and know that they had been fortunate in having the love of two or more sets of parents. Others would continue to hide the pain they had suffered through their parents' concern for their safety.

On 7 May 1945 the German Supreme Command finally surrendered. By this time many evacuated children had already returned to their families, the flow back to the cities having been set in motion in September 1944. Their parents were overjoyed, knowing that their children were safely home and would not have to leave again. Reg Castle can still see his mother, a quiet and gentle lady, after she had listened to the peace announcement on the wireless:

Together with my aunt she took a large Union Jack and climbed out onto the roof of the big house. I shall never forget the sight of those two ladies hoisting the flag to the top of the flag-pole amid great cheers and celebrations.

Other children, however, were still away in the countryside under the Government scheme. Many resented the fact that even after the war in Europe had ended they continued to he separated from their families. The truth was that although the evacuation process was much easier to execute in reverse, a major problem was housing. The bombing had taken its toll on many inner-city areas which, having not so long ago been emptied of children, were now bursting at the seams as the young people flooded back. It was not until March 1946 that the official resettlement programme was completed.

Yet the dancing in the streets on VE day was deceptive, for it hid the feelings of a large section of the nation. A militancy was beginning to grow among the members of a working class that had experienced the advantages of war in having a strong bargaining chip in the face of a Government that was prepared to concede higher wages rather than risk a disruption of the war effort. Now that peace was at hand, many were unwilling to return to the lifestyle that had been theirs before the war, a lifestyle of poverty that was reflected in the faces of children whose existence had been one that many thought had vanished with the age of Dickens.

The poor may have seen the countryside for the first time, but the countryside also saw the poor of the cities. It was a shock for both. Villagers who had thought they themselves were living a life of poverty found that they were opening their doors to children even poorer than their own. At the same time, wealthier families suddenly came into contact with children whose lives had been spent in the alleys of city slums. What they may have expected did not always appear. The majority were not dirty, rude, dishonest Faganites but children just like their own and, although tired and homesick, lovable none the less.

The evacuees' reactions to their experiences varied enormously. Some found the countryside dull, others developed a love of it that would never leave them. Those living in a wealthy environment for the first time were affected in different ways. Some would become radicals and fight to change the system. Others, having had a taste of the good life, would strive to join it. Whatever their feelings, they would change. Their accents would change too, so that it often became impossible to tell where they had originally come from. Religious beliefs would also be tempered, but above all it was their attitude towards authority – along with that of their parents – that would never be the same again. As the First World War had destroyed the sense of loyalty of millions who had felt cheated on their return from France, so, in the Second World War, the evacuation shattered many people's belief that authority was there to be blindly obeyed. The evacuees had suffered the humiliation of being treated like cattle as they waited to be picked out and carried away by strangers. Mothers who had received calls for help from their children had rushed to their aid and, in defiance of the Government, had brought them home again. The confidence of the working class grew. They were ready to shape the country's destiny.

Encounters with new faces and places had heightened people's awareness that there was a class structure in Britain that favoured a minority. The word spread – from returning evacuee to parent, from parent to friend. From concerned 'borrowed parents' in the countryside to village neighbours, a whole nation woke up to the injustice of a system that had prevailed for too long. It was time for a quiet revolution.

Both major political parties recognized the need for change, but it was the socialists who were entrusted with bringing it about. Churchill had been idolized as a leader in war, but few could forget that he was part of the regime that was responsible for the plight of the masses.

A coalition Government had defeated Germany. The moment for the first peacetime election had arrived. The wartime Government had included a large number of socialist MPs, and now they were to be given the responsibility of carrying out the wishes of the majority. Better housing was needed, an educational system that would give everyone the opportunity to learn and a health plan that guaranteed no one would suffer for want of medical care.

Britain voted against Winston Churchill and turned towards socialism. Britain would never be the same again.

Neither would its evacuees.

PART FOUR

The Memories Live On

9

'I'd never do it to my kids'

It is now almost 50 years since the beginning of the evacuation. It was an operation that shaped and charged the lives of all those who took part. Some have been left with scars that will never heal, others with memories that they will cherish to the end of their days.

Evacuees whose lives at home had been restricted by the poverty of their surroundings found themselves part of a whole new world. Some were encouraged to study, did so and qualified for university. Now, as lawyers, judges, surgeons and leaders in all fields, they owe a debt of gratitude to their wartime 'borrowed parents', whose loving homes were able to foster an awareness of life outside the environments they had left. The kindness shown to them opened a door to a new future, a door that would have remained closed had it not been for the evacuation.

Yet the fact remains that others were wounded so badly that they still carry the pain with them.

In the accounts that follow, the writers look back on their own experiences in their own way. Each is different, but one thought stands out: it was an unforgettable happening.

The first three letters are linked, and share loving memories. Dawn Hogbin, who was an evacuee, recalls:

I was chosen by a wonderful woman and her family to share her home when the world around seemed to be in utter chaos.

The children from schools in New Malden, Surrey left on a train in April 1944 for an unknown destination. We arrived in the evening, very tired, in the Rhondda Valley, South Wales. We were all taken to a school where someone would select us. It was very hard to understand the people as they spoke with a different dialect.

The thing that stands out most on that day is my determination not to be separated from my six-year-old sister. As most of the other children were being taken my hopes were getting bleak, as it seemed no one wanted two children. Finally a lady with the most cheerful disposition agreed to take us both. She told us to call her Auntie Bessie and her husband Uncle Percy. They had two young children, Shirley and Brian.

That first night my sister and I shared a camp-cot (as only one had been supplied by the Council). Deanne threatened to run away and I was afraid to sleep for fear that she would.

After a few days we began to adjust to the way of life. The quiet nights, no air raids, going to school and finding that friends from home were billeted down the street. One boy died when he threw himself from a rock on a mountain because he was so unhappy. I enjoyed school except for Welsh lessons, which I couldn't grasp. When the teacher realized the futility of it she allowed me to read a book instead.

Edmondstown was a mining town and Uncle Percy a coal miner, but Auntie Bessie really stretched the good rations and we always ate well and loved the Welsh cakes.

Relatives of Mr and Mrs Keates took my three-year-old brother as he was too young to be evacuated with the school. He was well looked after and spoiled by the teenaged boys of the house. But my heartfelt thanks go out to the Keates family who shared so much with two children during such a terrible time in wartime England. Thanks that cannot be expressed in words.

Percy Keates, Dawn's foster uncle, remembers:

We collected Dawn and Deanne from Craig-yr-sos School, Penygraig, in April 1944. Bessie went along with the intention of taking only one evacuee, but Dawn and Deanne were so frightened and they would have been heartbroken if they had been separated, so she gave in and took the two home. Bessie remembers singing jovial songs all the way home to cheer the girls because they looked so unhappy and frightened.

Both of the girls stayed with us until the end of the doodlebug period. Owing to the difference in ages the girls had to go to different schools. We had reports from both schools that they were getting on well and settling down.

They both seemed to have a good time with us.

Mary Anne Hogbin, Dawn's mother, writes from her present home in North Carolina, USA:

The war years, I think, will he stamped on my mind for the rest of my life.

We had the bombs, then the V1, which we called the doodlebug, then the V2. That was when the schools decided to evacuate the school-children.

I had two in school – my eldest daughter, Dawn, aged 12, and my daughter Deanne, aged six – and my son, Tony, almost three years old, in nursery school. My husband was in the Royal Air Force, and I was working for Parnell Aircraft all the time.

Before the children left we were told that we would not be informed as to their destination for at least a week. When we received a card, my eldest daughter said they were with a nice family – a Mr and Mrs Keates and their two children. Dawn said that on their arrival they were taken to a school and then people came to choose who they would take into their homes.

Then I heard that someone was willing to take my son, Tony. They were relatives of Mr and Mrs Keates.

It was very hard to adjust to being without the children, but their safety meant everything to me. They enjoyed their stay with the kind folks in Wales and my two daughters still correspond with them.

I will always be grateful to those kind people who took my family to their hearts.

Others were less fortunate. Margaret King was badly abused, and has never been able to forget her tormentor:

Now I am older I don't know, will I try and find him? I don't know that either. I feel even now great hate for him. I feel he has ruined my life to the extent that I trust no man. It made me very hard and determined that no man would hurt me again.

I now have a good third husband who knows I trust no man and he is very tolerant. I haven't been able to explain to him what happened, but he knows that it has to do with the war. After coming home from Norwich I can look back and see what sort of a child I was. I must have been a terrible child, and as I got older and married I tried to make up to my mother and be that person I really wanted to be.

My husband and daughters love me, and somehow the strength I have had to find makes them rely on me to help them through. Perhaps we are forced into becoming the people we become through circumstances that happen to us as children over which we have no control.

Fate!! Perhaps – because I could have had good foster parents, I believe many did – I was just unlucky.

Madge Dobinson (née Isaac) has happier memories, and her foster uncle must have had fond recollections of her, too:

On the death of Uncle Garfield we – my younger sister and I – were told by his solicitor that he had left us £200 each in his will.

Tommy McSorley survived wartime bombing and evacuation, and was then conscripted into the Army at the age of 18:

On active service in Italy in a United Nations peace-keeping force in 1948, the car I was driving in was blown up by a mine and as a result I had to have my left leg amputated.

I wouldn't have missed my time as an evacuee for anything, for it added such a great deal to my character. It helped me to look after other people as much as myself and put me on my own two feet, so to speak.

Michael Clark's memories are mainly happy ones:

We could not understand these strange people who for some reason we were sent to live with, but as the years have gone by I realize just what diamonds they were.

Doris Ward (née Roker), on the other hand, does not look back on her experiences as an evacuee with pleasure:

Even after nearly 50 years, I remember these events with a sense of pain.

Ann James (now Bowes), along with her sister Amba, suffered considerably during the evacuation years. She feels that the authorities were largely to blame:

I suppose that the evacuation of children from London had to be carried out in haste, and there were things wrongly handled. One of those was in the choice of the people in authority. Every time we were moved to a fresh billet, as it was called, the same man drove us in his car. Each time he sat me in the front passenger-seat, and Amba sat behind, and each time he would put his hand down the waist of my knickers and fondle my bottom. I endured this without complaint, hating every moment. That sort of thing could not go unnoticed for long these days.

We stayed for most of the war in the last billet, with a Salvationist family with grown-up children, who took in paid lodgers, foster children and evacuees. I think that was the time when I first became very cynical about overt 'do-gooders'. We were unhappy there. We were properly fed and clothed (although we didn't always get our fair share of food rations) and everyone told 'Nanny' as we called her, what a wonderful, kind and noble woman she was. Yet we were often unfairly criticized, hit for minor offences (or what were considered to be offences), kept away from school if Nanny needed some help and generally made to feel like second-class citizens. I can still remember the feeling of injustice when Nanny's granddaughter, who was fussed and spoilt, told lies just to get us into trouble.

We were also sexually abused; we were not raped, but we were interfered with and compelled, ourselves, to interfere with one or two of the adults in the family. We never spoke of this to each other. It was many years after we were back at home that we discovered that both of us had suffered in the same way. I was, and still am, astonished at the lack of integrity.

We did go once to what I suppose was a 'short-stay' home. This was a hostel run by a matron and a nurse, and was a well-run place. There were six girls there; it was orderly, quite strict and I suppose rather like a boarding school. I liked it there and would have been happy to remain there. *More of that type of home would have been ideal.*

In all, Amba and I stayed in five homes... The first was a caring home with two girls in the family, but we had to leave there because the mother got ill, I think. The second home did not feed and clothe us adequately, so that our mother asked for us to be moved (which was probably welcome to the people who had us, since we had been stealing and eating their store of pears, which was not discovered until almost the entire stock was eaten – but I say, in mitigation, that we were hungry and had grown quite thin). The third was the hostel and the fourth a very short stay with a childless couple where I think we were contented. The last was with the Salvationists...

I do not want to make it sound as though my sister and I were paragons of all the virtues. I am sure that we were as naughty as we were allowed to be and that it must have been difficult for people to take strange children into their homes. It takes a very special sort of person to show love to children not their own and to try to replace natural parents.

But when problems did arise, there was so much fuss made of it. I can recall a 'crime' I committed where my mother was actually sent for, when the matter could have been sorted out without worrying her... There was also the time when Amba broke her leg and this was a punishable offence. It was treated almost as though she had done it on purpose to spite someone, and she had

371

to take herself, alone, to the hospital. *This will show you that there was a coldness in our lives, and I don't think that that coldness stretched to the natural members of the family. We were children who were, you might say, bereaved, albeit temporarily, and it is not everyone who can cope with that...*

Evacuation away from one's parents is something which, in my opinion, should not have happened. It certainly destroyed something in me which I was never able to replace. I loved my mother, who died a couple of years ago. She was wonderful, yet I know I never showed her the love and affection she was due and which I felt, and it took me a very long time after we were reunited to be able to kiss and hug her without feeling embarrassed. Although I would never have allowed my children to be parted from me in the same circumstances, I do not blame my mother for having had us evacuated.

She had been deserted by my father two years before the war and had volunteered to run a home for evacuated children in the country, on the condition that she could have her own children at that home, but the authorities could not guarantee being able to grant that condition. So she stayed in London, working in a hospital and saving for the day when she could have us back...

Our mother made sure we had a pleasant home and a good education, and did everything reasonably within her power to make us happy.

She put us above everything else, even turning down a subsequent proposal of marriage, and when she sent us into the country for the duration of the war, she was thinking of us first and foremost.

Nevertheless, she did not know how unhappy we were. We were always careful not to let her know (apart from one occasion when I stole the price of a postage stamp to write to her surreptitiously to plead that we be allowed to come back to London – our letters home were always vetted). She visited us as often as she could, usually on a Sunday, and I'm sure it broke her heart every time she left us...

I was always so glad that we were only evacuees and not foster children and that we had a loving mother who would take us home one day to live with her. And how marvellous it was when that day came.

Like many evacuees, Greta Herring (now Reid) never really understood why her parents sent her away, especially since they kept her baby brother with them throughout the blitz. At first, Greta shared her foster home with another little girl:

She was so unhappy that she became sick and her folks came and took her home. Thus I was left alone with two strange but kind people.

Mr Walters was a gamekeeper to the local squire and used to take me around to his rabbit snares together with my beloved, dearest friend, Rob, the English sheep-dog. The feelings I showed to this dog set a format which has stayed with me to this day when I can shower my affections on my cat much more easily than on my husband of 32 years.

I used to serve Rob tea in my playhouse (a section of the chicken-house that was scrubbed for my use). Mr Walters even gave me an old alarm clock to play with. I also trained Rob to play 'in and out the window' and to climb on one end of the see-saw, also provided by Mr Walters.

Auntie Edna had been a kennel maid. She evidently loved me very much. She showed it by making me eat everything good for me, including tripe and fatty bacon and cabbage! I soon grew quite chunky and she sheared off my ringlet, so that my parents were quite shocked at the change in me. I also grew quite reserved and resentful, and found it harder each time to embrace my parents and the sweet little brother they always took home with them when they left me behind.

Freda Risley (now Costa) finally left her foster home to return to her parents on VE day, 8 May 1945. She had been evacuated to Wadebridge, in Cornwall, where she was taken into the home of a Mrs S. Despite the kindness of this woman, Freda finds the experience difficult to put to one side:

374

The whole experience marked me for life. Until fairly recent years I suffered bad bouts of home-sickness if I was away from home for any time; I find it exceptionally difficult to trust anyone other than my husband; for a large part of my young adult life I suffered badly from depression and feelings of rejection. I am angry that the whole scheme was so ill thought out and put into operation – they were messing about with children's lives, for God's sake, how dare they give it so little thought.

I thought at the time, and I still think, that because they needed our mothers to work long hours in munitions, evacuation served a dual purpose – it got us away from the big towns and it also provided cheap childcare.

The war – and the war effort – was para-mount and I think this is why we only hear good experiences. I don't deny these experiences; anyone lucky enough to have been billeted with Mrs S. in Wadebridge and people like her has only good experiences to relate. But there was another, darker side and I think it has been covered up and I'm bitter about it.

I still get upset – old newsreels showing evacuees with those damned luggage-labels round their necks still make me weep.

On the positive side, since I work with child-ren, I've learned invaluable lessons. I never take an adult's word against a child's at face value; I respect what kids have to say, I credit them with more understanding and awareness than is general. *I know why battered children never tell, and I'm pretty good at spotting when something is wrong. Children trust me – it helps in my work. But was the evacuation experience worth it to have gained understanding? On balance – no. It brought too much misery at the time and its effects ruined large parts of my life for too long.*

It would be a mistake to generalize about the children who were evacuated from the cities. Not all were poor – though most of them were – and not all were dirty or had antisocial habits, as Raymond Dawes points out:

All London evacuees did not wet the bed. On the contrary, my own baptism into this disgusting cult did not occur until I was forced to share the bed with an incontinent Yorkshire 10-year-old called 'ower George'. I would gladly have swapped those warm sodden midnight sheets for the daily dicing with the doodlebugs which I had enjoyed on my paper-round down south.
I have never slept with a man since.

Raymond also remembers the difficulties that lay in trying to adjust to an alien environment:

I was in the second form at the local grammar

school and the whole lot of us were shipped up to the mining towns south of Doncaster. There was nothing enriching about the experience. We should have been warned about the 'culture shock', but the concept had not been formulated in 1944.

I was doubly disadvantaged in that, apart from my innate loathing of football, I also wore glasses. I was the last to be selected from the cattle market which was conducted in the Masonic Hall of that dreary little town. True, I was a slum kid too – but a snobbish slum kid, like the rest of us scholarship boys. 'Ower George' became such a bore with his football and bed-wetting that I was finally obliged to turn him over to the form bully who had, thankfully, travelled north with us. This was the accepted way of dealing with the unruly natives, as soiling one's own doorstep could make life very difficult with the foster parents.

I barely survived evacuation. I was nearly drowned in the canal, was dragged by a local bus and nearly crushed by a train in a coalmine. I came home with chronic asthma and went straight into hospital. The V2 rockets were arriving. Bliss.

The invitation to write prompted Lenny Harris, like many others, to put his thoughts and memories down on paper for the first time. He writes from Australia, where he now lives. It's worth retracing his story, since it follows a path that so many of us also trod. So give us your hand, Lenny, as once again we board that bus that will take us to the nearest railway station. Don't forget the bag and, I've forgotten, what was in it?

One tin of Carnation milk, one packet of dry biscuits and one tin of bully beef. With lots of other kids we got on the train for Yeovil in Somerset. We went from Yeovil to the small village of Ash. Then at the school – a little church school – I, with my three sisters (we left seven other brothers and sisters in London), was put on a horse and wagon and taken to a hamlet called Milton. When we got there – it was about three miles – they put us in an empty cottage and we stayed there until it was getting dark, and then someone came. I think he was the local evacuees man. We had eaten our food. I remember it was very good, as in London we never had much to eat. I was always very hungry.

This man took us down the lane to a big farm-house. I remember the oil-lamps in the windows of the cottages as we passed them. We went round to the back of the farmhouse to the back door. Up till now it was a good adventure. The man banged on the big door with his walking-stick. When the door opened, this lady with an oil-lamp in her hand was there. She had her hair in a bun at the back of her head, and around her neck was a velvet band with a pearl in the front, and she had a long black thick dress on, with pointed-toed shoes or boots. She frightened the life out of me.

We went in the kitchen and it had an oil-lamp hanging up on a chain from the ceiling, with guns, duck wings and warming-pans of shiny brass hanging from the walls, and a very big fireplace. It was like stepping into another world. I remember I was afraid.

We had a wash and were taken up a big stairway to a long passage with rooms all the way along. My room was about three doors along. The lady walked in front with the oil-lamp. She looked about 10 feet tall and shadows were flickering everywhere. It seemed about 200 yards long but of course it wasn't. She opened the door and there was a canvas folding bed with some blankets and a pillow. She and my sisters said 'Bye', and she locked the door (I think that night was the most terrifying one of my life). In the room was all old furniture covered with white sheets. As my eyes got used to the light I thought I saw all the things moving and looking at me. I remember I did not move in that canvas bed, but as the nights went on I got more brave and started looking under those sheets, and it helped.

In the mornings we got up and had our breakfast of cold milk and potato fried like a pancake. It was very cold. We had our meals in the milkhouse.

This was the first time I saw cows, dogs,

chickens, ducks and turkeys. I can remember most of the sheds – cow stalls, sties for pigs – and most things to this day. I liked the farm and in about a week I was milking my first cow and got to know the men working on the farm. There was Jack Derrick, his brother Bill and their dad, a Mr Fred Cornelius, his daughter Mary and old Mr Milton. The farmer was Mr Moley. The name of the farm was Falconers Farm.

One day I rode the front horse on the binder-reaper cutting corn – that was great. With my sister we picked up apples and they made cider out of them. It was good to eat apples when you liked. For dinner at night before bed we had rabbit, and sometimes we had chicken – that was the best I've ever eaten. Compared with London, we lived like kings. One day I got mad and chucked a stone at my sister and Jack Derrick got me and gave me a good hiding. A few days later my sisters went to live with someone else in Ash.

I had to go to school with the farmer's old shirt on (one of those ones that look like striped pyjamas), with no collar, and when it was raining I had to put a big sack bag over my shoulders. Of course the kids at school laughed at me, but my big sister looked after me. I walked across the fields to school.

I had trouble with wetting the bed and I knew that Mrs Moley was getting mad with me so I did not get a drink after about three o'clock, but I got so thirsty I would drink the dog's water.

One day I was playing with a kid on a haystack and the kid picked up a two-prong pitchfork and stabbed me through the leg. I must have been lucky, I got it out all right, but they had to call the doctor and he sent me to a home called 'The Nest' with about 20 other problem kids, all boys.

That was a bad time – I was there about nine to 12 months and the same time on the farm. I look back now and think 'The Nest' was like Charles Dickens's Oliver Twist – that was a cruel place. One boy died there and he slept next to me. I was too afraid to say anything about what happened that night, and never have. But things got better after we had new people to look after us, and one day my sister from London came to take me home to London on the train. I was glad to get out of 'The Nest'.

In London, bad luck again. The bombing started to get bad, so after about four weeks I had to go back – but not to 'The Nest'. When I got to the little farm where my sister was evacuated, there were three kids there of their own – Donald, Joan, and Joyce. My sister was called Joan, too, but they called her Rose. This was a real good place and to this day I call it 'home' in England. Their name was Vickery and they had a hawker wagon with great horses and an old Bedford truck. I liked going to the villages all around, selling pots and pans and paraffin oil for the cooking and lighting.

I was riding Mrs Vickery's bike – too big for me – and fell off, cutting my leg badly, and worse, I *lost an eye. I got over it, but the doctors said I'd have to go back to 'The Nest', so I ran away. I got to Yeovil and on a goods train to Leeds, but the police got me and took me back. But, thank God, not to 'The Nest'.*

A few years later, in a bad fire at Vickery's in the oil store, I managed to get Donald Vickery out. He was badly burned, but he lived and I'm happy about that.

I rang him in England a few weeks ago – the first time for 25 years. I hope I'm not being too silly, but I would like to see those places again and think of all those wonderful people and characters at that time.

To Betty Window (née Worley) it all still seems like a dream:

I see different parts of the evacuation on television and I still don't see the actual sadness. I see them with parents waving goodbye with happy faces ... all along I think I must have imagined it.

The passage of time has given David Owen a clearer perspective:

I have taken years fully to appreciate the experiences that unquestionably have shaped my attitudes and values.

In more obvious and concrete terms, the direction my life has taken was determined by the unforgettable teacher at the one-room school in the village. Her name was Grace Priestly. Mrs Priestly encouraged and influenced me at a critical time as she prepared me for the infamous 11-plus exams, which I sat in March 1942.

As a result I gained entrance on a full scholarship to Christ's Hospital, and subsequently a scholarship to McGill University [in Montreal, Canada].

For Gloria McNeill (née Needler), as is so often the case, music has become the key that unlocks the door to some of the most potent memories:

Every time I hear Vera Lynn sing 'Goodnight children everywhere' I see a forlorn 11-year-old curled up in a corner of a strange bedroom, hiding tears behind the pages of The Blue Fairy Book. *I don't think I ever got over that unbelievable loneliness.*

Joan Hellyer (née Johnson) now runs an antique fair and talks to a lot of other ex-evacuees:

They all say, 'We will never get over it. We all have phobias.' We were all left with some mental scar because of it. On the other hand, those two years that I had were an academic gift.

Joan Porter (née Gordge) looks back and

sees both drawbacks and benefits:

I live with the results of three years of middle-class input, which helped to estrange me from my family but opened my horizons and heightened my expectations.

Jocelyn Jackson (née Murphy) identifies clearly the influence that evacuation had on her life:

I trace my own lifelong interest in the environment, natural history, hill-walking and outdoor activities to the initial shock of total immersion in a rural environment. It is the only part of my childhood that I remember with any clarity.

Cecil Green thought his foster home was wonderful, but wasn't so favourably impressed by the billeting procedure:

I'm still in touch with my foster mother, but the system was like Russian roulette. We went from the railway station in a car. We were taken to a house and the billeting officer said to this woman, 'Do you want two boys or two girls?' and she said, 'Two boys,' and that was the fostering arrangement.

Cecil later became a social worker in foster home care.

Catherine Yorke (née Borthwick) finds the

general attitude to evacuees annoying:

In the years since, I have been irritated by references to evacuees who thought that milk only came in bottles and thought that baths were for storing coal. For me it was mostly an unhappy three years, and doodlebugs and rockets proved much less worrying. At least with them I was home, and that was all that mattered.

Pat Smith (née Senior) recognizes that her being evacuated might have saved her life:

Waldron Road School was bombed to the ground during the blitz, so possibly if I hadn't been evacuated I wouldn't be here to tell the tale.

Rita Symons (née Friede), who is Jewish, recalls that evacuation led to her being introduced to all manner of things:

In the foster home I learned to eat pork and bacon, which I had never had before, and I developed a real taste for it. What I got out of the experience was that I learned to say, 'I can!' rather than 'Cannot!'

Ray Turner's mother and father acted as foster parents. Ray remembers two little boys who spent time with his family:

David died in his middle twenties. I don't know

what became of Bill. But I do know that during their time with our family they portrayed many characteristics and qualities that were an excellent example to me. And I also know that had I, as a young sheltered boy, been in their situation, 'in a strange land', I should not have acquitted myself one half as well.

Malcolm Jeffrey remembers his 'second mum' very affectionately:

She was great. I always wrote to her and I understand that she received a letter from me while I was in Palestine. She was dying at the time and said to her daughter, 'He never forgot me,' and I won't!

Eugene McCoach feels that as a child he was not fully aware of his foster family's kindness:

It was only in later life that I fully appreciated the extent of the generosity of the people of Helensburgh in opening their homes to the people of Clydebank.
Perhaps even in some small way they learned something of our lifestyle in that although we may not have been rich, we were, on the whole, honest and mannerly. In a small number of cases where people were living alone, or were a retired couple, a new lease of life was opened and it gave them something worthwhile to do.

Doris Pritchard (née Thompson), on the other hand, writes:

I met a German Jewish woman, who had come to England at the beginning of the war, who told me how badly she had been treated by the English, and I said, 'Don't worry, we in England were treated just as badly by our own people.'

Patsy realizes what a powerful effect her experiences as an evacuee have had on her:

I think that none of us who were sent away from our homes as small children has been fully aware of the tremendous impact that it had upon us. I have a great deal of strength and independence which I have laid to that time of my life. What I have failed to come to grips with is my inability or unwillingness to form close ties with other human beings.

For Imelda O'Connor (née Kirwan), writing about evacuation has been a cathartic exercise:

I have enjoyed writing this as it has got rid of the bitterness I have always felt at being separated from my family. My father died in his sleep six months after I returned home. I realize now how good so many people in Ireland were to me.

Doreen Dixon (née Caldwell-Barr) believes that what she witnessed as an evacuee influenced her politically:

I went to Wales and saw worse poverty than my own. I think I became a socialist as a result of my experience.

Peter Shillingford, who was evacuated to Surrey, is convinced that the experiences he and his companions shared made them part of a 'special generation':

I ended up at Sutton Place, the Duke of Sutherland's home near Guildford. It was the event of a lifetime for me. I'm sure I wouldn't have enjoyed my life half so much if I hadn't gone there. And I'm sure I wouldn't be the person I am today.

There were 20 of us; there was a schoolmaster in charge of us and we lived the life of Riley. We were all tearaways from London. We used to ride into Woking. One boy would go by bus and he'd collect all the tickets off the floor of the bus and give the stubs to us so that we could claim the fare, which was quite a regular bit of pocket-money for us in those days.

We lived in the servants' quarters of the big house and we were looked after by a steward who was the butler. It was full of suits of armour and tapestry on the wall, and when the Duke

388

wasn't in residence – which was frequent – we used to wander all over the place. All the various rooms were our playgrounds. They had wild gardens, French gardens and English gardens, lily ponds and ornamental gardens.

One of my greatest friends down there was an old poacher and he taught me how to poach and I can still do that today. I kept my mother quite well-provided with food in those days. Every weekend I used to cycle home to London from Woking with a bag full of rabbits and all kinds of vegetables that I liberated down there.

There were all kinds of funny liaisons that were going on, strange people who would suddenly appear at the swimming-pool when the Duke of Sutherland was there.

We were very independent, literally no mothering at all. The food was provided but we looked after ourselves from there on. I got a huge independence out of this at a very early age. I was an old man at 14. I could look after myself at all levels. We had a load of skills that we could add to the cunning we brought with us. If we had gone through the educational machine that existed in those days, I'm sure we would have finished up just as products of the established order. As it was, we turned out a huge variety of independent people. I am sure we were a special generation because of it.

I think that the evacuation changed a whole generation of people. The expectations of the poor were raised. We had a heightened awareness of the economic differences. I don't think any of us would ever have been able to understand the level of life that some of the larger families of England had going for them in those days compared with ours. We wouldn't have known that it existed.

The Duke of Sutherland at this time had about four other establishments. The servants must have had a rather cushy life while the Duke was gone, and then they had 20 of us hoisted on them and all the aggravation that went with it. They all had their problems with us. The gamekeepers found that their gin traps disappeared every time they laid them.

Kenneth Barber also thinks that evacuation changed him, but not necessarily for the better:

The whole experience made me very vicious, and my father used to say, 'If you don't calm your temper you'll be hanged one day.' I think the experience made me very resourceful, but often when things go badly it flashes in front of your eyes again. It's easy enough to say, 'Get on with it!' but sometimes you can't, can you?

Back in London, when the sirens went, my mother used to stay in bed and I'd say, 'Mum! Mum! Come on down to the shelter. The bombs is dropping.' She used to swear and say, 'If Hitler wants me out of bed, he's got to f... ing well bomb me out of bed.'

Pauline Adams (née Simpson) can only speculate as to exactly how she felt:

I can never understand why, as a normal 12-year-old, I should have kept my mum's first letter to me, which I still have. I can't remember knowingly keeping it, but perhaps it was because in it she explained that the only reason she let me go was because 'I loved you and wanted you to be safe.'

Margaret Done (née Scicluna) would not have missed the experience of being an evacuee 'for anything':

I learned to appreciate so many things in life and even today I much prefer the country to the town.

For years and years after I came home I kept in touch with my foster parents and I still visit Ulverston [in Cumbria], my second home. I am sorry to say that my foster parents are now no longer with us, but they will always have a special place in my heart.

The first family I stayed with, and mostly my second, they did a wonderful job of looking after me and it must have been from love, it certainly can't have been for the 37½p the Government gave them. They taught me a great deal and I owe them a debt I can never repay. They took me into their homes, an unknown entity, and

391

moulded me, and for that I will be ever grateful.
Each family in turn took the place of my own parents and did the job they weren't able to do. They brought me up to respect all things and property. They certainly taught me right from wrong; I couldn't ask for more. I didn't always agree with them, I often kicked over the traces, but with give and take on both sides it worked out well. I am still using their guidelines and I will always be glad they took me in, an eight-year-old Salford evacuee.

Patricia Kingswell (now McPhail) was sent to Bingley, in Yorkshire, and she is still trying to remember the names of the people who took her in:

They were the most wonderful people – an older couple with a son who was a POW and a daughter who was in the WAAC. The wife used to cook for Lord somebody-or-other and she was a super cook. I wish that I had kept in touch with them, but the years roll by and you just do these things.
Being evacuated had its good and bad sides. I'm not as close to my family as the rest because I spent my formative years away from them. My mother, who is now dead, and I unfortunately remained miles apart. On the positive side, being evacuated made me independent.

Patricia left for Canada when she was 19

and has never been back to England.

Muriel Horak (née Marco) explains why she lost touch with those who had cared for her:

By the time the thought crossed my mind to contact the people who had been so kind to us I could not go, because it would have meant talking about the death of my mother and brother in March of 1945 – V2 rocket – and I couldn't do it. By the time I could talk about it it was too late. Please say a thank you for those of us who appreciated those who opened their hearts and their houses to us. Sometimes it was circumstances and not ingratitude that prevented us from expressing our thanks at the time.

Jean Dark (née Fraser) notes that when most people talk about war they are concerned only with battles:

They never think of the devastating effect on children who are deprived of a normal child-hood.

Ron Larby remembers how delightful it was to enjoy such freedom of movement:

How many other children get to play as part of their everyday life in the ruins of a Norman castle ... King Arthur's at that!

Margaret King, who was sexually abused, found no such freedom, and is still haunted by her experiences:

I tried so many times to talk to someone. I am now 52 years of age and this is the first time I have told anyone. I knew how much he hurt me and as I got older, I kept trying to get someone who would listen. I was then (unknown to me at the time) to be hurt so much with hate for a man that it has followed me all my life. I have no respect for men. I have now been married three times (I will admit to nice men) and have four smashing kids. My two eldest boys I have I don't see now as I have fallen out with them (men again have hurt me a great deal). My two daughters I love very much. I have to fight my fear of any man doing what that man did to me.

Being an evacuee saved my life from bullets but gave me another fear for the rest of my life. I'll never forget the horror of it and am sure to find this man sometime in my life.

Peter Gardner's parents have often told him that it was one of the biggest decisions of their lives:

…to send us away and not know whether we would be left as orphans. They said it was matched only by their decision to have their children vaccinated against diphtheria in 1942.

Patricia Smith (née Patmore) remembers 'with horrifying clarity the devastation this separation from home and family caused':

I try to equate it with my relationship with my own children, and have often thought how I would have reacted myself had I been a mother with young children at the time.

One of the most difficult things for many children was fitting in again once they were back with their families, as Joan Porter (née Gordge) recalls:

I never really became part of the family again. I am now a social worker. A strong will and inner strength have helped me to become a survivor. My first instinct is to shield others from pain.

When Vivienne Martin (not her real name) returned home, she certainly felt she didn't belong any more:

I could have stayed with the Hunts – they wanted me to and I had a job offered me. But to be honest I thought of home with Mum and Dad going dancing and generally having a good time. Oh, dear, I could never have been more wrong. Mum seemed to resent me ... to me, it was strange. I had been looking forward to coming home and it seemed they didn't want me. They said I was a snob and stuck up and they didn't like the way I spoke, so it seemed that they wished I had never come home.

I started work, and the people at work kept saying to my sister, 'Oh, she's not like you, she's very stuck up, she thinks she's too good for us,' and the trouble was, I did think that, I thought they were loud and common *and very rude.*

Many children who were badly treated later found that their experiences led to their being rather intolerant. Geoffrey West, whose home is now in New Zealand, writes:

I find this is true in the area of sexual deviants, even in milder forms. I am cynical towards people who claim to be Christians yet lack any underlying care for other people.

I find the all-pervasive English class system intolerable. I am sure my rather unforgiving attitude in these matters stems from my time spent as an evacuee. Yes, I can truly say, my experience as an evacuee was traumatic. TRAUMATIC, an emotional shock that has long-lasting effects. No doubt people will look forward to a reunion but to stand around reminiscing about the good old days when we were evacuees is the last thing I want to do.

June Addison (née Evans) now recognizes what she gained from her evacuation years:

Our parents surrendered us for our protection. Nobody knew where we were going or to whom. What did we learn from this? Independence to trust people, a love of the country which has stayed with us. My brother and I both lacked the basic writing and spelling skills but we agree we are late learners. Charles is a consulting engineer with a degree in engineering, a B.Sc., is an accomplished pianist and is studying English literature. I became a registered nurse. We are both married and each have two sons and two daughters.

David Cornelius was evacuated to Cornwall at the age of five. He stayed with a middle-aged couple until 1945, and now remembers:

...the incredible kindness of the couple who, perhaps to their surprise, adopted me for the duration of the war. I can't say enough about them and their kindness or the influence they had on my life. Certainly it was them I emulated as a role model and it was partially the burning desire to live like them that led me from London to Canada.
Some time ago we were watching one of those documentary programmes on TV about that part of the war, and I said to my three children, 'I was one of those children.' It was only then that I realized the impossibility of my allowing them to be parcelled up and sent away and

began to feel something of how my parents must have felt.

Jean Talbot (now Chapman) was evacuated from a children's home at the age of six to Gainsborough in Lincolnshire, where she was badly treated:

As I write this letter I'm still searching for the sister who went with me over 40 years ago. I have not seen her since.

I am now a mother and grandmother and shudder when I think of my evacuation. I thank God none of my children and grand-children will have to go through what I went through. How I survived to tell this tale I shall never know.

When Aldyth Rapley (née Griffiths)'s father died in 1986, among his papers Aldyth came across a postcard she had sent to her mother from the youth hostel where she had been billeted as an evacuee:

I hadn't dated it, but it was written on a Monday and I think it must have been on either the 11th or maybe the 18th of September, for we were only at the hostel for a short time.

It is yellow with age now and the pencil somewhat faded (there were no ball-point pens in those days), but I can still read what I wrote:

Dear Mother

I am not at all jolly as it is a horid old pig sty. I recived your letter this morning (monday) I have seen Mrs Edwards, Grace and Goronwy and Blanche. The Rathbone are up there. Joyce & Peggy Barker are with Mrs Edwards they live in Leopold Rd and I should have stayed at Rathbone. Please come as soon as you can I am freting and I have cried three times.

Lots of love Aldyth

Give my love to Evan and Dada.

On the top of the card, next to the address, I had written, 'I am going to come home if I can.'

10

Back to the Past

It is only natural that ex-evacuees should feel the pull of the areas that have played such an important part in their lives. For those who look back on happy times, revisiting the places to which they were evacuated can be sweetly nostalgic and a source of great pleasure.

Those who have painful memories, on the other hand, often have no wish to return, believing that a part of their lives that was so brutal is better buried and left in the past. Yet there are those who have found the urge to return so overwhelming that they have gone back in spite of everything and, even more important, have faced the people who were so cruel to them when they were children. Only those who have themselves been the victims of child abuse can fully understand the courageousness of such an action. Many of those who have made the pilgrimage have done so in the hope that a return to the scene of their childhood nightmares might repair some of the psychological damage they have suffered and enable them to live the rest of their lives in peace.

David Nelson (not his real name) was severely abused for three years after being sent to stay in a small village in Dorset at the age of eight:

I first returned to West Milton on a motor cycle in 1958. It was exactly as I remembered it. I spoke to no one. I saw the school and church exactly as it was. I returned every couple of years to try and lay the 'ghost' that has haunted me ever since. I met the woman Mrs Storm [not her real name]. I just knocked on the door and when she answered it I recognized her instantly.

I told her who I was – I was polite – and said I'd come to visit her. She told me that she'd never had evacuees, yet she invited me into the house and plied me with tea and cakes. I mentioned many names from those days and with no hesitation she told me what they were doing.

Her husband had died – a decent chap but frightened to death of her.

When I left Mrs Storm after four hours she said it was good to see me after all these years and for me to call again. Meanwhile she would tell her daughter! (And she didn't recognize me?)

I returned again last year. Mrs Storm is dead.

I have three daughters and a son. I brought them up with my experience in mind and kept a vow made to myself at 11 years of age, which was that they would have a very happy childhood.

One correspondent's sister was evacuated to Llanaber, a tiny village near Barmouth on the west coast of Wales, and recently made a return visit:

She stood by the cobbled wall looking at the old childish scrawls, including her own... C.E.A. LOVES F.F. She wept for the lost years.

Tommy McSorley went back to Ballinluig in central Scotland, where he had been billeted:

Within minutes of my arrival the word had spread by bush telegraph throughout the village that big Tommy had arrived, and we all had a marvellous time down at the local.

When Derek Trayler revisited Norfolk with his son, he was surprised at the way history repeated itself:

Three weeks after I arrived I had to go into hospital to have my appendix out. This gave me my moment of fame when the national newspaper stated that the first evacuee to go into hospital had had an operation and was recovering.

The strange thing is, I took my son back to visit Norfolk when he was the same age as I was when I went there, and he ended up in the same hospital having his appendix out.

Vic Atkinson went back to Hartland, in Devon, and found that nothing seemed to have changed. As a child he had been badly treated by the two ladies who had taken him into their home:

Something drew me like a magnet until I found the graves of the two ladies ... I forgave them!

G.A. Ritchie has discovered that one woman who was cruel to her is still alive, along with her husband. All the same, she is happy to visit a friend who lives next door to them:

Kathy is still a great pal and when I went down last she took me around to the school. The school hadn't altered at all and she said, 'I want to show you something.' Tears came to my eyes as she lifted the desk-top. Our names were still written on it.

Ralph Rogers went back to visit his foster mother as an Army officer, determined to prove that he had made good:

I turned up on the doorstep in my officer's uniform and she invited me into the lounge. It was the first time I'd ever been in there. I went in my new service dress and her first words were, 'Oh, hello. I see you are still cleaning your teeth properly.'

Even after 33 years' absence, Joyce Wheeldon recognized all the old familiar places as soon as she got to the High Street, and had no trouble finding the road where she had lived as an evacuee:

I boldly went up and knocked on the door of number 11. No one in, but someone next door came out and I asked about Mrs Oliver. She was working just down the hill, and the neighbour hurried down the hill to fetch her. She wasn't told anything about her 'visitor' so when she saw me she was looking at a complete stranger.

Over a cup of tea I gave her one or two clues as to who I was. Eventually she jumped up and said, 'Oh yes, of course. I remember you three, oh what lovely kids you were.'

As we left she was telling everyone, 'This is my 'vacuee.' I felt about 14 years old again.

William John Cambridge returned to Up-lyme, in Dorset, for a farm holiday with his family. It was 30 years since he had left:

On my mentioning to the farmer's wife, Mrs Alford, that I was there in the early part of the war and stayed with old Mr and Mrs Turner, Mrs Alford said, 'Why, the old girl is still alive.'

We went next day to see her and sure enough, there she was, large as life and 99.

She lived to a few weeks short of her 102nd birthday. A tough old bird indeed. Must have been something in the porridge.

Renée Selvage (née Bickerdike) arranged to meet a friend she had not seen for 40 years:

I was home with a broken ankle but was able to get about. I had time off from work so I arranged to meet my friend Lilian.

We recognized each other straightaway. She was off work with a broken arm. We had a lovely day together.

Ronald George Evans went back to Not-tingham after many years to find that the people he had been billeted with now ran a public house:

When I went in to pay them a visit they were too busy to talk about old times, so I had a drink and left for home, never to return again.

Betty Wilson was a foster mother during the war. A few years ago, the oldest of three girls she had looked after paid her a visit:

She came with her own little family to let them see where she stayed and went to school when she was evacuated here.

To my regret I was not at home and she left no address. I do wish she had, because I shall never forget my three little girls.

Patricia Robertson (née Sawyers) decided to go back to Broughton in Northamptonshire, where she had been billeted in a pub, to find her 'Aunt Edna':

That was quite a day, I can tell you... I knew exactly where the pub was, only it had gone and a block of flats was there now. I got so panicky my husband remarked that maybe I had made a mistake. But I knew I was right. Across the road was the village green with four swings. The first swing had been 'mine'. For so many years it had squeaked a little song and I would sit for hours on it. Over we went and I sat down on the swing and sure enough it sounded the same. I was laughing and crying and we all pumped on the swings.

I was determined to find out where the pub had gone. I knew there was another pub up the road and thank goodness it was still there. I asked the man inside what had happened to the Green Dragon. He looked at me as if I was nuts. 'Oh that was pulled down years ago.' 'Where's Aunt Edna gone?' I said. His eyes went wide. 'My God, are you Pat?' 'Yes,' I said. 'Well, Edna Johnson is living in a senior citizens' flat down the road,' he said.

So off we all ran. We found the place and I can tell you my legs were like rubber. I went up to the door and knocked. She opened it and said, 'Good God, it's Pat!'

Violet Goode (née Sutton) is now married and lives in Australia. In 1976 she returned to England with her husband, hired a car and set off to see if she could find the woman who had been her foster mother:

I had often told my husband of my life in Cornwall and how Mr and Mrs James had been so good to us. The last time I had seen them was in 1944, leaving them and us in tears. That was 32 years ago with no contact.

We finally reached the village, but I didn't recognize it. So we stopped the car, my husband saying, 'You ask in the small shop and I'll ask the woman waiting across the road at the bus stop.' He went across and said, 'Do you know if there is a Mrs James living around here?' She replied in true Cornish, 'I'm Mrs James. Which one do you want?' My husband said, 'The one who looked after two evac...' He never finished. She looked across and said, 'Is that Violet? ... Yes, it was my Mrs James... All the years rolled back.

I know how she felt. Thirty years after leaving my Welsh smithy's family, I went back.

Much had happened in the intervening years. After various jobs, during a period as a professional musician, I had met my wife, Doreen. She was a nurse, and felt, as I did, that our future lay outside Britain. We left to live in Canada.

Our three children were 14, 13 and three when we decided to return to the UK to visit Doreen's parents in Bristol. On a sightseeing drive in the country, it suddenly occurred to me how close I was to South Wales and my wartime home. Off we went, the excitement building as I explained for the first time to my children how, long before they had been born, their father had gone away from home to live with strangers.

The village was not easy to find, but eventually a sign appeared with the magic words, 'Cross Hands'. We made our way into the village, which now seemed strange. The mountains of slag that formed its backdrop were now covered in grass.

We drove slowly under the railway arch that crossed the main street looking for anything that might give me a clue to the whereabouts of the house in which I had spent so many happy hours. Suddenly it was there, still lying quietly in the shadows of the working-men's club.

I pulled the car gently into the kerb and turned off the ignition. My wife and children sat staring at the cottage. It looked much smaller than I remembered.

Doreen suggested that I approach the house alone to find out if it was the right one. I opened the car door, walked up the short path to the whitened doorstep and knocked.

A woman in her fifties opened the door and stood staring at me. I explained that I had lived in the house during the war and had now returned to show my children.

'But I'm Rachel,' she cried, 'the daughter of the house ... we were playmates.'

We hugged each other and laughed. 'If only Mum and Dad could be here it would be perfect,' I said.

'But they are.' Rachel pushed me back to an arm's length. 'They're in the kitchen.'

'But I was sure they'd be...'

'Not them, boy. They're too tough for that, though they're over 90 apiece.'

I quickly went back to the car to fetch Doreen and the children, and we followed

Rachel into the tiny, dark kitchen where I had spent so much time. Mr and Mrs Roberts sat at the table staring at us, as Rachel explained to them, in Welsh, who we were. We hugged – although, to be honest, I don't think they remembered me. I had been a child who had occupied such a small part of their long lives.

All too soon it was time to leave. As we stood at the door, the old man reached into his pocket and, as is the native custom in Wales, pressed a coin into the hand of each of my children.

For better or worse, evacuation had the effect of splitting families and groups so that they would never be reunited. Children whose original homes were places where they had been abused or ill-treated slowly adjusted to a new life in caring homes where they were loved and accepted as part of the family. Their foster parents knew that when the time came to part it would be difficult – for both them and the children – and many made attempts to adopt the new members of their families. Some succeeded, some did not.

Children who were returning to homes where they were not loved found it particularly traumatic now that they had experienced life in homes where they had been shown affection. For them, evacuation had brought two kinds of fear: in the beginning, the anxiety they felt about leaving the familiar for the unknown, and now, paradoxically, a dread of returning to the life they knew and remembered. Unable to cope with their 'new' life back at home, some ran away and returned to their foster parents. Others stayed but could not adjust. Although their own families welcomed them back and tried their best to make them feel at home, the pull of another family, elsewhere, was a strong one.

Evacuees whose parents had remained in the cities must have understood that the lives of their mothers and fathers might be in danger, but the loss of one parent or both was still utterly devastating. The love and understanding of many foster parents filled the void in bereaved children's hearts as they stepped forward to accept them as new sons and daughters.

The sight of the coin being pressed into the hand of my son, Vincent, caused a lump to form in my throat. Vincent was 14 years old – the same age at which, many years before, another young boy, standing on the same spot, had found a small horseshoe being pressed into his palm. Inscribed along the side were the words, 'with love, the Roberts family'.

I still have the horseshoe today – a

memento of a time long past that will help this ex-evacuee remember the years he spent with borrowed parents for the rest of his life.

The publishers hope that this book has given you enjoyable reading. Large Print Books are especially designed to be as easy to see and hold as possible. If you wish a complete list of our books please ask at your local library or write directly to:

Magna Large Print Books
Magna House, Long Preston,
Skipton, North Yorkshire.
BD23 4ND